Children's Film
in the Digital Age

Children's Film in the Digital Age

Essays on Audience, Adaptation and Consumer Culture

Edited by KARIN BEELER
and STAN BEELER

McFarland & Company, Inc., Publishers
Jefferson, North Carolina

ALSO BY KARIN BEELER
___

Seers, Witches and Psychics on Screen: An Analysis of Women Visionary Characters in Recent Television and Film (McFarland, 2008)

Tattoos, Desire and Violence: Marks of Resistance in Literature, Film and Television (McFarland, 2006)

ALSO BY STAN BEELER
___

Dance, Drugs and Escape: The Club Scene in Literature, Film and Television Since the Late 1980s (McFarland, 2007)

LIBRARY OF CONGRESS CATALOGUING DATA ARE AVAILABLE

Children's film in the digital age : essays on audience, adaptation and consumer culture / edited by Karin Beeler and Stan Beeler.
    p.   cm.
    Includes bibliographical references and index.

    ISBN 978-0-7864-7596-4 (softcover : acid free paper) ∞
    ISBN 978-1-4766-1840-1 (ebook)

    1. Children's films—History and criticism. 2. Film adaptations—History and criticism. 3. Childhood in motion pictures.
I. Beeler, Karin E. (Karin Elizabeth), 1963– editor. II. Beeler, Stan, editor.
    PN1995.9.C45C465 2015
    791.43083—dc23   2014041469

BRITISH LIBRARY CATALOGUING DATA ARE AVAILABLE

© 2015 Karin Beeler and Stan Beeler. All rights reserved

No part of this book may be reproduced or transmitted in any form or by any means, electronic or mechanical, including photocopying or recording, or by any information storage and retrieval system, without permission in writing from the publisher.

Cover image © iStock/Thinkstock

Printed in the United States of America

McFarland & Company, Inc., Publishers
Box 611, Jefferson, North Carolina 28640
www.mcfarlandpub.com

To our daughter Amy,
a child of participatory culture

Acknowledgments

We would like to thank all of the contributors, who shared their fascinating views on recent developments in children's film. We also thank the University of Northern British Columbia (Canada) for supporting our research through travel funding for conferences where we communicated some of the initial ideas for this project.

We are grateful to our daughter Amy, whose interest in film studies, television studies, fandom and digital culture has allowed us to redefine the way we study film and other media. The films and shows she has viewed on her mini DVD player, videogame devices, home computer and, more recently, her handheld devices have provided her with hours of entertainment and an education in the art of storytelling across different media.

We look forward to finding out how this generation of children will contribute to the visual narratives of the future.

Table of Contents

Acknowledgments   vi
Introduction
    Karin and Stan Beeler   1

Section One:
Childhood, Adults and Films for Dual Audiences

No Place Like Home: Circumscribing Fantasy in Children's Film
    Julian Cornell   9

Songs for the Older Set: Music and Multiple Demographics in *Shrek, Madagascar* and *Happy Feet*
    Stan Beeler   28

The Fantastic Childhood Imagination Through an Adult Lens: A Todorovian Approach to Tim Burton's *Alice in Wonderland*
    Heather Rolufs   37

Asterix & Obelix vs. Hollywood: A Pan-European Film Franchise for the "Family" Audience
    Noel Brown   49

Section Two:
Film Adaptation and Transmedia Forms

Re-Mixing *The Chronicles of Narnia*: The Reimagining of Lucy Pevensie Through Film Franchise Texts and Digital Fan Cultures
    Naomi Hamer   63

An Evolutionary Journey: *Pokémon*, Mythic Quests and the Culture of Challenge
    Lincoln Geraghty   78

Diary of a Wimpy Kid: Film Adaptation and Media Convergence
for Children
    KARIN BEELER   89

Nurturing Young Cinephiles: Martin Scorsese's *Hugo*
    DAN NORTH   98

Section Three:
Cultural and Consumer Contexts for Children

Russian Animated Films and Nationalism of the New Millennium:
The Phoenix Rising from the Ashes
    MICHEL BOUCHARD *and* TATIANA PODYAKOVA   109

Cosmopolitan Endurance: Migrant Children and Film Spectatorship
    STEPHANIE HEMELRYK DONALD   133

Dubashi: Indian Film, Cross-Cultural Communication and Screenings
for Children
    SWARNAVEL ESWARAN PILLAI   148

Branding Blackness: Disney's Commodification of Black Culture in
Song of the South and *The Princess and the Frog*
    LYDIA E. FERGUSON   160

The Commodification of Ms. Penny Proud: Consumer Culture in
Fat Albert and the Cosby Kids and Disney's *The Proud Family*
    DEBBIE OLSON   172

About the Contributors   189
Index   191

Introduction

Karin and Stan Beeler

The relationship between the film industry and the youthful segment of its audience has always been complex, perhaps because children are participants in film as actors, diegetic subjects as well as a large target audience. Moreover, as the technology involved in the distribution of film has evolved, children have become a significant economic factor in a successful production. As an audience segment, children are no longer dependent upon parental schedules for access to the medium; instead of waiting for a family outing to the local cinema, children can access their favorite films in the comfort of the home. For this reason, films for children and the distribution and consumption of these films through DVD sales, television rebroadcast or adaptation, and the digital distribution market (iTunes, Netflix, etc.) have become an important part of the production and reception of film over the last few decades. As an area of scholarly inquiry, screen studies—including both film and television studies—has begun to pay closer attention to participatory culture and to how the new technology and radically altered viewing platforms demand different ways of discussing film.[1] Our volume presents some of these innovations and approaches in the interpretation of films produced for and about children.[2]

Childhood and youth studies are interdisciplinary areas of scholarly study that are becoming more prominent in the United Kingdom, Canada and the United States and may include considerations of the impact of technology or media on children as part of a conference program or research center. Popular culture and screen studies scholars have also been involved in sessions on children and visual media. For example, a 2005 special issue of the U.K. journal *Screen* focused on "The Child in Film and Television." The Mid-Atlantic Popular and American Culture Association features a "Children and Childhood Studies and Popular Culture" area in its annual conference, and Canada is home to the Centre for Research in Young People's Texts and Cultures (CRYTC). However, despite these developments, there is still a need to bring communities of scholars together to engage in the discussion of children's film and their roles within the film and as viewers of film and as participants in transmedia culture. During a 2014 Society for Cinema and Media Studies conference session on "The Materialities of Fantastic Media," Matt Hills, author of *Fan Cultures* (Routledge 2002), suggested that children's fandom and their perspectives were still an underrepresented area of study in screen studies.[3] This volume will explore how children's film must be re-examined alongside recent developments in the production of film for children. Recent children's films take into account the effect of multi-media opportunities on the child audience and the role of participatory opportunities and their pedagogical implications. Essays in this collection also address how childhood is inscribed within film and linked to various national/cultural and consumer contexts. Releases of films over the last fifteen years in the multiplicity of available formats also reflect a reconceptualization of film genres (e.g., fantasy), audiences (children and adult) and the impact of technological advances like 3D film upon adaptation.

As mentioned, digital technologies and other modern modes of film delivery have had a significant impact on the way that contemporary children experience film. As Henry Jenkins has pointed out, there has been a "cultural shift as consumers are encouraged to seek out new information and make connections among dispersed media content" (*Convergence Culture* 2006, 3). The delivery and experience of film has shifted from a rather self-contained cinema event, which was normally received under the supervision of adults, to a highly interconnected multimodal production that often does not include parental supervision. Young children may bypass the feature film itself and opt to watch or interact with these special features on DVD, television or tablet. Children's DVDs and Blu-ray discs have facilitated the child viewer's fascination with characters' narratives through the special or bonus features that accompany the feature film, thus facilitating a higher degree of media literacy among younger viewers. Sometimes animated shorts or simple games extend the narrative presented by the feature film.[4] More recently digital copies and "streaming" with bonus features (e.g., Disney Movies Online) have offered yet another way of consuming film. Outtakes or bloopers that make up these bonus features (either in a DVD/Blu-ray format or as online extras) lay bare the medium of computer animation and increase a viewer's media literacy.

Not only have children's films incorporated more self-conscious references to multiple digital media in the actual shows (*The Lion King 1½*, *Diary of a Wimpy Kid*), but current films in the DVD/Blu-ray or digital copy environment are experienced by viewers (children and adults) in conjunction with a multitude of online sites and resources/products to facilitate different—transmedia—

modes of consuming and producing content. Videogames, merchandise, films as adaptations of cartoon-novels (e.g., *The Diary of a Wimpy Kid* phenomenon), or graphic novels available in print or ebook versions (e.g., *Paranorman*) and film websites have drawn in the viewer to become part of this interconnected process of "media convergence" (Jenkins 3).

It is important to note that the child or the construction of the child in film is an important facet of our collection. While not every film that features a child character may be designed for younger audiences, it is worth considering how the construction of the child contributes to the child/adult dichotomy that occurs in film and, occasionally, its transmedia ramifications. For example, Karen Lury's *The Child in Film: Tears, Fears, and Fairy Tales* (I.B. Tauris 2010) elaborates on the impact of the figure of the child in film. James Bennett's and Tom Brown's *Film and Television after DVD* (Routledge 2008) includes Brown's study of theme parks based upon film and how they appeal to the child viewer. *Children's Films: History, Ideology, Pedagogy, Theory* by Ian Wojik-Andrews (Garland 2000) was published over a decade ago and presents some useful information on how to define a children's film but did not address the proliferation of film through digital technologies and various media delivery systems that have affected any future consideration of children's film. John Stephens' edited collection *Ways of Being Male: Representing Masculinities in Children's Literature and Film* (Routledge 2002) is an analysis of a very specific issue in literature and film with a greater focus on the literary than the filmic experience. *Diversity in Disney Films: Critical Essays on Race, Ethnicity, Gender, Sexuality and Disability* (2012) focuses exclusively on Disney films, one of the most pervasive branches of the children's film experience. Films that are designed for different audiences (child/adult) or which break down the boundaries between audiences have also become an important phenomenon worthy of scholarly consideration.

Although the studies mentioned have provided a valuable insight into the representation of children, the aim of our collection is to provide a more comprehensive examination of a variety of children's films (by venturing beyond the North American film), primarily those that have been released since the 2000s as DVDs or Blu-ray or digital copies. We have also chosen not to restrict our study to animated children's film; this book also includes consideration of live action movies as well. The essays will appeal to scholars interested in film across a number of disciplines while engaging with and furthering some of the important considerations raised by scholars such as Henry Jenkins (*Convergence Culture*) and Barbara Klinger (*Beyond the Multiplex: Cinema, New Technologies and the Home*) since their publications on convergence culture and the post-cinema experience have *not* focused solely on films for children.

The essays in this collection are divided into three key sections. The first unit addresses "Childhood, Adults and Films for Dual Audiences," and the essays explore the fact that material generally categorized as children's films are often not focused solely upon a single demographic audience.

Julian Cornell's "No Place Like Home: Circumscribing Fantasy in Children's Film" deals with the pedagogical implications of films that have been designated as appropriate for children. Cornell points out that "given this daily contact with television, film and literature, the intermingling of entertainment and pedagogy, the media profoundly shape children's lives, not just in terms of forming their consciousness of themselves, but in helping them understand what it means to be a child in society." In other words, adult expectations concerning the containment of fantasy in children's film are often a significant determinant in the creation and marketing of films such as *The Polar Express* (2004) and *Ice Age* (2002).

Stan Beeler's "Songs for the Older Set: Music and Multiple Demographics in *Shrek, Madagascar* and *Happy Feet*" is a study of the function of music in contemporary animated features. This essay discusses the ways in which filmmakers use nostalgic selections of adult music to broaden the demographic appeal of children's films. This technique makes parents and grandparents comfortable with animated features by providing them with a familiar classic rock soundtrack that can evoke a more mature level of interpretation.

"The Fantastic Childhood Imagination Through an Adult Lens: A Todorovian Approach to Tim Burton's *Alice in Wonderland*," by Heather Rolufs, is a case study of Burton's adaptation of the classic children's novel. Rolufs analyzes the film as "a complex blend of live action and animation, fairy tale and fantastic tale, and adaptation and reinvention." She presents an intriguing theoretical discussion on the differing nature of fantasy for the children and adults that make up this film's mixed audience. The immersive aspect of the fantastic world in *Alice in Wonderland* that is available to viewers through the film's 3D technology appeals to the child viewer, while other aspects of the narrative create nostalgia for childhood that targets adults watching the film.

The final essay in this section, Noel Brown's "Asterix & Obelix vs. Hollywood: A Pan-European Film Franchise for the 'Family' Audience," presents a European effort to appropriate the stylistic appeal of Hollywood family films. Brown suggests that "*Asterix & Obelix vs. Caesar* and *Asterix & Obelix: Mission Cleopatra* ... were conceived of as Hollywood-style 'family' blockbusters designed to appeal not only to children, but to the broadest possible cross-section of mass audiences." Of these two films, *Mission Cleopatra* appealed to a broader spectrum of consumers with its use of "big international stars," computer-generated effects and intertextual references that chiefly draw "on the collective cultural memory of potential consumers across the world, with few jokes playable solely to Francophone audiences."

The second section, "Film Adaptation and Transmedia Forms," is comprised of four essays about multi-media approaches to storytelling. Naomi Hamer's "Re-Mixing *The Chronicles of Narnia:* The Re-Imagining of Lucy Pevensie Through Film Franchise Texts and Digital Fan Cultures" is an intriguing study of more recent developments in the adaptation of C.S. Lewis' children's novels *The Chronicles of Narnia*. Hamer notes that "while all adaptations of Lewis's text involve the translation of textual discourse into a new context or format, the recent Disney/Walden Media film exemplifies the translation of discourse across a number of media forms simultaneously in the context of a branded franchise." Her investigation includes not only the initial efforts on the part of the filmmakers, but also the audience responses through "digital fan cultures"; the designers of fan videos and fan fictions expand upon the film discourse by blurring the real identity of Georgie Henley, who played Lucy, and the fictional identity of Lucy Pevensie.

"An Evolutionary Journey: *Pokémon*, Mythic Quests and the Culture of Challenge" by Lincoln Geraghty is a look at the entirely modern evolution of a narrative, from the Pokémon Japanese trading cards, to computer games, then on to the more conventional formats of television and feature films. Geraghty acknowledges that the transmedia aspects of the Pokémon franchise are important, but chooses to "focus more on the relationship between transmediality, the collecting ethos (catching and training Pokémon) and how this informs a culture of challenge as seen in the various films that depict Ash, Pikachu, and friends."

Karin Beeler's "*Diary of a Wimpy Kid*: Film Adaptation and Media Convergence for Children" continues the discussion of multi-media adaptation and storytelling with this look at film adaptations of Jeff Kinney's popular novel series, which first appeared as an online version in 2004, then as a series of print-form novels and finally in film adaptation. She also explores the impact of Kinney's companion text *The Wimpy Kid Movie Diary: How Greg Heffley Went Hollywood* (2011), which "serves as an educational tool to make children even more media savvy" since it helps them engage in a unique intertextual and intervisual play with the film. Beeler concludes that the *Diary of a Wimpy Kid* multimedia phenomenon clearly shows how text and film converge in an interconnected way, allowing multiple entry points to different media and in a different order whether one accesses the characters or storylines through Jeff Kinney's cartoon novel, through the films and their DVD/Blu-Ray bonus features or through Kinney's companion movie book and official website.

The final essay in this section is Dan North's "Nurturing Young Cinephiles: Martin Scorsese's *Hugo*." North has selected a interesting example of a film which is superficially both about and for children, yet "mobilizes discourses concerning the preservation of cinema's celluloid heritage, even as it embraces the new media technologies that are superseding it." *Hugo* is an adaptation of Brian Selznick's novel/picture book *The Invention of Hugo Cabret*, and the director, Martin Scorsese, has employed a range of modern digital filmmaking techniques to convey his personal fascination with the history of film. North's analysis of Scorsese's creation of "an aesthetic of wonderment" indicates that the director's spectacle of visual effects operates at a diegetic level for characters within the film and for young spectators watching the film.

The third section, "Cultural and Consumer Contexts for Children," explores the complex social contexts of films designated for children in American and international contexts. In "Russian Animated Films and Nationalism of the New Millennium: The Phoenix Rising from the Ashes," Michel Bouchard and Tatiana Podyakova seek to "provide a short history of animated films in both the Soviet Union and Russia and ... analyze the ways in which concepts of nation, nationality, and gender are both caricatured and reaffirmed in the (pseudo-)history presented in contemporary Russian animated films set in ancient Rus." The authors note that because of the unrestrained access to foreign films on DVD in post–Soviet Russia, animated films with a pro-nationalist message are subsidized by the Russian government. The reason for this is that these subsidized animated films, whether they are consumed as DVDs, Internet stream or theatrical release, are valued for the cultural message which is received by both children and adults. This essay is a valuable contribution to the discussion of children's film as a form of patriotic expression promoted by the state but also acknowledges that these films feature satirical or parodic depictions of characters in positions of power.

"Cosmopolitan Endurance: Migrant Children and Film Spectatorship," by Stephanie Hemelryk Donald, considers children as part of the diegetic world of film, as an audience component and, as film-makers themselves. It "discusses child responses to images of child migration in world cinema." The author considers the relationship of a child's perspective on a film to that of the film-makers and adult audiences. In contrast to more traditional studies, this essay does not assume that children are a passive and innocent audience. Hemelryk Donald's incorporation of an active workshop on film-making for the children involved in her study (U.K. children of Afghani backgrounds) proved that the audience of children were far from passive in their reception of films on migration. This study establishes some key parallels between migrant children as viewers of films about migration and as creators of film genres that incorporate the concepts of the journey, violence and insecurity.

Swarnavel Eswaran Pillai's "*Dubashi*: Indian Film, Cross-Cultural Communication and Screenings for Children" is a fascinating study of a film, *Dubashi* (*The Translator,* 1999), that was released in India on the cusp of the new millennium. The central figures of this film are a family of translators who work within the cultural framework of a nation with multiple languages. The film's means of distribution is of particular interest to our collection as it was screened in schools for a targeted audience of children. Funded by the Children's Film Society of India, *Dubashi* represents an effort to combine didactic elements with entertainment. The film also pays homage to the Italian neorealist classic *Bicycle Thieves* (1948) and reflects the potential of cinema to reach diverse audiences through translation/subtitles while still highlighting the themes of translation and interpretation that have been so central to the development of Indian cinema.

Lydia E. Ferguson's "Branding Blackness: Disney's Commodification of Black Culture in *Song of the South* and *The Princess and the Frog*" discusses the targeting of child audiences with results that are not as benign as those in the previous essay. Ferguson considers the negative representation of race in Disney films for children, using as her examples the infamous *Song of the South* (1946) and the more contemporary *The Princess and the Frog* (2009). After *Song of the South* Disney did not release a feature length film with African American protagonists until *The Princess and the Frog*, sixty-three years later. As Ferguson argues, the *Princess and the Frog* merchandise "has helped diversify the Disney Princess brand," but the film presents a problematic image of race for child viewers.

The final essay is concerned with the representation of consumer culture and race in film and television. Debbie Olson's "The Commodification of Ms. Penny Proud: Consumer Culture in *Fat Albert and the Cosby Kids* and Disney's *The Proud Family*" analyzes "how African American children are placed in a subject position that naturalizes the desire for full participation in American capitalist consumer culture as constructed and presented by the white media industry." She uses as her examples two television shows that were later adapted into feature length films. Olson indicates how the live action 2004 *Fat Albert* film is an "odd trip down memory lane" since it is replete with "cell phones, DVDs and rap music." In this sense it is geared more towards consumer culture than the original television series and therefore reinforces the avid consumption that is also promoted in *The Proud Family* television series and film adaptation.

These studies of film and related media experiences highlight the role of audience, film adaptation and specific cultural contexts in American and international films that are produced for children. Children have clearly become a key part of the participatory culture facilitated by a variety of media forms and consumer goods, an experience which can simultaneously provide educational opportunities for young cinephiles while still encouraging the future consumption of film, and in some cases, the creation of such visual narratives by young people.

Notes

1. Work by Henry Jenkins, *Convergence Culture: Where Old and New Media Collide* (New York: New York University Press, 2006) and Barbara Klinger, *Beyond the Multiplex: Cinema, New Technologies and the Home* (Berkeley: University of California Press, 2006) have contributed to this discussion.

2. In "DVD Screen Culture for Children: Theories of Play and Young Viewers," Karin Beeler indicates that play is an important component of the viewing experience for children. She argues that by "considering elements of unstructured and structured play, as well as the concepts of pretend play and point of view (POV) shots in the context of DVD viewing by children, scholars of film studies may also find themselves devoting greater attention to the kinds of media content that have previously been called mere add-ons." *Screening the Past* 32 (December 2011) (n.p.).

3. Hills' remarks were part of the general discussion following the presentation of papers in this SCMS conference session. March 19, 2014. Seattle, Washington.

4. Gary Trousdale's 2007 short film *Shrek the Halls* is a continuation of the diegesis of the *Shrek* films. It was first broadcast on television on November 28, 2007, then released as a DVD in 2008, which was included in some bundle packs of *Shrek the Third*.

Section One: Childhood, Adults and Films for Dual Audiences

No Place Like Home: Circumscribing Fantasy in Children's Film

Julian Cornell

> We must have towards that sacred thing, the mind of a child, toward that clean and virgin thing, that unmarked slate—we must have toward that the same responsibility, the same care about the impressions made upon it, that the best clergyman, the most inspired teacher of youth would have.—Will Hays, quoted in Bazalgette and Staples 94

Santa Claus and Hollywood have a long symbiotic relationship and not just Christmastime DVD and Blu-ray sales. As Hays' above sentiments indicate, the movie industry, like St. Nicholas, is a public guardian of childhood, of the innocent, pure, untainted child. As his star turns in *The Polar Express* (2004) and *Rise of the Guardians* (2011) show, Santa's life purpose is not just to administer presents to the worthy, but also to preserve a system of belief in innocence from the harsh vagaries of the world, to provide a bulwark for fantasy against reality. As Nicholas St. Nick explains to raw recruit Jack Frost in the latter film, the role of potent mythical figures such as himself and his cohorts—the Easter Bunny, the Tooth Fairy and The Sandman—is to manage children's identity by preserving their steadfast belief in their own innocence and distance from real world (i.e., adult) concerns. The same stewardship is apparently entrusted to politicians and pundits. Twice during his unsuccessful run for the presidency Senator Robert Dole castigated the American film industry for prioritizing excessive sex and violence over family friendly content, a kerfuffle so edifying it was deemed worthy of a June 1995 *Time* cover story. The senator praised both Disney's *The Lion King* (1994) and the James Cameron–Arnold Schwarzenegger action-espionage-comedy *True Lies* (1994), and one year later opined that 20th Century–Fox's science fiction epic *Independence Day* (1996) was patriotic, wholesome fare while *Natural Born Killers* (1994) and *True Romance* (1993) were beyond the pale of propriety. Dole was ridiculed for tabbing the ultra-violent *True Lies* and blithely destructive *Independence Day* as family films and reporters duly noted that both Schwarzenegger and Fox chief Rupert Murdoch were high profile advocates for the Republican cause (Lacayo 24). In both speeches, Dole's hackneyed encomiums were secondary to his confusion about what kinds of films were consonant with the Republican Party's "Family Values" platform (Masters 64).

While the candidate's comments could be dismissed as an obvious attempt to spark controversy and garner sound bite time on network news broadcasts, it is possible to situate the Senator's statements within the larger context of the culture wars of the 1990s that pitted the Republican old guard of Dole and George H.W. Bush against baby boomer Democrats President Bill Clinton and Vice President Albert Gore, Jr. Thus when Dole noted that there was more to a film than just an afternoon's diversion, he was tying the question of what constitutes family and children's entertainment to an ideologically inflected conception of American nationhood. When politicians like Dole and media pundits publicly debate the content and parameters of family and child "appropriate" films they raise such questions as: How and where does a culture locate its children, who can dictate that process of definition, and what is the purpose of entertainment for children? At the same time, Dole, unwittingly perhaps, stumbled upon another conundrum: Exactly what is a family film, or, rather, what movies are appropriate viewing for young children? Such questions have obtained for decades, but recent technological innovations, such as Blu-ray, on-demand video, Internet streaming and the multi-channel cable environment, along with the centrality of the children's film to the American film industry—successful children's films often prove lucrative at the box office and are important to Hollywood's bottom line—suggest that such questions are more relevant than ever.

As Dole and Hays (and St. Nick for that matter) indicate, a children's film is assumed to have *value* for society; it is valued if it can serve a readily apparent cultural-pedagogical function—the same one assigned to educators, clergy and authors—to turn children into citizens. If, as Altman contends, "film genres are functional for their society" then children's film is a genre defined by its purpose and intention, more than by subject matter, narrative conventions, thematic structures and visual vocabulary (Altman 26). The children's film is a conscious intervention in the construction of a particular type of spectator, one assumed to be influenced profoundly by the viewing experience. The audience, child and parent, is presumed to get something out of the film in excess of pleasure or entertainment, and that is a lesson, a moral, a sense of identity, a life enhancing pedagogical experience. Thus, in the children's film, ideological/pedagogical effects are normally overt, rather than sublimated as in many films of other genres.

Of course, Hays and Dole were merely reiterating the long held belief that potentially entertaining and pleasurable texts for children should also serve pedagogical purposes. Shavit argues that the idea that books for children should contribute to their spiritual welfare and education has not changed substantially since the mid–eighteenth century. Though specific ideas about children and what is appropriate for them to read, or see, have given historical and social co-ordinates, the notion that books have to be pedagogically appropriate and contribute to the child's emotional and social development remains the dominant force in cultural production (Shavit 26–27). What has also changed little, given the focus on moral, ethical and educational outcomes, is that an overwhelming number of narratives for children highlight personal heroism, individual growth and identity formation rather than historical process or collective agency.

Central to such pedagogy is the very idea of innocence itself. As Rose notes, children's literature of the eighteenth and nineteenth centuries was influenced frequently by the educational philosophies of John Locke and Jean-Jacques Rousseau, who held that rather than being born marked with original sin, the child entered the world *tabula rasa,* beginning life in an innocent state. Influenced by Rousseau and Locke, nineteenth century American intellectuals and educators began to insist that the child's entry into the adult world must be carefully managed and regulated, their innocence preserved as long as possible to guard against a difficult and fraught transition to adulthood (Jackson 17–18).

While innocence indicates lack of experience in matters economic and historical, knowledge socially constituted and acquired through interaction with the world, Rose emphasizes that it is in the relationship of sexuality, that which is innate, to innocence where the mundane, political uses of innocence are both thrown into sharpest relief and where language is rendered most ambiguous. For when Freud undermined prevailing notions of childhood's sexual innocence, he challenged adult sexuality, identifying how child's "sexuality (bisexual, polymorphous, perverse) threatens our own at its very roots. Setting up the child as innocent is not, therefore, repressing its sexuality—it is above all holding off any possible challenge to our own" (Rose 4). Children's literature acts to conceal the uncertain boundaries between adult and child sexuality identified by Freud. Thus innocence, as a discursive trajectory, reveals itself as "not a property of childhood, but as a portion of adult desire" a yearning for fixity in terms of identity, for coherence in subjectivity (Rose xii). This enables children's literature and film to define childhood in terms of opposition with adulthood, rather than in terms of continuity or contiguity. Innocence emerges as a site of truth, which can be marshaled in an attempt to preserve a society's imperiled values, as children are "innocent and can restore that innocence to us" (Rose 43–44). Dole and Hays' appeals to that kind of innocence reflect a similar process.

The site of childhood innocence can be configured topographically, as a place where the culture's purest, oldest, essential values are maintained, kept free of the corrupting influence of (post)modernity. Thus, because of the cultural equation of children and innocence, childhood can be figured along both spatial and temporal axes. Woodson suggests that childhood, is a "temporary and temporal classification" and like race and gender "acts as a set of power relationships" mapping "ideological (and moral) assumptions in the conceptualization of what it 'is' to be a child as well as what it 'ought' to be" (Woodson n.p.). Childhood is primarily defined as a "specific kind of space" which is created by figuring children as other to adult, as being constituted by the very places that are reserved for exploration and play. The spatial dimensions of childhood are reflected in the preponderance of animated films in children's entertainment; whether hand drawn or computer generated, animation's asymptotic relationship to reality is marshaled to create vivid experiential cinematic places where concerns, anxieties and prevailing dilemmas about childhood are played out, figured spatially. More than merely providing visually intriguing backdrops against which narrative action can transpire, these animated worlds, can act as sites of the reaffirmation of innocence or the discovery of identity. It is only by reaching Santa's metropolis following a treacherous journey from Grand Rapids, Michigan, to the North Pole on Christmas Eve on the titular train, that the unnamed protagonist of *The Polar Express* (listed in the credits as Hero Boy) can have his vacillating belief in Kris Kringle validated and his fading innocence about a central story of childhood's mythical character returned to him. The Hero Boy is then rewarded for both his virtuous actions and his faith by being granted any gift he desires. He eschews the opportunity to acquire a hip toy in favor of a bell from Santa's sleigh, a modest token of his inherent goodness embodied in his retention of innocence. The evocative, shimmering animated environment of *The Polar Express* acts as a fantasy site where it becomes possible for innocent belief to be reaffirmed, where a narrative about childhood and storytelling— characterized by innocent conviction and uncomplicated belief, separate from harsh realities and cynicism—can reverse the trajectory of the journey from innocence to knowledge (the film begins with the protagonist researching the North Pole and Santa's existence, finding only evidence of Claus' status as fable). The North Pole figures prominently in *Rise of the Guardians* as well, but in a film that meticulously creates beautifully detailed visions of several cities, such as New York City and Moscow, it is significant that the place where belief about childhood myths can be reestablished is not an actual urban area, but is instead the fictional middle American small town Burgess. In an idealized, mythical

America, the child denizens of this ideologically resonant site vanquish the Boogeyman Pitch Black alongside the mythical quintet of Jack Frost, Santa Claus, the Tooth Fairy, the Easter Bunny and the Sandman. Led by Jamie, the one child who still retains steadfast belief in childhood's stories, the innocence of the children is reclaimed from the peril of despair, cynicism and trauma represented, indeed proffered by the Boogeyman (who is desperate to have children believe in him instead of the benign protectors of innocence).

Temporality implicates topography. Childhood is connected with time in a different way than adulthood. Children will age and mature, but childhood, as a space, is delimited, divorced from time itself, outside of history. As the years accumulate and time passes, children leave the space of childhood and enter the world of adulthood but childhood, as a place, remains fixed. In cultural narratives such as films, children can be defined by their transient residency along these spatio-temporal co-ordinates, in this space characterized by innocence. As Bazalgette and Buckingham note while, "childhood is often seen as another world" a place "we have all visited," the passage of time renders that space "inaccessible to us except through the distortions of memory" (Bazalgette and Buckingham 1). Perhaps not coincidentally, canonical children's literature and film is often referred to as time-less, indicating a desire to view childhood as standing apart from historical process.

For adults, the putative innocence of childhood also exists as a specific form of cultural memory—nostalgia. As Giroux argues, nostalgia, when expressed as childhood innocence through corporate entertainment "excludes the subversive elements of memory" which removes it from the "historical, social and political context that defines it as a process of cultural production that opens rather than closes down history" (Giroux 47). Thus, innocence for adults can be said to express a desire to exist outside and before history and culture. Innocence, and, by extension, the child, is fixed temporally and spatially, simultaneously providing a site of cultural origin and standing outside of culture, naturalizing culture by existing outside history while residing in a primordial past and fixing the present by simultaneously containing the past and the future. For example, Giroux argues that Disney "almost synonymous with the very notion of American popular culture" engages in an overt "politics of innocence" in order to "secure its moral and pedagogical legitimacy" (Giroux 45). Disney products utilize innocence to "aggressively rewrite the historical and collective identity of the American past" and an attempt to "produce specific, knowledge, values and desires," which masks the "institutional and ideological power of a $4.7 billion multi-national conglomerate that wields enormous influence pedagogically and politically" (Giroux 45).

Since childhood innocence is a text, childhood itself is frequently the meta-narrative of the children's film, possessing a specific trajectory, one that must be continually articulated on the one hand, and strictly controlled and policed on the other. As Bazalgette and Buckingham remark, media's address to the child "is about instructing children in the ways of the adult world and their eventual place within it" (Bazalgette and Buckingham 3). Many children's films instruct the child in just that—how to be a child, how to fulfill adult expectations and desires for and about childhood. For example, the original version of *Willie Wonka and the Chocolate Factory* (1971) has an overtly didactic narrative. In four distinct scenes, a child violates Wonka's directives and prohibitions and is gruesomely punished for being impulsive, impetuous or just plain selfish. Each sequence ends with the Lilliputian-like Oompah Loompahs singing a song which reinforces the moral of the scene for the children in the theater—do not be greedy, do not eat too much, do not be a brat, do not watch too much television, delay gratification. Charlie, the good child, only violates a prohibition when his grandfather insists that he do so, and his innate innocence and goodness are reinforced by both his poverty and his willingness to relinquish his invaluable candy prize to atone for his guardian's misdeed. The film is an example of educational children's film in that it has a plainly stated moral lesson. The *Toy Story* films even situate the innocence of the child within the commodity itself and to express it in terms of the toy, the locus of much child desire and fantasy. In the first *Toy Story* (1995), Buzz Lightyear is that innocent; he is the child-like figure who is ignorant of his purpose, of his identity, while Woody experiences a similar state of being in *Toy Story 2* (1999). Since the child spectator knows that Buzz is a toy (even though the character himself is initially, blithely unaware of his true nature), the child is placed in the position of an adult, of having more knowledge than the innocent. The child is reflected back upon itself by the narrative; childhood, the state before knowledge and self-identity, is presented as the text for the child, and as a process which requires the acquisition of an identity, albeit one that exists ambivalently alongside innocence. For instance, in *Rise of the Guardians*, the narrative delineates the journey to self-knowledge of Jack Frost, depicted as a boy of about fourteen who can control the winter elements but suffers amnesia regarding his true identity. As part of his battle with the Boogeyman (known in the film as Pitch Black) Jack learns (courtesy of the Tooth Fairy's archiving of his baby teeth—a compelling symbol of the physical and emotional maturation of the child) that three hundred years prior he had sacrificed his life to save his little sister, and the God-like Man-in-the-Moon, touched by his martyrdom, transformed him into an immortal winter sprite albeit at the expense of his memory. Initially reluctant to join the other, more adult guardians, and dismissive of their concern with preserving childhood, since he is invisible to children (a symbol of their lack of belief in Jack Frost as a mythical figure on par with better known mystical beings), Jack eventually comes to accept his rightful place as a protector of innocence by defeating the Boogeyman. Along with knowledge about his origins, Jack also learns that his talisman, his "center" as St. Nick calls it, the defining trait of childhood as a state of being and idea that he will specifically guard and symbolize is Fun. Where Claus is Virtue, Sandman is Dreams, Bunny is Hope and The Tooth Fairy is Memory, Jack is Play; in his journey to knowledge, Jack emerges as the protector of another essential component of innocence.

Less overtly, films such as *Babe* (1995), *Madagascar* (2005), *Toy Story*, and *Rise of the Guardians* are also about childhood. *Babe*, an ingenious hybrid of live-action and computer generated animation, is an apparently simple tale of one piglet's search for its life's purpose. Through compelling animal point of view shots, innovative use of anthropomorphic special effects and an interpretative voice over, the film engages in the construction of the subjectivity of an innocent. The film, unlike the source novel by Dick King-Smith, depicts a childlike being's journey from innocence to knowledge. Babe learns her horrifying purpose and rejects it, refashions a new one for herself that upsets the established social order (though not patriarchy). Though there are no children in the film (there are two teenagers in a brief holiday scene) the story is, on a basic level, about childhood. Unsurprisingly childhood is constructed as a journey from innocence to knowledge, to finding one's purpose as a defining component of childhood itself. Indeed, childhood is the space that one leaves once a purpose has been found. This construction of childhood as text for children is characteristic of the Hollywood children's film. The narrative of *Toy Story* is essentially about Buzz's acceptance of his identity and reality; *Toy Story 2* details Woody's similar journey from innocence about his past, to knowledge about his place in the world; the striking and sobering *Toy Story 3* (2010) directly confronts mortality. In a sense, childhood is the text itself, the meta-narrative of the children's film, regardless of whether the protagonist is a child or an animal.

Life lessons, and a didactic narrative mode which enables their transmission, are part of the adult audience's expectations of what a film should provide in excess of entertainment, to manage and contain, constrain even, the evocative fantasies of the fully realized cinematic environment. To be appropriate for the child viewer, the film must define place for the child, should teach the young viewer what defines childhood. In a sense this component of the genre, the coming of age tale, presents childhood to children as a space which one moves away from as they gain knowledge about the world. They also find that their present state of being, childhood, is incomplete, inferior to adults in terms of knowledge and power and self-definition. Thus, they learn their relationship to the adult world and what is expected of them. Santa's invocation for each of the young main characters in the climactic moments of *The Polar Express* emphasizes virtues that define the proper child for adults (self-esteem and confidence, humility, patience, community, friendship, belief in stories told to them), gentle admonitions underscored by the Conductor who imparts similar practical wisdom as he helps the children board the train for their ride home.

Often the premium placed upon didactic mode, clear morals and positive outcomes are at odds or in conflict with other aspects of the given film, particularly thrills and pleasure. Since films for children are also intended as entertainment, they address their young audience members, first and foremost in terms of adventure, fantasy and play, and, less apparently, in terms of desire for freedom, self-definition or anxiety, regarding their role in the family or place in the world. Structurally, play and adventure precede the moral and educational components of narrative. Much of the running time of *The Polar Express* is given over to a series of perils involving the train careening wildly out of control or the children falling quickly through space, adventures whose computer generated subjective camera mimics the point of view of first person video games and amusement park rides. When these thrills are exhausted, the moral is imparted; the climax of the series of chills and spills is a "lesson learned," to quote one the Conductor's final lines of dialogue. Some films delineate the correlation between fun and pedagogy through opening sequences that configure play as preceding didacticism. In another example, *Toy Story 2* begins with an extended sequence in which Buzz Lightyear plummets to an alien planet and does battle with a phalanx of androids. As Buzz falls to the planet's surface, the film shows a radical point of view, which mirrors the perspective of flight simulators. Buzz evades the robots and duels their mastermind Zurg, only to be vaporized. The sequence is then revealed to have been a video game, being played by Rex, the neurotic dinosaur. This material seems superfluous to the plot, which concerns Woody and his discovery of his true identity. Structurally, the sequence positions the child as participatory in the filmic experience, articulated simultaneously as play (video game) and adventure (Buzz's inter-galactic mission). Play in the film is thus configured as an extension of the child's own play and imagination. All four of the theatrical *Ice Age* films begin and end with a character who serves a key narrative purpose yet exists completely apart from the main characters Sid the Sloth, Manny the Mammoth and Diego the Smilodon. In a series of inventive and amusing vignettes, a sabertooth squirrel (identified in the credits as Scrat) goes to absurd and comical lengths to accumulate and stash acorns. Scrat's sequences end with his obsessive pursuit of sustenance accidentally setting off the cataclysmic ecological change that will motivate the plot of the central narrative, each one involving the three male friends embarking upon a physical journey away from impending disaster while becoming better and more effective father figures. The Scrat-Acorn episodes commence the films on a light and humorous note, which precedes a danger filled, death-defying adventure and its lessons which continually return to the affirmation of patriarchy. Crucially, these types of openings address the child in terms of entertainment, spectacle and pleasure, not in terms of educational or moral value. In order to teach delay of gratification, the films must first demonstrate pleasure, and then frame it through lessons.

This is conveyed through the distinct rhetorical strategies of the genre, analogous in many ways to children's literature. Rose contends that children's literature originally had a narrational voice that was overtly adult and didactic as authors consciously laid bare their pedagogical intentions. Thus, children's fiction started with the simultaneous containment of two distinct modes of address, sharply divided and readily apparent, expressed in the same words, but constituting separate languages. In the twentieth century, this mode of address, has gradually given way to increasing narrativization, dispensing with the overtly pedagogic voice. Instead "adult intention has more and more been absorbed into the story and, apparently, rendered invisible" (Rose 59). The children's film can be characterized as having not only this type of invisible, dual mode of address, but also a reflexive sense of that duality. There is the cognizance of the particularity of the audience in the address, but also the acknowledgement that the two primary segments of the audience, children and parents, will apprehend the film in markedly different ways.

For Shavit many canonical children's stories (e.g., *Alice in Wonderland*, *Gulliver's Travels*, *Robinson Crusoe*, fairy tales), began as adult literature giving them an ambivalent status. These works are ambivalent in that they are not only open ended and flexible, but "belong simultaneously to more than one system" of literature, (belong to both children's and adult's canons), and "are read differently (though concurrently)," by these two groups of readers, who "diverge in their expectations, as well as in their norms and habits of reading" (Shavit 66). In order for the ambivalent text to be included in the canon of children's literature, it must have a certain level of *sophistication*; to facilitate this, a writer must address "the text both to children and to adults and [only] by pretending it is for children can the writer make possible the dual acceptance of the text" (Shavit 67). The manner in which the book addresses each component of the audience is different, but must be contained in the same language. The text contains at least two different, co-existing models, systems of convention, expectation and narrative structure; one is established, conventional and addressed to the child, while the other, addressed to the adult reader, is more original, sophisticated, and based upon distortion, adaptation, parody or renewal of the conventional models (i.e., intertextuality). The child likely ignores the less conventional model, while the adult can decode both (Shavit 68).

Contemporary children's films mirror Shavit's notion of sophistication. Since the 1990s in particular, children's films have seen a deployment of the divergent mode of address, but one that acknowledges the presence of adult spectators. Adults are addressed in terms of irony and reflexivity, via generic intertextual relays. Even more crucially, intertextual references to popular culture and to cinema history, often ancillary to plot and character development, are meant to appeal to adults' superior cultural knowledge. This has the additional effect of reinforcing childhood innocence for adult spectators, of separating them from children through jokes young viewers are not expected to fathom. As Rose argues, children's entertainment "sets up a world in which the adult," as generator of knowledge and text, "comes first, and the child comes after (reader, product and receiver), but where neither of them enter the space in between" (Rose 2). Intertextual filmic references reinforce the notion that interpreting narrative is a function of adulthood and specific, learned cultural knowledge. Examples are literally innumerable: *Ice Age* (2002) structurally mimics John Ford's *3 Godfathers* (1948); *Rise of the Guardians* makes visual and story references to superhero team-up films. In *Toy Story 2*, for example, when Buzz hops from one stone to another *Thus Spake Zarathustra*—the main theme from *2001: A Space Odyssey* (1968)—is heard; Buzz's persona is derived from Captain Kirk of *Star Trek*; the sequence where Woody learns that he is a valuable toy from the 1950s is shown as a parody of Kinescoped black and white television shows; Far-Far Away, the villain Farquard's fiefdom in *Shrek* (2001), is a parody of Disneyland; the mating calls of the Emperor Penguins in *Happy Feet* (2006) are a series of classic rock hits, with the protagonist Mumble's parents meeting and coupling to dueling strains of Elvis Presley's "Heartbreak Hotel" and Prince's "Kiss."

Perhaps no children's film was as pivotal in this regard as Disney's *Aladdin* (1992). Many visually evocative rousing musical set-pieces in the film are built around Robin Williams' seemingly improvised riffing, finding visually ingenious equivalents for his kinetic stand-up routine, careening from impersonations of one pop culture icon to another (Ed Sullivan, Groucho Marx, Jack Nicholson, Elvis, Arsenio Hall, Robert DeNiro as Travis Bickle, Ethel Merman, William F. Buckley, et al.—persons with which young children are likely unfamiliar.) These free-form transformations are visualized in terms of a plasticity that enables the Genie to continually morph from one character to another. Wojcik-Andrews suggests that the Genie reduces all of twentieth century pop culture "to a series of one-liners" rendering his omnipotence as "harmless innocence" (Wojcik-Andrews 214). This type of playful semiotic mixing reconstitutes popular culture in terms of its very inappropriateness to the children's movie as one source of humor for the adult audience. A recurring gag in *Shrek* involves the titular character and his friend Donkey making sexual innuendos about the unctuous Lord Farquard's anatomical inadequacies, while both *Shrek* and *Shrek 2* (2004) utilize popular songs with very adult themes—Leonard Cohen's "Hallelujah" in the former and Nick Cave and the Bad Seeds' "People Ain't No Good" in the latter to articulate moments of crisis and loneliness for the main characters. Several of the featured musical numbers in *Happy Feet* were made famous by performers noted for the sexual and/or androgynous aspects of their star personae (Prince, Freddie Mercury, Elvis Presley, P!nk, Salt-n-Peppa, etc.). Such content serves to underscore the child spectator's lack of knowledge about popular culture, an innocence which is constructed *by* the film and the larger culture; thus, the films sanction the adult to imagine the child as innocent, to construct childhood as separate from adults in terms of cultural and cinematic knowledge.

Adults are also addressed in terms of sophistication by the genre's reliance upon special effects. Part of the appeal of *Babe* for adults was that the computer generated effects made it look as if the animals were really talking; in the *Toy Story* films, the impressive computer generated images (CGI) provided a fully realized environment and compelling characters, and the same is true of the claymation puppets of *Wallace & Gromit: The Curse of the Were-Rabbit* (2005), the striking fantasy realms of the heroes *Rise of the Guardians*, the arctic landscapes of *The Polar Express* and the isolated island village of *How to Train Your Dragon* (2010) (whose flight and water effects are simply stunning). Special effects and the technological innovation they demonstrate become a primary text in the adult address of the children's film, legitimizing the children's film for the older spectator. Adults realize the movies' technical achievement, the asymptotic relationship of the spectacle to reality, rather than fantasy, which is the province of children.

Still, what prevents an adult spectator from responding to the film in exactly the same manner as a child is the recourse to the genre's social function—to provide life lessons for kids. The didactic mode of address, the presentation of the moral at a narrative's dénouement, is where child and adult viewing experiences are expected to merge. While as Hays and Dole demonstrate that it frequently is assumed that the moral lessons imparted are meant for the children, it is equally possible to conceive of the didactic mode of address being intended for adults. As Rose argues, to claim that the message of a children's cultural product is just for children is to confuse adult intention with the child imagined by the text (Rose 1). Didacticism is meant, not only to construct the child, but the adult by extension. While a life lesson may or may not be transparent to the child, they are assumed to be unable to separate it from the entertainment and pleasure, from the free-play of fantasy. What the child learns from the children's film is that fantasy and pedagogy, entertainment and edification are not separate but intermingled and interdependent. Parents may also recognize the social assumptions about the regulation of play and desire in children; thus the didactic address re-assures the adult spectator that the film has value above pleasure for the child.

More importantly, the didactic address allows adults to manage children's pleasure. As the films address the child spectator in terms of entertainment and play, there is always the danger that the fantasy elements will exceed established social boundaries. As they construct the child and childhood there is always the possibility that children will read the films differently, finding pleasure in the wrong places, and behavioral models in the denigrated, outlaw roles, or ignore the moral outcome in part or entirely due to the thrills occasioned by the overwhelming special effects action, particular those that are repeatable due to their similarity to video games and amusement park rides. According to Thacker, there are numerous ways in which children derive pleasure from the text. Re-reading, or re-viewing, one of the primary ways children express pleasure in relation to texts is a form of re-writing, a process by which the reader engages the author and the narrative. Thacker states that pleasure is not located in, "the fulfillment of expectation, but [in] *the ways in which expectations are fulfilled* that create the pleasure of self-aware readers" (Thacker 4, emphasis in original). The easy availability of modern distribution technologies, from DVDs, to Internet ready Blu-ray players, on-demand streaming and cable multiplexing have enhanced the relationship between the child and the text, facilitating re-viewing and re-experiencing the same pleasures which, as Thacker's analysis implies, is a key pleasure for many children. This has also enabled the fetishization of a given text by the child. Thacker suggests that it is in the use of the text where the child locates its pleasure, in its ability to engage with text and to re-write through re-reading, and thus repeated, re-viewing (Thacker 7). In other words, the child reimagines, fantasizes even, its relationship with a given text or film. A didactic mode would seem to mitigate against the possibility of children deriving solely pleasure from spectacle, and would manage and direct such re-watching through a concomitant redeployment and reinscription of pleasure within the framework of pedagogy.

As Thacker suggests, the pleasure that the child derives from re-reading and re-writing indicates an active and subjective awareness of desire that can be sanction the construction of the self through an engagement with the text by which "the reader can perform the role of author" [Thacker 7]. Constituting the self through the exertion of authority over the meaning of the text which is achieved through rereading, also can be seen as a means by which children "test and challenge" the symbolic order of language. For Thacker, "texts that invite the reader to play with meaning, to question the authority of the author's voice, or to think for themselves in a "writerly" way are threatening to a society that wishes to construct the child as conformist and obedient" (Thacker 9). Similarly, when a culture produces entertainment artifacts, it engages the spectator at the level of desire and anxiety. In children's culture, according to Steinberg and Kincheloe, desire needs to be colonized, to take a subordinate position to the repression of that desire in order to construct both conscious and the unconscious identity of the child (Steinberg and Kincheloe 8). By building fully realized dream-like, fantasy worlds, such as the ones in *Toy Story, Ice Age, Rise of the Guardians, Shrek, How to Train Your Dragon, Happy Feet*, et al., worlds which often create a space where pleasure, adventure and desire meet, entertainment culture presents the possibility of a more intense, more fulfilling experience than that offered by schooling or other public spheres. Fantasy offers the child access to their unconscious in a potentially uncontainable way. Many critics, such as Wojcik-Andrews, Giroux, Bazalgette, Staples, Steinberg and Kincheloe, all note that contemporary children's entertainment attempts to channel this fantasy into consumerism and commodification, what Zipes in *Breaking the Magic Spell* termed the "instrumentalization of fantasy" (Zipes 104).

When evocative and glimmering fantasy spaces are created for children outside the family structure, there is always potential for subversion. Neil Sinyard suggests that Hollywood films must contain such fantasy; the most feasible resolution is to treat adventure as a temporary aberration, to return the child comfortably to the bonds of family (Sinyard 19). Fantasy is also related to leisure time, and children have to be taught how to work leisure time in our society, to utilize imagination in a productive fashion. In order for children to manage the subversive, fantasy must exist within proscribed limits. The canonical film *The Wizard of Oz* (1939) is perhaps the starkest and most edifying example of this process. A dense, multilayered and resonant text, *The Wizard of Oz* is ultimately about fantasy narrative itself—about how fantasy works for the individual and for society through wish-fulfillment, empowerment and containment. The film expresses in oppositional terms how fantasy operates in terms of adult prescriptions for childhood, holding in tension the desire for change and the sobering acknowledgement that freedom is impossible because of society's demands, which children learn, over time, to internalize. Fantasy is great, but must be circumscribed by a pre-existing value system that structures the way in which children and by extension adults are supposed to experience and evaluate fantasy. But even more importantly it tells us about fantasy itself—the multiple, one might say infinitely possible readings that are proof of how fantasy works, how it is potentially empowering and dangerous and how social institutions, in this case Hollywood, work to contain it. As Rushdie wonderfully delineates in his BFI monograph, *The Wizard of Oz* demonstrates how fantasy can be so subversive, so formidable, that it resists even the most strenuous attempts to contain it within the demands of cultural pedagogy. For Rushdie, the film's cloying ending is untrue to the film's anarchic spirit, as the empowering fantasy of Dorothy's sojourn in the Land of Oz is so compelling, so evocative that it resists the literal circumscription by the narrative's framing story and the renowned assertion that "there is no place like home" (Rushdie 56). No place, perhaps, save fantasy itself.

Children's films reveal adult assumptions about the role of fantasy in children's lives. Instrumentalizing fantasy is one strategy to manage children's pleasure, but, perhaps a more potent way is to encode pleasure into narrative and reading, and to render it in socially acceptable, didactic forms. Rose argues that fantasy is rationalized by removing it from the domain of the unconscious, which is often irrational and non-narrative, and then adapting it to a pre-determined, culturally specific notion of narrative cohesion, subjective identification and story-telling. This move serves to unite fantasy and realism in service of a particular narrative form, to make fantasy coherent and amenable to moral and ethical concerns (Rose 64–65). In a sense, this necessitates retention of realism in fantasy, which aids in containment. The conceptualization of fantasy in the children's film can be understood in terms of its interplay with realism (where realism is also understood to mean the relationship of the narrative to real world adult and child concerns, on the one hand, and the utilization of the continuity editing aesthetics of the mainstream, commercial film on the other). In aesthetic terms, there is the desire that animation should approximate reality as well, which, as noted, is part of the adult address in the films such as the *Toy Story* movies, *Babe, How to Train Your Dragon, Happy Feet, Ice Age* and *Rise of the Guardians,* to name but a few. The contemporary technologically marvelous blockbuster, special effects driven and CGI generated, provides an overwhelming, kinetic spectacle and experience that creates a vivid, fully realized fantasy world, but also utilizes and approximates the visual style and language of live action, mimicking the realist aesthetics of the mainstream Hollywood film. The recourse to realism—visual, psychological, spatial and temporal—contains the fantasy within known limits by figuring them against well-worn narrative patterns and didactic intentions. While many children's stories feature strong magical elements, it is their relation to realism, to children's lives, and to conventional narrative patterns, that is key in the children's film. Fantasy in the children's film is not about transgression but about free associative play, within proscribed limits, those with some relation to the real, to lived experience. Again, this type of containment is the basis of the overt assumption that a children's film must administer a pedagogical function. Leisure and fantasy must serve society or they would be destabilizing. In a conventional manner, the potentially liberating fantasy of a film such as *Happy Feet*, where Mumble struggles against prejudice, bravely attempting to chart his path in the world, is redirected in the latter part of the film to be a more conventional story of a son's struggle to win his father's approval and to become a hero for his community (Mumble's dancing and charisma alerts the world's leaders to the dangers of overfishing, thus leading to a ban on harvesting in polar waters), a hypothetically empowering fantasy constrained within the reestablishment of the family unit. Mumble not only earns his father's respect but is able to marry Gloria, the penguin of his heart song's desire.

One recurring narrative element of children's film, and a fantasy that requires containment, lest it pose a challenge to the didactic intentions of the genre is the rebellion against authority. Typically children's films have an authority figure against whom protagonists must measure themselves. One way that they test this boundary is through disobedience, rather than rebellion. These films allow for the expression of child desire, the wish to rebel against authority figures, but simultaneously contain these same fantasies within proscribed limits. The acclaimed *How to Train Your Dragon*, like *Happy Feet*, demonstrates the boundedness of such desire. The awkward Hiccup, like Mumble, is an outcast who desires no more than his father's love and who must defy his society's ideological foundations; he strives to prove his worth as a Viking King's son. While undergoing basic combat training, Hiccup befriends a fearsome dragon enemy, a Night Fury he dubs Toothless. He domesticates him and learns the secrets of dragon biology and psychology, knowledge that enables him to vanquish all bestial foes. Because this knowledge contradicts the heritage of the community, its entire social organization and reason for being, Hiccup's decision to show compassion for the marauding creatures is a violation of the father's law and power. At the conclusion of the film, Hiccup's knowledge and bravery and friendship with Toothless facilitates the defeat of the tyrannical Dragon Lord—the Red Death. This empowering fantasy—where the son proves the father wrong and usurps his authority—is contained by recourse to familiar narrative resolutions. Hiccup wins the heart of Astrid, established in the opening voice-over as the object of his desire, through masculine mastery of nature and knowledge, while also becoming a respected member of the community cherished by his father; the closing voice, which parallels the first but reverses the negative tone, details Hiccup's new found affection for his island home. Thus, the desires expressed at the outset of the film are all achieved by the end, Hiccup's desires for difference are not for rebellion but for acceptance, not on his own terms, but on the ones established at the start as the norm. Rebellion is fine, appropriate even, as long as it remains within limits of fantasy and has some desirable end result.

The children's film deployment of innocence presents an interesting conundrum. In order to present childhood for the child and adult spectators, the narrative must first display and subsequently trouble the same innocence that is the essence of childhood in the first place. In fact, one of the defining characteristics of the children's film is that the innocence depicted creates the conditions for its own erasure. Part of the dynamic tension in the children's film is that this innocence is rendered spatially and temporally, a space and time where the child exists before history and culture, but the film must move the child out of this time-space in order to provide the didactic lesson, and to appeal to adults' need to contain child pleasure and desire. In order to establish Mumble as savior for his community, for all man and penguin-kind even, *Happy Feet* whose promotional materials depict a light story about a dancing sea bird, also includes a bracing and melancholic narrative that presents four perilous different life and death obstacles Mumble must overcome to garner the love of his parents, future mate and community. The dramatic and intense storyline depicts the potential erasure of his community while it also raises racial issues (the different polar species are vocalized in terms of ethnic and racial identity, with some troubling stereotypes, particularly in Robin Williams' dual voicing of African American and Latino characters) and features a brief scene of psychosis when the hero is interred in an aquarium, producing a narrative constituted by adult subject matter. Mumble's travails follow a similar trajectory to Hiccup's where innocence is forever lost in the passage to adulthood, his appealing naïveté sacrificed in pursuit of knowledge about the diminishing food supply. And yet, the magical utopian resolution, where Mumble's charm and tap dancing leads to the salvation of his community and the planet demonstrates again the subtle limits of fantasy—the son's challenge to the father and patriarchy ends in marriage and child rearing (a baby penguin dances with the hero and Gloria in the finale indicating their successful union) and the transgressive figure's reabsorption into his society.

As noted, innocence can not only be construed as an adult rendering of childhood topographic terms, but as a space of being that is outside of time and history, that is timeless. It is a bounded space circumscribed by its ahistorical nature; it exists at this juncture of time and space. But, as Woodson argues, childhood is a power relation organized around knowledge, bound up in terms of pleasure, wish fulfillment, desire and lack of cultural experience. At issue is transgression, particularly of metaphorical boundaries; these are, in one sense, social boundaries, but in another they are physical. Childhood's bounded-ness forms a meta-discursive space for the articulation of an ideologically constituted configuration of childhood defined by innocence. In the children's film, boundaries are critical, indeed, the bounded-ness and the testing of borders is a crucial narrative structure device. Some examples of border crossing in children's film include the dangerous spaces outside the good home in *Toy Story*, or the identity confusing Al's Toy Barn in *Toy Story 2*; the piglet's refusal to be confined to the trough and barn in *Babe*; *Happy Feet* requires Mumble to cross several forbidding Antarctic milieus and swim all the way to Sydney; each of the four *Ice Age* films begins with Scrat causing an environmental disaster that forces the three protagonists to migrate to safer climes; in *Madagascar*, the narrative is motivated by the expressed wish of Marty the Zebra to leave the safety and predictability of New York City's Central Park and return to the Wild, the idealized idyllic natural habitat that he has never seen and for which he and his domesticated pals are spectacularly unprepared. When a naïve and ill conceived escape attempt from the zoo goes awry, Marty and his companions—Alex the preening celebrity Lion, Melman the neurotic, hypochondriac giraffe and Gloria, the motherly, practical hippopotamus—are dispatched to a wildlife preserve in Kenya (though they run aground in the titular island nation due to the meddling of four stowaway penguins.) Though unready for life in the Wild, in the paradise of Marty's dreams, it is in this natural environment, apart from the modern urban metropolis, that each of the main characters learns their true identity and reclaims their animal i.e., innocent nature. In these cases, the borders are rendered spatially and temporally; crossing these physical markers leads to a diminishment or destruction of the innocence of the child-like figure, and enables their forward progression toward adulthood.

Movies remain powerful forces in the socialization of children, even more so today, given the proliferation of media, and distribution mechanisms for viewing and re-viewing. Children's culture is not only the site of formative interchange with the adult world, it is also a recurrent, important space for interaction with peers. Given this daily contact with television, film and literature, the intermingling of entertainment and pedagogy, the media profoundly shape children's lives, not just in terms of forming their consciousness of themselves, but in helping them understand what it means to be a child in society. Films and cultural artifacts for children comprise what Steinberg and Kincheloe term *cultural pedagogy*, "the idea that education takes place in a variety of social sites including but not limited to schooling" (Steinberg and Kincheloe 4). The sites of children's cultural pedagogy are those places where power is structured and deployed, where desire is engaged, consciousness constructed and fantasy contained. Steinberg and Kincheloe insist upon the commercial nature of cultural pedagogy, structured by market ideologies, where "patterns of consumption shaped by corporate advertising empower commercial institutions as the teachers of the new millennium" (Steinberg and Kincheloe 4).

These critics have identified how the representational practices of children's entertainment profoundly shape children's lives in contemporary America; instrumentalization of children's fantasy and play is not confined to easily identifiable character types, themes and visuals, rather it is embedded in the very structures of films for children. Children's films present children with an identity and a subjectivity, destabilize them and then restabilize them in a particular manner, and in a given ideological framework which allows for a reinscription of adult authority and knowledge. In a genre where the return to home and to safe space is the only appropriate resolution, where behavior modeling is not just the overt theme, but also the underlying structural logic, children's films engage in a pedagogy of fantasy containment.

Works Cited

Aladdin. Dir. Ron Clements, John Musker. Walt Disney Pictures, 1992. DVD.
Altman, Rick. *Film/Genre.* London: British Film Institute, 1999. Print.
Babe. Dir. Chris Noonan. Universal Pictures, 1995. DVD.
Bazalgette, Cary, and David Buckingham. "The Invisible Audience." *In Front of the Children: Screen Entertainment and Young Audiences.* Cary Bazalgette and David Buckingham, eds. London: British Film Institute, 1995. 1–14. Print.
Bazalgette, Cary, and Terry Staples. "Unshrinking the Kids: Children's Cinema and the Family Film." *In Front of the Children: Screen Entertainment and Young Audiences.* Cary Bazalgette and David Buckingham, eds. London: British Film Institute, 1995. 92–108. Print.
Cave, Nick, and the Bad Seeds. "People Ain't No Good." *The Boatman's Call.* Reprise Records, 1997. CD.
Cohen, Leonard. "Hallelujah." *Various Positions.* Columbia Records, 1984. CD.
Giroux, Henry. "Are Disney Movies Good for Your Kids?" *Kinderculture: The Corporate Construction of Childhood,* 2d ed. Shirley R. Steinberg and Joe L. Kincheloe, eds. Boulder, CO: Westview, 1997. 31–52. Print.
____. "Memory and Pedagogy in the *Wonderful World of Disney.*" *From Mouse to Mermaid: The Politics of Film, Gender and Culture* Elizabeth Bell, Lynda Hass and Laura Sells, eds. Bloomington: Indiana University Press, 1995. 43–60. Print.
Happy Feet. Dir. George Miller. Warner Bros. Pictures, 2006. DVD.
How to Train Your Dragon. Dir. Chris Sanders, Dean DeBlois. Aardman Animation, 2010. DVD.
Ice Age. Dir. Chris Wedge, Carlos Saldanha. 20th Century–Fox, 2002. DVD.
Ice Age: Continental Drift. Dir. Steve Martino, Michael Thurmeier. 20th Century–Fox, 2012. DVD.
Ice Age: Dawn of the Dinosaurs. Dir. Carlos Saldanha, Michael Thurmeier. 20th Century–Fox, 2009. DVD.
Ice Age: The Meltdown. Dir. Carlos Saldanha. 20th Century–Fox, 2006. DVD.
Independence Day. Dir. Roland Emmerich. 20th Century–Fox, 1996. DVD.
Jackson, Kathy Merlock. *Images of Children in American Film: A Sociocultural Analysis.* Metuchen, NJ: Scarecrow, 1986. Print.
Lacayo, Richard. "Violent Reaction: Bob Dole's Broadside Against Sex and Violence in Popular Culture Sets Off a Furious Debate on Responsibility." *Time* 12 June 1995: 24–31.
The Lion King. Dir. Roger Allers, Rob Minkoff. Walt Disney Pictures, 1994. DVD.
Madagascar. Dir. Eric Darnell, Tom McGrath. DreamWorks Animation, 2005. DVD.
Masters, Kim. "Dole's Bomb Squad." *Time,* 12 August 1996: 64. Print.
Natural Born Killers. Dir. Oliver Stone. Warner Bros. Pictures, 1994. DVD.
The Polar Express. Dir. Robert Zemeckis. Warner Bros. Pictures, 2004. DVD.
Presley, Elvis. "Heartbreak Hotel." RCA Victor, 1956. CD.

Prince and the Revolution. "Kiss." *Parade: Music from the Motion Picture Under the Cherry Moon*. Warner Bros., 1986. CD.
Rise of the Guardians. Dir. Peter Ramsey. Paramount Pictures, 2012. DVD.
Rose, Jacqueline. *The Case of Peter Pan or the Impossibility of Children's Fiction*. London: Macmillan. 1994. Print.
Rushdie, Salman. *The Wizard of Oz: BFI Film Classics*. London: BFI, 1992. Print.
Shavit, Zohar. *Poetics of Children's Literature*. Athens: University of Georgia Press, 1986. Print.
Shrek. Dir. Andrew Adamson, Vicky Jenson. DreamWorks Animation, 2001. DVD.
Shrek 2. Dir. Andrew Adamson, Kelly Asbury, Conrad Vernon. DreamWorks Animation, 2004. DVD.
Sinyard, Neil. *Children in the Movies*. New York: St. Martin's, 1992. Print.
Steinberg, Shirley R., and Joe L. Kincheloe. "No More Secrets: Kinderculture, Information Saturation, and the Postmodern Childhood." *Kinderculture: The Corporate Construction of Childhood, 1*. Shirley R. Steinberg and Joe L. Kincheloe, eds. Boulder, CO: Westview, 1997. 1–30. Print.
Thacker, Deborah "Disdain or Ignorance? Literary Theory and the Absence of Children's Literature." *The Lion and the Unicorn* 24 (2000), 1–17. Print.
3 Godfathers. Dir. John Ford. Metro-Goldwyn-Mayer, 1948. DVD.
Toy Story. Dir. John Lasseter. Pixar Animation, 1995. DVD.
Toy Story 2. Dir. John Lasseter. Pixar Animation, 1999. DVD.
Toy Story 3. Dir. Lee Unkrich. Pixar Animation, 2010. DVD.
True Lies. Dir. James Cameron. 20th Century–Fox, 1994. DVD.
True Romance. Dir. Tony Scott. Warner Bros. Pictures, 1993. DVD.
2001: A Space Odyssey. Dir. Stanley Kubrick. Metro-Goldwyn-Mayer, 1968. DVD.
Wallace & Gromit: The Curse of the Were-Rabbit. Dir. Nick Park. DreamWorks Animation, 2005. DVD.
Willie Wonka and the Chocolate Factory. Dir. Mel Stuart. Paramount Pictures, 1971. DVD.
The Wizard of Oz. Dir. Victor Fleming. Metro-Goldwyn-Mayer, 1939. DVD.
Wojcik-Andrews, Ian. *Children's Films: History, Ideology, Pedagogy, Theory* New York: Garland, 2000. Print.
Woodson, Stephani. "Exploring the Cultural Topography of Childhood: Television Performing the 'Child' to Children." *Bad Subjects* 47, January 2000. Web.
Zipes, Jack. "Breaking the Disney Spell." *From Mouse to Mermaid: The Politics of Film, Gender and Culture*. Elizabeth Bell, Lynda Hass and Laura Sells, eds., Bloomington: Indiana University Press, 1995. 21–42. Print.
―――. *Breaking the Magic Spell: Radical Theories of Folk & Fairy Tales*, rev. and expanded ed. Lexington: University Press of Kentucky, 2002.

Songs for the Older Set: Music and Multiple Demographics in Shrek, Madagascar and Happy Feet

Stan Beeler

Since the year 2000, technological, social and demographic changes in North America and the United Kingdom have combined to develop a rapidly expanding market in film intended for children in theatrical release, on DVD and digital distribution (Netflix, iTunes, etc.). One might consider social changes the motivating force behind the evolution in distribution strategies that are accommodated through technological innovations. Parents in the twenty-first century are substantially more reluctant than their forebears to allow their children to attend a public venue without their direct supervision, so an afternoon or evening at the theater has become a regular ritual for many families. In fact, the family audience has become a significant component of the otherwise rapidly declining numbers of theatrical release attendees. This change in audience demographics has not escaped the attention of the multi-level corporations responsible for film production and marketing, and it has resulted in some alterations in the content and marketing of contemporary children's films. Films like the *Shrek*, *Happy Feet* or *Madagascar* series, although perfectly acceptable for children, have a level of cultural commentary with political, social and even sexual themes that can entertain adults. Often this second level of meaning is conveyed with music, both diegetic and non-diegetic, that is aimed at the older component of the audience.

Early in the twenty-first century, film trade publications like *Variety* began to note that the large Hollywood studios had become aware of the economic benefits of producing films aimed at a family audience. In 2002 Charles Lyons points out that "though the family event film is by no means new, studios have discovered lately that the up side of such pics can be more significant than that of teen-driven event pics.... And a family pic can be hyped to kids on the Internet or through McDonald's or Burger King promotions, product placement, merchandising, music and cross-promotions on MTV or Nickelodeon" (Lyons 69). The fact that family films can be cross-marketed and also provide revenue streams from the sale of ancillary merchandise meant that the precarious economic aspect of film production could be ameliorated somewhat through a number of methodologies.

The first, and perhaps the most obvious mechanism for ensuring the economic success of a film is the standard strategy of adaptation. As Linda Hutcheon has noted, "A best-selling book may reach a million readers; a successful Broadway play will be seen by 1 to 8 million people; but a movie or television adaptation will find an audience of many million more" (Hutcheon 5). If an existing children's book, comic or graphic novel is adapted to film, it brings with it a pre-existing audience who will be predisposed towards the new film and any ancillary products that are associated with the film adaptation:

> "They cross platforms," says Jane Startz.... "As a parent, if I were going to buy some spinoff product from a movie, I think it would be great to have something based on a book."
>
> As one analyst puts it, "It's not a question of profit maximization. It's a question of loss minimization. A property that already has some recognition is appealing to a vertically integrated machine where you have the pieces in place to create merchandise and a theme-park ride. The movie doesn't have to hit a grand slam [Bing and Dunkley 69].

As the above suggests, it is important to make the film attractive to both segments of the audience in order to maximize the profit. To ensure its initial success, children must be entranced by the characters and situations in a film, but their parents hold the purse strings and are more inclined to buy toys and trips to theme parks if they are favorably impressed by a film. Films like *Shrek*, which is an adaptation of a picture book by cartoonist William Steig, gain resonance because of the perceived superiority of the written word as an educational tool.

The positive effect of literary antecedents upon the marketing of a film is not absolute. Hutcheon points out that although association with the print media has a positive effect upon the reception of a film, the adult audience still demonstrates some reluctance to validate the film. She notes that this resistance to adaptations in visual media has not, however, resulted in a serious impact upon the success of these adaptations: "[A]ccording to 1992 statistics, ... 85 percent of all Oscar-winning Best Pictures [are] adaptations[.] ... adaptations make up 95 percent of all the miniseries and 70 percent of all the TV movies of the week that win Emmy Awards" (Hutcheon 4). Moreover, parents, as gatekeepers to their children's entertainment, often react favorably to the validation of entertainment through industry awards and prizes.

Although the venial need for films that appeal to both children and their parents may appear to be a new phenomenon brought about by the social concerns mentioned above, before television gained popularity in North America, animated films were an integral component of the double feature marketing of theatrical releases; animated features were commonly shown in theatres—along with newsreels—before the standard adult oriented double billed live action features. This placement encouraged an adult audience yet allowed children access in a de facto form of parental guidance category. Shull and Wilt summarize the economic imperatives behind the earlier split-market cartoons as follows:

> The cartoon industry could not afford to make only "kiddie" cartoons because its product would then be severely restricted in its appeal: to Saturday matinees in neighbourhood movie houses. Cartoons were an integral part of virtually all motion picture theatre programs for more than 30 years until the demise of the double feature system in the 1960s [Shull and Wilt 9].

The *Shrek* series of films has been remarkably successful in fitting the bifurcated demographic that has re-emerged in contemporary theatrical releases, and an important component of this appeal is the judicious use of popular music in the soundtrack. The original *Shrek* film appeared in 2001, and the first song that is heard begins just after the title character departs his outhouse to the anachronistic sound of a flush toilet is "All Star" by Smash Mouth. This song appeared on the popular music charts in 1999, just two years before the film's release and is aimed squarely at an adult demographic. Its lyrics recommend seizing the day and taking pleasure in the world, despite any perceived personal limitations. It seems strange to begin a children's film with a song based upon a theme of *carpe diem* with lyrics rhapsodizing the process of maturing. While the bouncy music plays, Shrek takes inordinate joy in his unique form of the quotidian pleasures of a solitary middle-aged existence. Children in the audience will revel in the visual representation of the "monster's" odd personal habits—using pages of a book for toilet paper, bathing in mud, flatulence in the bath, eating slugs and eyeballs—as the song's lyrics keep the adult component of the audience firmly grounded in the need to enjoy life while you have it. The initial joy of partaking in Shrek's fiercely independent existence is primarily motivated by the tempo and lyrics of the music. However, as Jane Caputi suggests, we soon see that "Shrek has become isolated in his swampland home. Lonely and somewhat embittered, he is emotionally immature and has no relationships with others" (Caputi 27).

As the narrative progresses and the confirmed bachelor/ogre develops then loses a relationship with the lovely princess Fiona, the complexity of the musical messages increases. To express the emotional depth of this pivotal point in the film it employs a song of lost love, "Hallelujah" (written by Leonard Cohen and performed by John Cale) in combination with cinematographic techniques worthy of a live action film intended for adults. Although the cinematography is subtle, and the level of metaphorical reference is appropriate for an adult film, the animated images are such that the youth component of the audience can maintain their interest despite the slow music and unhappy characters. The scene that employs "Hallelujah" is presented as a montage employing parallel editing to present Shrek as he wanders, his once-comfortable demesne confronted by symbolic representations of his empty life in counterpoint with Fiona's less than joyful preparations for impending nuptials with Lord Farquaad. Shrek's image is shown in broken reflection in a puddle of water on the ground with the connotation of his shattered life without Fiona. (Darren Aronofsky's decidedly adult film *Black Swan* [2010] employs the trope of a shattered mirror image in a similar fashion.) After presenting a distraught Shrek contemplating his own partial image spread across multiple reflective surfaces, the cross-cut moves to multiple images of Fiona reflected in a chandelier. However, her reflection consists of numerous, yet individually complete images, rather than a single, broken reflection. The subtle implication is that Fiona is considering a number of possible futures while Shrek is considering his life as incomplete without Fiona. This fits with Fiona's available choices; going through with marriage to Lord Farquaad or continuing her relationship with Shrek. Before the scene cuts back to Shrek's location, Fiona is shown with an overlay of window-panes in a grid over her face. The cage-like effect is symbolic of her feelings of entrapment that are engendered by her impending nuptials. Her social situation as a princess has made the option of remaining with Shrek much less viable. A similar technique is used in the opening scene of Sam Mendes' *American Beauty* (Mendes 1999). The protagonist of that film, Lester Burnham (Kevin Spacey) is shown reflected in the grid pattern of a spreadsheet on a computer monitor, indicating his feeling that he is trapped in a job that he loathes. We then are treated to cross-cuts of first Shrek and then Fiona sitting at one end of matching long, empty tables. One might compare this to Orson Welles' symbolic technique in *Citizen Kane* (Welles 1941) in which the deteriorating relationship between Kane (Orson Welles) and his wife Mary (Agnes Moorhead) is represented by increasing their distance from each other in a montage of breakfast conversations spanning several years. Rather than using Welles' technique of background conversations, the Shrek montage employs a stripped down arrangement of Cohen's poetic lament, "Hallelujah," in the background. It is fairly obvious that the lyrics of the song have been bowdlerized in the film version, although the general principle behind the modifications is not completely transparent; we do not know if it has been cut for reasons of duration, thematic relevance or to spare the sensibilities of children. Although this heartsick lament for a lost love remains substantially intact and is accessible to the adult component of the film's audience, the subtle theological elements—which also would not be readily available to the children—have been removed to maintain a secular, "on topic" presentation. Despite these alterations, the demographic bias to parents is maintained by both the choice of music and the artist. Cohen's initial 1984 release was not particularly popular, but cover versions by John Cale (1991), Jeff Buckley (1994), Rufus Wainwright (2003) and k.d. lang (2004) attest to the lasting popularity of the music. The Buckley version was used in the film, but Wainwright's nearly identical interpretation appears in the cross-marketed soundtrack compact disk. The choice of a relatively modern cover of older music is aimed at a much broader spectrum of adults than the opening Smash Mouth song, which would be familiar to younger parents, but not the older component of the audience. Cohen's music was popular among the Baby Boomers who would comprise a large proportion of grandparents dragooned into accompanying children to the film while parents might find the modern versions of "Hallelujah" by Cale and Wainwright more familiar.

The principle of using contemporary covers of "boomer music" is maintained in *Shrek* in the final scene of the film. Shrek and Fiona are married to the strains of the 1966 Neil Diamond/Monkees hit "I'm a Believer" (Monkees) (Diamond). The cover is by Smash Mouth with some vocals by Eddie Murphy, who voiced the Donkey in the film. The lyrics are on-topic for their use in the film, and not quite so adult-oriented as "Hallelujah" and "All Star." The visual elements of the wedding scene are similarly upbeat and accessible to both children and adults with one brief reference to the Macarena that may have political implications for the older American demographic.[1] The fact that a Monkees/Neil Diamond hit does not play to the intellectual abilities of the adults on the level of lyrics or visual complexity should not be surprising to anyone, but its familiarity to the older generation certainly sends a welcome to certain members of the audience. *The Monkees* TV series ran from 1966 to 1968 and was aimed at a demographic slightly older than the youngest component of *Shrek*'s audience. Nevertheless, *The Monkees*' combination of pop music and humor puts the live action series in a category similar to *Shrek* and other animated features that are the subject of this chapter.

As the use of the Monkees' song would suggest, another aspect of the techniques used to entertain the older portion of these split demographic films is the tendency to constantly reference other, more adult, films and television in combination with music that would appeal to an older crowd. Sometimes this is done in parodic form, but often the allusion is simply homage.

George Miller's 2006 Antarctic adventure *Happy Feet* (Miller and Coleman) is a prime example of this pattern. The opening diegetic medley sung by Norma Jean (Nicole Kidman) and Memphis (Hugh Jackman), the parents of Mumble (Elijah Wood) the protagonist, is comprised of covers of "Kiss" (Prince 1987) and "Heartbreak Hotel" (Presley 1956). The release dates of the original songs span a full generation (31 years) and would be familiar to an adult audience including both parents and grandparents of the children in attendance. The names of Mumble's parents, Norma Jean and Memphis, are intended to evoke stars of a bygone era. Norma Jean Mortenson was the original name of Marilyn Monroe (a star of films aimed at a decidedly adult audience) and Memphis was the hometown of Elvis Presley. Presley's films, although not as risqué as Monroe's offerings, were also aimed at a more mature demographic than *Happy Feet*'s primary target. The animated images created to represent the voices are designed to be similar to Monroe and Presley. Although these two figures would be more directly accessible to the oldest segment of the film's audience, their ongoing popularity would assure that even younger parents would understand and appreciate the reference. The fact that Mumble, Norma Jean and Memphis are all voiced by stars who made their reputations in contemporary features intended for adult audiences is consistent with the split-audience strategy of this film.

The opening medley of *Happy Feet* ends with a direct visual reference to another famous penguin film that was released the year before: the documentary *March of the Penguins* (Jacquet 2005). In *Happy Feet* the courting penguins are shown in a back-lit shot with heads and necks curving to form a perfect valentine heart shape. The documentary original of this stylized reference has a similar shot in which two penguins curve their heads together in a heart formation during a pre-mating grooming ritual. Although the popular music selected for the soundtrack of *Happy Feet* is predominantly aimed at the older demographic, the adult messages concerning ecology and the environment embedded in the narrative of *Happy Feet* do not rely as much on the music as the more subjective, emotional messages that are central to the *Shrek* films. Rather than attempting to use the music to directly convey its adult concepts, *Happy Feet* employs songs from the Beatles, the Beach Boys, the Jackson 5, Queen, and Stevie Wonder which serve to enhance a comfortable sense of familiarity for the adult audience; rather like a golden oldies radio station. Despite targeting the older members of the audience with its song selection, this music which was most popular in the 1960s, '70s and '80s, manages to entrance all of the multiple demographics of this film's audience.

The year before *Happy Feet* appeared, Eric Darnell and Tom McGrath's 2005 comic masterpiece *Madagascar* impressed audiences of all ages with its stunning visual design and witty use of filmic and musical references. Although the animal stars of *Madagascar* are familiar cartoon style figures, the island landscape of the film is based upon nineteenth century painting:

> For the bigger picture, Darnell turned to Henri Rousseau, the turn-of-the-(last)-century artist best known for his large, naive jungle paintings.
>
> "The thing about Rousseau that struck me was how he organized plants," Darnell said. "He still created a very exotic jungle in the paintings that he did, but there was a formality to it, and a composition, in the way things were structured within the frame, that was exciting to me" [Rosen].

This combination of references to art most commonly found in museums with popular culture of the twentieth and twenty-first centuries is typical of this film. Parents will be pleased by the reference to "high art" while their children will revel in the pure visual pleasure of the talking animals.

The music that is employed in the film is also designed to attract the older demographic. After the characters of the four New York City zoo animals that are the protagonists are introduced, we are shown the zebra Marty (Chris Rock) breaking out of the zoo and strutting down the streets of New York to the strains of the Bee Gees' 1977 hit "Stayin' Alive" (Bee Gees). The song first appeared as a film soundtrack in the opening credits to John Badham's paean to the disco era, *Saturday Night Fever* (Badham 1977). The scene from *Madagascar* is a precise homage to its equivalent in *Saturday Night Fever* with the exception of the protagonist; Marty the Zebra has replaced John Travolta. As the cocky lead characters strut in beat-matched splendor down the street, they encounter an attractive woman wearing a zebra patterned jacket. In both films the protagonist turns and slowly checks out the woman and then returns to his path. The visual reference to the 1977 film is unmistakable, but the placement in a "children's film" twenty-eight years later is proof positive that the filmmakers have more than a single demographic group in mind. In fact, it is more likely that *Saturday Night Fever* would be familiar to the grandparents of the primary audience than to the parents.

However, *Madagascar* does not neglect the younger parents in its clever web of references to other films. After the animals have been shipwrecked on the eponymous island, the lion Alex (Ben Stiller) has a dream about food that directly references Sam Mendes' 1999 film *American Beauty* (Mendes). In Mendes' film a dream sequence presents the protagonist, Lester Burnham (Kevin Spacey) lying on his back looking up at a naked teenaged girl on the ceiling. She is in a bed of rose petals that gently flutter down toward the bemused dreamer. In the *Madagascar* version, Alex the lion (Ben Stiller) dreams that he is lying on his back and looking up into a shower of juicy, red steaks while gently moving his arms from shoulder to hips. He is startled awake to find himself gently tasting the haunch of his friend Marty, the zebra (Chris Rock). The music, although not exactly the same in both films, is similar enough in tempo and instrumentation to impart an otherworldly air to the parodic animation. The two scenes are thematically similar in that they both represent a dream of forbidden desire, yet the animated version never once hints at sexuality in a way that would impinge upon the consciousness of the younger component of the audience.

As seen in the above examples, children's films regularly use popular music from an earlier generation to superimpose a more complex psychological narrative upon the more direct diegetic pleasures of a children's animated feature film. A wealth of intertextual references are applied to animated features through music and visual allusion to enhance the viewing experience for adults without directly presenting material that would be disturbing for the primary audience of young children. Although one might assume that popular music in contemporary adult film is always carefully selected to fit a single, highly specific demographic and target audience, anachronistic musical elements are, in fact, not uncommon. Filmmakers are well aware that musical taste is an important indicator of community and cultural bonding, yet music associated with a given cultural group or demographic is often re-purposed for another group through changes in style, artist, instrumentation or simple cultural context. Occasionally the effect that is produced by the deliberate use of music outside of its normal cultural context may be termed cultural dissonance. Cultural dissonance is the sense of discomfort arising when one's cultural environment undergoes a change resulting in behavior that does not coincide with one's cultural identity. When a film uses music that is not obviously appropriate to the age group of the expected demographic, it can enhance the emotional impact of the narrative through this sense of discomfort. In other cases, anachronistic music is employed to add a sense of period to a performance, much in the same way that classic automobiles or women's fashion can add to the authenticity of a period drama. For example one might consider the use of music to set the scene for Marty McFly's (Michael J. Fox) trip to the 1950s in Robert Zemeckis' 1985 film *Back to the Future*. I would suggest that there is a third possibility for the use of music that has not been specifically developed for the primary audience of a film. The animated films that are the focus of this chapter do not intend to develop a sense of discomfort in their audience, nor do they use music to develop the illusion of historicity. Because they aim at an audience that spans several generations, these animations rarely use the original artist's version, opting for a more contemporary arrangement that does not jar the sensibilities of the parents while instilling a sense of the familiar in grandparents. In fact, these films also attract a reasonable number of patrons from the much-desired fifteen to twenty-five unmarried demographic. I suspect, however, that these members of the audience are, like young parents, satisfied with the contemporary arrangements of the classic rock tunes. Since the children attending the films (the ostensible primary audience) are not likely to be avid contemporary music fans, it is unlikely that they will demonstrate any preference for their "own music" and walk out of a film that does not incorporate the works of Raffi or the Wiggles. Instead, they become acculturated to the simple pleasures of their parents' younger days.

Notes

1. In 1994 the Spanish duo Los del Rio released "Macarena" and it went on to international success. It became the unofficial theme song for the 1996 U.S. Democratic convention in which President Bill Clinton was selected by his party to run for a second term in office.

Works Cited

American Beauty. Dir. Sam Mendes. DreamWorks, 1999. Film.
Bee Gees. "Stayin' Alive." Bee Gees/Reprise, 2007. Audio Recording.
Bing, Jonathan, and Cathy Dunkley. "Kiddy Litter Rules H'wood." *Variety* 385.7 (2002): 1. Print.
Black Swan. Dir. Darren Aronofsky. Fox Searchlight, 2010. Film.
Caputi, Jane. "Green Consciousness: Earth-Based Myth and Meaning in Shrek." *Ethics & the Environment* 12.2: 23–44. Print.
Citizen Kane. Dir. Orson Welles. Warner Home Video, 2001. DVD.
Diamond, Neil. "September Morn'" / "I'm a Believer." Columbia. Audio Recording.
Happy Feet. Dir. George Miller and Warren Coleman. Warner Bros., 2006. Film.
Hutcheon, Linda. *A Theory of Adaptation.* Routledge, 2006. Print.
Lyons, Charles. "Family Pics Get a Fix." *Variety* 385.7 (2002): 69. Print.
Madagascar. Dir. Eric Darnell and Tom McGrath. DreamWorks, 2005. Film.
March of the Penguins. Dir. Luc Jacquet. Buena Vista, 2005. Film.
Monkees, The. "I'm a Believer." Rhino, 2004. Audio Recording.
Presley, Elvis. "Heartbreak Hotel." RCA Records, 2002. Audio Recording.
Prince. "Kiss." Rhino/Warner Bros., 2007. Audio Recording.
Rosen, Lisa. "A Jungle's Classic Roots." *Los Angeles Times* 8 May 2005. *LA Times.* Web. 19 January 2014.
Saturday Night Fever. Dir. John Badham. Paramount, 1977. Film.
Shull, M.S., and D.E. Wilt. *Doing Their Bit: Wartime American Animated Short Films, 1939–1945.* Jefferson, NC: McFarland, 2004. Print.
Shrek. Dir. Andrew Adamson and Vicky Jenson. DreamWorks, 2001. Film.
Smash Mouth. "All Star." Interscope, 2005. Audio Recording.

The Fantastic Childhood Imagination Through an Adult Lens: A Todorovian Approach to *Tim Burton's* Alice in Wonderland

Heather Rolufs

Tim Burton's *Alice in Wonderland* (2010) is a twenty-first century film adaption of Lewis Carroll's literary novels: *Alice's Adventures in Wonderland* (1865) and *Through the Looking Glass* (1871). Burton's "re-imagined" take on Carroll's classic tales is an intriguing exploration of multiple fantastic "realities" and states of "being" for both the child and adult viewer. The film tells the story of Alice (Mia Wasikowska), a nineteenth-century girl who feels trapped in a Victorian life filled with tradition and convention. In frustration, she wanders off and falls into a rabbit hole. This rabbit hole transports her to "Underland," a place where her childhood "nightmares" are reality and she is expected to slay the monstrous Jabberwocky and restore the white queen to the throne. The resulting adventure is Alice's quest to find the courage and belief to make the impossible possible and to free herself from her self-imposed traps experienced in the "real" world. Her hesitation is expressed numerous times throughout the film. The memory of her first visit to "Underland" as a child finally allows her to believe the impossible is possible. For children, the movie provides a visual and aesthetic immersion into a 3D experience where they are "plunged into a world whose laws are totally different from what they are in our own [world] and in consequence that the supernatural events which occur are in no way disturbing" (Todorov 172). For a child viewer, the "plunging down the rabbit hole" experience is not unbelievable; Tzvetan Todorov's fantastic suspension of belief—acceptance of the supernatural—is an almost automatic response for the child viewer (52). For the adult viewer, however, reason is never far from the mind, and uncertainty regarding the existence of "Underland" becomes a more ambiguous and psychologically dualistic experience. Child-like innocence is replaced by life experience for adults; thus, as Buckingham and Bazalgette state, childhood is "often seen as another world," one that "[adults] have all visited," but which "has become inaccessible to [them] except through the distortions of memory" (iiv). They further suggest, "[f]or most adults, there is an 'essence' of childhood that is unknowable, mysterious, even magical," and, therefore, "[adults] can only recapture it vicariously, through the imagination and, perhaps more commonly, through accepted and conventional ideas of what constitutes childhood" (iiv). As a result, the film functions on two levels, the first is the entertaining visual adventure experienced by the limitless imagination of the child viewer, and the second is the adult viewer's struggle with feelings of loss through a nostalgic childhood imagination and the realization of the limitations within "reality."

Consequently, Tim Burton's *Alice in Wonderland* is an example of how children's films, and more specifically children's fantasy/fairytale films, are constructed to communicate on multiple levels to multiple audiences. By examining constructions of "reality" in *Alice in Wonderland* through aspects of Todorov's theory of the fantastic, we can see critical ways of analyzing the film's portrayal of the child's power of imagination to make the impossible possible, and the "limits" of adult nostalgia: the "hesitation experienced by a person who knows only the laws of nature confronting an apparently supernatural event" (Todorov 25). Ultimately, this analysis will demonstrate how children's fantasy films are developing both increased complexity and critical relevance for film studies, and add acute value beyond what the distinctions of "childhood" and "fantasy" dictate.

In order to write critically about fantasy, including cinematic fantasy of the twenty-first century, the term itself needs to be defined and explained. Tzvetan Todorov (1973) is arguably the first to set a definition for what is now termed the fantastic in his text, *The Fantastic: A Structural Approach to a Literary Genre*. He states:

> [i]n a world which is indeed our world, the one we know ... there occurs an event which cannot be explained by the laws of this same familiar world. The person who experiences the event must opt for one of two possible solutions: either he is the victim of an illusion of the senses, of a product of the imagination—and the laws of the world then remain what they are; or else the event has indeed taken place, it is an integral part of reality—but then this reality is controlled by laws unknown to us.... The fantastic occupies the duration of this uncertainty.... The fantastic is that hesitation experienced by a person who knows only the laws of nature, confronting an apparently supernatural event [25].

Todorov distinguishes the fantastic from two other modes, the uncanny and the marvelous. While these modes have some of the ambiguity of the fantastic, ultimately they offer a resolution governed by natural laws (the uncanny) or the supernatural (the marvelous). Other theorists like C.N. Manlove and Eric Rabkin expand on Todorov's definition. In *Modern Fantasy* (1975), Manlove suggests fantasy is, "a fiction evoking wonder and containing a substantial and irreducible element of the supernatural with which the mortal characters in the story or the readers become on at least partly familiar terms" (1). Rabkin, in contrast, states in *The Fantastic* (1976) that

> [t]he fantastic is a quality of astonishment that we feel when the ground rules of a narrative world are suddenly made to turn about 180°. We recognize this reversal in the relations of the character, the statements of the narrators, and the implications of structure, all playing on and against our whole experience as people and readers [41].

Alternatively, W.R. Irwin, Brian Attebery, and Rosemary Jackson credit Todorov while focusing more directly on fantasy narrative. Irwin contends in *The Game of the Impossible* (1976) that fantasy is a subgenre "based on and controlled by an overt violation of what is a generally accepted as possibility; it is the narrative result of transforming the condition contrary to fact into 'fact' itself" (4). In *The Fantasy Tradition in American Literature* (1980), Attebery indicates that, "[a]ny narrative which includes as a significant part of its make-up some violation of what the author clearly believes to be natural law—that is fantasy" (2). Lastly, Jackson states in *Fantasy: The Literature of Subversion* (1981) that

> [t]he Fantastic traces the unsaid and the unseen of culture: that which has been silenced, made invisible, covered over and made "absent." The movement from the first to the second of these functions, from expression as manifestation to expression as expulsion, is one of the recurrent features of fantastic narratives, as it tells of the impossible attempt to realize desire, to make visible the invisible and to discover absence [4].

While these theorists offer a very basic historical lineage of the fantasy genre Attebery and Jackson also consider the cultural, social and political implications of the fantastic, a divergence from and expansion upon Todorov's stricter definition.

The relevance of fantasy, literary or cinematic, has been a continuous uphill battle in relation to critical study within academia. Many held what Butler argues is a "Suvinain perspective," a reference to Darko Suvin's perception that

> [f]antasy is less concerned (if at all) with any cognitive requirements and its estranging qualities receive little rationalization or creditable explanation: they simply happen and are accepted (or not, if one is a character like Alice refusing to accept the nonsensical behaviour of the inhabitants of Wonderland) within their fictional world [Butler 21].

In addition, critics also maintain the attitude that the "so-called 'realist' mode of writing is somehow more profound, more morally committed, more involved with real human concerns than a mode of writing that employs the marvelous"; thus, conveniently forgetting that what is now considered the "real" world, "was for many centuries regarded as the world of appearances" (Swinfen 11).

The result of these views is a serious lack of critical academic study of fantastic material—especially anything that has "mass market" appeal. The qualifying of what is considered "worthy" fantasy is demonstrated by fantasy theorists as well. For example, Zipes suggests that, "what is fascinating about the academic approach to fantasy is that there is an attempt to qualify what is high and low fantasy, as for instance, Robert Boyer and Kenneth Zahorski, who have established themselves as the priests of high fantasy," and, therefore, limiting the sources of fantasy to what is considered "high quality" fantasy (188). A result of this disparaging view of the genre, various forms of literature, comics, and films have been excluded from academic exploration—especially children's fantasy/fairy tale films.

The general consensus by theorists critical of the genre is that fantasy is merely escapism, "without any meaningful content or social function" (Butler 3). Critics like Schatz openly dismiss film fantasy due to its lack of political potential: "we see films that are increasing plot-driven, increasingly visceral, kinetic, and fast paced, increasingly reliant on special effects, increasingly 'fantastic' (and thus apolitical)" (23). Escapism in fantasy is often considered negative, but as theorists like Worley point out, fantasy as meaningless escapism is a misconception, because "fantasy is inextricably defined by reality; how else can one define what doesn't exist except by what does?" (4). Perhaps, though, it is the negative perception of escapism that needs to change. Ursula Le Guin poses this question: "from what is one escaping, and to what?" (179). Le Guin's question opens up the genre to one of its true purposes, as Hashmi, Kirkpatrick, and Vermillion suggest: "we might be better served by understanding [fantasy] as a certain perspective toward present social, cultural, and economic realities, an orientation that can cross discourses and genres" (1). Consequently, fantasy can be viewed as a "method of approaching and evaluating the real world" rather than just "a means to escape from the contemporary world" (Swinfen 230). With that said, the importance of "escapist" film resides in how it represents cultural, political and economic issues that stem from reality. For instance, Guillermo del Toro's fantasy film *Pan's Labyrinth* (2006)—which arguably contains some *Alice in Wonderland* influences albeit darker and more adult—is set in 1944 Spain just after the Civil War and presents numerous feminist, religious, and political issues for critical analysis; the film's complexity makes it more than mere "childish" escapism. When it comes to fantasy/fairy tale films that are directed towards children and families, how the films incorporate ideologies that children absorb requires critical analysis to better understand how and why the films influence their audiences into accepting cultural norms.

As previously stated, fantasy/fairy tale films have been generally dismissed and ignored in academic study, which is surprising given how archetypes and motifs have been cinematically adapted from fantastic sources. Zipes argues in his foreword to *Fairy Tale Films: Visions of Ambiguity* (2010) that: "aside from a number of essays and a couple of books that touch on the subject, film critics, folklorists, and literary historians in America and Europe have not realized how much films owe to folklore and the fairytale" (ix). When it comes to fairy tales/fantasy films the most notable figures are Walt Disney and Lotte Reiniger, both of whom started adapting fairy tales and folklore to film in the 1920s. A large number of the North American/European populations first became familiar with fairy tales like *Cinderella*, *Sleeping Beauty*, *Beauty and the Beast*, and *Alice in Wonderland* through Disney's animated adaptations of the stories, rather than their literary progenitors. In itself, this indicates the importance influence of the fantasy genre, but these films, especially Disney's films, also dictate cultural ideologies. Ironically, Walt Disney started out in the 1920s adapting fairy tales by modernizing and experimenting with plots to "expose the ridiculous aspects of romantic love, fixed gender roles, the greatness of royalty, and so on" (Zipes xi). This did not last however, and Disney began to take a more conventional approach, adhering to the nineteenth century patriarchal ideology that many of the fantasy/fairy tale narratives encompass. Zipes argues that Disney practiced this type of conventional filmmaking until his death and, in doing so, developed a traditional structure that filmmakers continue to follow:

> (1) girl falls in love with young man, often a prince, or wants to pursue her dreams; (2) wicked witch, stepmother, or force of evil wants to demean or kill girl; (3) persecuted girl is abducted or knocked out of commission; (4) persecuted girl is miraculously rescued either by a prince or masculine helpers; (5) Happy ending in the form of a wedding, wealth, and rise in social status or reaffirmation of royalty. [Consequently,] in many ways, Disney's predictable fairy film schemata became classic in the same way that the Grimms's stories served as the model for most early collections of fairy tale films in the nineteenth century [xi].

There is no denying Disney's impact on cinematic fairy tale/fantasy adaptions; "it is virtually impossible for any filmmaker born after 1945 not to have seen or been exposed to a Disney fairy tale film as a result of the powerful marketing and distribution of all the products by the Disney Corporation" (Zipes xi). Yet, twenty-first century fairy tale filmmakers are not forced to singularly recognize Disney's versions, but given the widespread notoriety of his adaptations a certain amount of familiarity must be assumed, even if they oppose or simply disregard the Disney rendition. The twentieth, and especially the twentieth-first century, has seen a proliferation of fantasy/fairy tale films both in live-action and animation that have moved beyond Disney's conformist outlook by exposing audiences to genre mixing. This transition, in turn, "engenders new insights into art and life [which are] significant because they mirror possibilities of estranging ourselves from designated roles and conventional patterns of the classical tales" (Zipes xii). Similarly, Greenhill and Matrix state:

> [t]he mirror of fairy tale film reflects not so much what its audience members actually are but how they themselves and their potential to develop (or likewise, to regress). The fairy tale film's frame—not only the physical limits of what it actually shows but also its containment in time and—space allows an often-succinct and telling expression. Its metaphorical flexibility means that viewers can potentially return at different times and receive different, sometimes even contradictory, impressions of the film's meanings and intentions. Nevertheless, we suggest that within the genre of fairy tale film—apart from Disney—experiments, departures, and innovations predominate [Greenhill and Matrix 17].

When it comes to dark and twisted fantastic narratives or reinterpreted fairy tales, few do it better than director Tim Burton. His cinematic work, for the most part, has garnered very little critical analysis; moreover, "though Burton is often left out of this critical conversation, his films have indeed done as much or more to challenge the status quo" (Ray 199). Ironically, one Disney production that encompasses Greenhill and Matrix's conception of the modern innovative fairy tale/fantasy film is Tim Burton's re-imagined *Alice in Wonderland*. Carroll's *Alice's Adventures in Wonderland* and *Through the Looking Glass* have many incarnations and the "reinterpretation, incorporation, or transposition of these familiar stories, tellers create new tales to serve contemporary needs" (Tatar 1992). Burton, known for his somewhat eccentric, gothic, and slightly twisted style, has taken Lewis Carroll's literary novels, *Alice's Adventures in Wonderland* (1865) and *Through the Looking Glass* (1871), and applied his uniquely subversive awareness to this children's classic fairy tale/fantasy story, thus focusing more concretely on unsettling notions of nineteenth-century patriarchy by incorporating Todorov's fantastic modes of the uncanny and the marvelous. Tim Burton's vision of *Alice in Wonderland* incorporates more of the darker elements of classic folklore and fantasy by taking on the symbol of the "cautionary tales that follow audiences from childhood to adulthood" (Greenhill and Matrix 9). When we first are introduced to Alice in the film, she has had a nightmare about Underland and is telling her father about the "creatures" she saw in her "dream" (*Alice in Wonderland 2010*). The film then flashes forward thirteen years and Alice is now an adult, her father is dead and her mother is trying to make the best life for Alice she can by marrying her off (*Alice in Wonderland* 2010). The scene with the young Alice operates on two levels as it foreshadows the events to come and emphasizes the father's dialogue: "'[y]ou are mad. Bonkers. Off your head. But I will tell you a secret, all the best people are'"; a statement Alice repeats at various times throughout the film (*Alice in Wonderland* 2010). The film straddles both the uncanny "[an] experience of limits" (Todorov 46) and the marvelous "acceptance of the supernatural" (52). Alice believes her time in Underland is an *uncanny* dream for most of the film and questions her own sanity:

> MAD HATTER: "Still believe this is a dream, do you?"
> ALICE: "Of course, this has all come from my own mind."
> MAD HATTER: "Which would mean that I'm not real?"
> ALICE: "I'm afraid so, you are just a figment of my imagination, I would dream up someone half mad."
> MAD HATTER: "Yes yes, but you would have to be half mad to dream me up?"
> ALICE: "I must be then. I'll miss you when I wake up" [*Alice in Wonderland* 2010].

This is a key element in Todorov's definition of the uncanny, where the character or the reader justifies what they see as madness or a dream. This scene is pivotal as it is near the end of the film and both the child and adult audience has begun to believe Alice has gotten over her "hesitation" and accepted that Underland is not an *uncanny* dream, because "pinching" did not do the trick, and she is still stuck in this marvelous reality. For the adult audience especially, Alice's conversation with the Mad Hatter (Johnny Depp) reaffirms her hesitation about believing that these events are *merely* in her head and she almost seems to prefer this, than to accept the impossible alternative. Alice's "moment of truth" arrives in her final conversation with Absolem where she confronts not only her past visit to "Wonderland," but also her realization that she is her "father's" daughter:

> ALICE: "My father was Charles Kingsley and he had a vision that stretched halfway around the world and nobody ever stopped him. I'm his daughter. I'm Alice Kingsley."
> ABSOLEM: "Alice, at last, you were just as dimwitted the first time you were here. You called it Wonderland as I recall."
> ALICE: "Wonderland.... It wasn't a dream at all. It was a memory. This place is real and so are you and so is the Hatter."
> ABSOLEM: "And the Jabberwocky. Remember the vorpal sword knows what it wants. All you have to do is hold on to it. Fairfarren Alice perhaps I'll see you in another life" [*Alice in Wonderland* 2010].

Through most of the film, Alice has been passive and let others dictate her direction and, to a certain extent, her identity. Since she fell down the rabbit hole, she has been told that she is the "wrong Alice" and that she does not know who she is. In the scene above, the audience is finally introduced to the "real Alice," the one who knows who she is and that she has to take charge of her life. She finally accepts that Underland is—marvelously—real and that the only limitations are those you place on yourself. The foreshadowing throughout the film presents Alice as unhappy with the expectations her conventional and traditional life. When Alice says to Absolem that her father, "'had a vision that stretched halfway around the world and nobody ever stopped him'" and then continues: "'I'm his daughter. I'm Alice Kingsley,'" she is deliberately separating herself from her female relatives and relating and identifying with her late father (*Alice in Wonderland* 2010). This scene illustrates Alice's break with conformity and the realization that she can do/be whomever she wants, that she *can* make the impossible possible. The scene also solidifies the idea that "the fairy tale has to teach its child [viewer] a lesson about the real adult world, and our enjoyment of the pleasures of fairy tale imagination has to be justified by its ultimate performance of duty" (Bacchilega and Rieder 33). As a result, the relationship between the real world and the fairy tale world is always connected by the "relationships between children and adults ... about make believe versus reality in relation to pleasure versus duty and childhood versus maturity" (Bacchilega and Rieder 33). Unlike other films, such as Andrew Adamson and Vicky Jenson's *Shrek* (2001), which targets both adult and child audiences through multiple levels of meaning or adult-only humor, Burton's *Alice in Wonderland* manipulates the tension that exists between the adult and child in all audiences to produce meaning. Adult Alice remembers her past visit to "Wonderland" and realizes it is memory, not a dream. The openness of her child-like imagination helps her adult-self accept the "reality" of Underland and what it symbolizes— possibility. The film's climax—or "fraptious day"—is Alice's day of reckoning where she slays the Jabberwocky, not only freeing the inhabitants of Underland from the tyranny of the Red Queen but also symbolizing Alice's ability to upset normative gender ideologies by donning armor and setting out to slay the "dragon." She is not the damsel in distress; she does not need a masculine figure to come and save her; she takes her destiny into her hands and meets her adversaries directly. Ray argues that, "Burton's heroines indeed possess a lioness's share of agency. They tell their own stories and resolve their own problems. They do not rely exclusively on men or authority figures" (216). This coincides with Attebery's idea that a female initiation or coming of age fantasy should at first be "recognizably grounded in the biological and social reality of [the] woman's life" before a series of events transcend that reality or in Alice's case, before she falls down the rabbit hole (291). The Jabberwocky represents both the Red Queen's tool to control the masses in Underland, as well as a manifestation of nineteenth-century patriarchal repression in Alice's reality. Alice's desire to break away from the conservative and traditional gender roles enforced by Victorian society gives her the strength to do the impossible:

> ALICE: "Six impossible things, count them Alice. One: there is a potion that can make you shrink. Two: there's a cake that can make you grow."
> JABBERWOCKY: "So my old foe, we meet on the battlefield once again."
> ALICE: "We've never met."
> JABBERWOCKY: "Not you, insignificant bearer. My ancient enemy, the vorpal one."
> ALICE: "That's enough chatter."
> ALICE: "Three: animals can talk. Four: Alice, cats can disappear. Five: there's a place called Wonderland. Six: I can slay the Jabberwocky" ... "Off with your head!" [*Alice in Wonderland 2010*].

The film was given a PG (parental guidance suggested) rating, meaning "some material may not be suitable for children." In this scene, in particular, the audience can see why. Not only does Alice cut off the CGI Jabberwocky's tongue after issuing the statement: "That's enough chatter," but she also cuts off his head after shouting: "Off with your head" (*Alice in Wonderland* 2010).

Other CGI creatures were also fighting during the battle and the audience sees needles in eyes, rocks flattening bodies, and other violent examples. What is interesting about violence in the realm of fantasy is that it somewhat acceptable for children due to the fact that it is fantastic. In a sense, Todorov's definition of the fantastic helps categorize films for particular audiences and creates its own rating system. The rating FV (contains fantasy violence) is one way the television and film industry is differentiating between violence and fantasy violence. Butler continues along this line by writing "once again fantasy is being used in relation to something being less real and thus perhaps, not to be taken as seriously, the inference being that FV is (more) acceptable violence" (30). Add 3D special effects into the mix and one has a whole new kind of immersion into fantasy violence. William Brown argues that, "3D cinema is often thought to be realistic as a result of its immersive capacities" (262). Fantasy alone is immersive, but by adding the 3D element Todorov's fantastic takes on a new dynamic for the audience: "[t]he fantastic therefore implies an integration of the reader into the world of the characters; that world is defined by the readers own ambiguous perception of the event narrated" (Todorov 31). The audience becomes immersed with the characters not just psychologically or emotionally, but through the creation of a more visceral visual experience. The 3D glasses are a symbol of Todorov's condition of fantastic hesitation as "3D viewers are inescapably aware that what they are seeing is a construct—even if the digital animation is perceptually realistic" (Brown 264). Brown's statement is supported by Perry Nodelman's theory that, "fantasy does not really persuade us of the existence of the world it describes; it only allows us to pretend it exists ... we experience the pleasure of its otherness by pretending not to be different from it" (177–78). While the film's effects and characters are definitely geared toward families, Tim Burton's *Alice in Wonderland*, like many of his films, incorporates darker gothic elements along with fantastic violence. As a result, Burton's *Alice* narrative is directed slightly more towards the adult viewer in terms of the complex ideologies and theoretical approaches Burton integrates. By making a film that is aesthetically pleasing and fantastically immersive for children, while simultaneously providing a complex narrative that challenges the adult mind and creates a sense of childhood nostalgia, Burton illustrates how his films can entertain and inspire. Essentially, fantasy is about possibility, as Tamora Pierce argues, "[fantasy] opens the door to the realm of the 'What If,' challenging [viewers] to see beyond the concrete universe and to envision other ways of living and alternative mindsets" (180). Burton's *Alice in Wonderland* incorporates all of these elements, suggesting the critical relevance of fantasy/fairy tale films and the important need for further examination of the genre in regards to how these films engage both child and adult audiences.

In conclusion, Tim Burton's *Alice in Wonderland* is a complex blend of live action and animation, fairy tale and fantastic tale, and adaptation and reinvention. He has taken a story and modernized it for contemporary society by constructing Alice as an intelligent heroine who does not fit the cookie cutter Walt Disney fairy tale model. Burton's Alice solves her own problems and does not rely on the "handsome prince" to save her. The scene at the end of the film where Alice is standing alone on a ship waiting to set sail to places unknown is invigorating. The slippage between Todorov's marvelous reality and Alice's reality is beautifully accomplished when Absolem lands on her shoulder, thereby keeping his promise to see her in another life. This last scene blurs the lines between fantasy and reality and suggests all dreams and new unexplored frontiers are fantastic—in a Todorovian sense—at first, but the individual has the power to make them real. Analyzing Burton's *Alice in Wonderland* through a Todorovian lens provides insight into the different structures that make up fantasy narrative and shows how they are more than just child's play. Fantasy and fairy tales are more than mere escapism; they are deserving of critical study for how they represent societal norms, gender ideologies, and cultural paradigms. Todorov suggests, "by the hesitation it engenders, the fantastic questions precisely the existence of an irreducible opposition between real and unreal"; fantasy film and narratives do this by dissecting the very notion of the "real" and stripping it down to explore its meaning (168). Ultimately, whether fantasy/fairy tale films are asking or illustrating the right critical meaning should not be the main issue; instead we might wonder whether the audience is "seeing" or asking the right critical questions.

Works Cited

Alice in Wonderland. Dir. Tim Burton. Johnny Depp, Mia Wasikowska. Walt Disney Pictures, 2010. Film.
Attebery, Brian. *The Fantasy Tradition in American Literature*. Bloomington: Indiana University Press, 1980. Print.
____. "Women's Coming of Age in Fantasy." Egoff, et al. 288–300. Bacchilega, Cristina, and John, Rieder. "Mixing It Up: Generic Complexity and Gender Ideology in Early Twenty-First Century Fairy Tale Films." Greenhill and Matrix 23–42. Print.
Bazalgette, C., and D. Buckingham, eds. *In Front of the Children: Screen Entertainment and Young Audiences*. London: British Film Institute, 1995. Print.
Brown, William. "Avatar: Stereoscopic Cinema, Gaseous Perception and Darkness." *Animation, an Interdisciplinary Journal* 7.3 (2012): 259–271.
Butler, David. *Fantasy Cinema*. London: Wallflower University Press, 1988. Print.
Egoff, Sheila, et al. *Only Connect: Readings on Children's Literature*, 3rd ed. New York: Oxford University Press, 1996. Print.
Greenhill, Pauline, and Sidney Matrix, eds. *Fairy Tale Films*. Logan: Utah State University Press, 2010. Print.
____. "Introduction: Envisioning Ambiguity: Fairy Tale Films." Logan: Utah State University Press, 2010. Print.
Hashmi, M., B. Kirkpatrick and B. Vermillion. "Introduction." *Velvet Light Trap: A Critical Journal of Film and Television* 52 (2003): 1–3.
Irwin, W.R. *The Game of the Impossible*. Urbana: Illinois University Press, 1976. Print.
Jackson, Rosemary. *Fantasy: The Literature of Subversion*. London: Methuen, 1981. Print.
Le Guin, Ursula. "Escape Routes." Ursula Le Guin, ed. *The Language of the Night: Essays on Fantasy and Science Fiction*. London: Women's, 1975, 176–81. Print.
Lukasiewicz, Tracie. "The Parallelism of the Fantastic and the Real: Guillermo del Toro's Pan's Labyrinth/El Laberinto del fauno and Neomagical Realism." Greenhill and Matrix 43–59. Print.
Manlove, C.N. *Modern Fantasy*. Cambridge: Cambridge University Press, 1975. Print.
Nodelman, Perry. "Some Presumptuous Generalizations About Fantasy." Egoff, et al. 175–78. Print.
Pan's Labyrinth. Dir. Guillermo del Toro. Estudios Picasso, Tequila Gang Esperanto Filmoj, Sententia Entertainment, Telecinco. 2006. Film.
Pierce, Tamora. "Fantasy: Why Kids Read It, Why Kids Need It." Egoff, et al. 179–83. Print.
Rabkin, Eric. *The Fantastic*. Princeton, NJ: Princeton University Press, 1976. Print.
Ray, Brian. "Tim Burton and the Idea of Fairy Tales." Greenhill and Matrix 198–218. Print.
Shrek. Dir. Andrew Adamson and Vicky Jenson. Mike Meyers, Cameron Diaz. DreamWorks Animation, 2001. Film.
Suvin, Darko. *Metamorphoses of Science Fiction*. New Haven, CT and London: Yale University Press, 1979. Print.
Swinfen, Ann. *In Defense of Fantasy*. London: Routledge and Kegan Paul, 1984. Print.
Tatar, Maria. *Off with Their Heads: Fairy Tales and the Culture of Childhood*. Princeton, NJ: Princeton University Press. 1992. Print.
Todorov, Tzvetan. *The Fantastic: A Structural Approach to a Literary Genre*. New York: Cornell University Press, 1973. Print.

Worley, A. *Empires of the Imagination: A Survey of Fantasy Cinema from George Méliès to Lord of the Rings.* Jefferson, NC: McFarland, 2005. Print.

Zipes, Jack. "The Age of Commodified Fantasticism: Reflection of Children's Literature and the Fantastic." *Children's Literature Association Quarterly* 9.4 (1984): 187–190. Print.

____. "Foreword: Grounding the Spell: The Fairy Tale and Transformation." Greenhill and Matrix ix–xiii. Print.

Asterix & Obelix vs. Hollywood: A Pan-European Film Franchise for the "Family" Audience

Noel Brown

In 1999, *Asterix & Obelix vs. Caesar* (Claude Zidi; Fr. "Astérix & Obélix contre César"), the first in a much-heralded series of live-action adaptations of the French *Astérix* comics (1959–), was released to an expectant European market. A French, German and Italian co-production budgeted at approximately U.S. $45 million, it constituted the most expensive French-language film ever made. The film eventually recouped more than U.S. $100 million at the global box office, with enormous returns in key central and western European territories, despite widespread critical disapproval and dismal returns in North America. Three further films have since been released—each of them expensively made, popular with audiences, but widely denigrated by critics: *Asterix & Obelix: Mission Cleopatra* (Alain Chabat, 2002; Fr. "Astérix & Obélix: Mission Cléopâtre"); *Asterix at the Olympic Games* (Frédéric Forestier and Thomas Langmann, 2008; Fr. "Astérix aux Jeux Olympiques"; and *Asterix and Obelix: God Save Britannia* (Laurent Tirard, 2012; Fr. "Astérix et Obélix: Au service de sa Majesté"). This essay will focus largely on the first two films in the franchise, *Asterix & Obelix vs. Caesar* and *Asterix & Obelix: Mission Cleopatra*, arguing that they were conceived of as Hollywood-style family blockbusters designed to appeal not only to children, but to the broadest possible cross-section of mass audiences. It will argue that their success is largely attributable to an appropriation of traditionally Hollywood strategies of mass audience address, with the emphasis on spectacle, broad comedy, and transparent (but emotionally fulfilling) narratives supported by highly visible promotional campaigns. This chapter examines the extent to which the *Asterix* film franchise constitutes effective local resistance to Hollywood's near-hegemony of the children's/family entertainment markets.

The *Asterix* films must be seen in context of a number of social, cultural and commercial factors, most notably (1) the decline and subsequent resurgence of French cinema in the 1980s and 1990s; (2) concern in Europe over the dominance of Hollywood films (and U.S. culture more broadly); (3) the strong push during this period for a unified European industry able to resist/compete with Hollywood; and (4) the enormous popularity of the *Astérix* comic books among multiple demographics. The seeds were effectively sown in the mid–1980s, when French cinema attendances declined precipitously, and Hollywood strengthened its grip on the local market (Marie 230). Anxiety over the proliferation of popular American entertainment in Europe—and fears concerning the possible loss of local cultural tradition—led to a series of protective countermeasures; most notably, attempts to sustain and stimulate the European film market through funding and distribution bodies, such as the European Union's MEDIA program, instigated in 1987, and the Council of Europe's Eurimages, established in 1988.

These aspirations were reaffirmed when the European Community was reconstituted as the European Union through the signing of the Maastricht Treaty in 1992, which pledged to "contribute to the flowering of the cultures of the Member States, while respecting their national and regional diversity and at the same time bringing their common cultural heritage to the fore" (Miller et al. 185). The notion of a common market for popular European culture—which itself mirrored economic and political stances positioning Europe as a counter-balance to the U.S.—was strongly motivated by commercial impulses, with a potential unified market of 320 million people. France's peculiarly adversarial stance towards cultural imports was localized in 1993 with the assertion of the so-called "cultural exception," which held that cultural products should be exempt from free trade agreements. Nevertheless, French cinema's resurgence during the mid–1990s—both in attendance and production—ultimately stemmed more from massively increased investment by television companies (particularly Canal Plus). Its subsequent strengthening has prompted scholar Rémi Fournier Lanzoni to venture that, "despite their popularity among French audiences, American movies do not, as they do for the rest of the European market, pose a commercial or financial threat to the French film industry" (356–57).

That point remains open to debate. Despite the "cultural exception," France is not immune to the effects of "globalization," with a recent *Time* magazine article grimly announcing "the death of French culture" (Morrison). At the heart of the matter are ongoing debates as to whether Hollywood's global dominance is attributable more to long-term competitive advantages supported by barriers to entry, or its films' globally appealing narrative transparency. Arguing that "the trend towards U.S. dominance [of global cinema] is indubitable," Toby Miller and his co-authors in *Global Hollywood 2* point to aggressive strategies of protectionism, supported by Federal government, and linked to broader expansionist agendas. At the same time, they contend, Hollywood condemns—and, via government intervention, legally opposes—attempts on the part of foreign markets to establish import barriers, on the grounds that they contravene established trade agreements (17, 28). In contrast, critics such as Scott Robert Olson suggest that economic and political explanations for Hollywood's near-hegemony are insufficient "without consultation of such crucial factors as local taste, consumer perception, marketing strategies, currency exchange rates, and, most importantly, the attributes of the product itself" (xi). While conceding that "Hollywood does not hold a monopoly on the production of transparent texts," he insists that its unparalleled global success reflects "a fairly unique bond between text and audience." Olson defines transparency as "any textual apparatus that allows audiences to project indigenous values, beliefs, rites, and rituals into imported media" (xi, 4).

My own position lies somewhere between these poles. My research into the Hollywood "family film" deals with the universalistic (across barriers of culture, nationality, age and ethnicity) aspects of the genre, especially since the 1980s. Family films have been a leading Hollywood genre since the early days of sound production (Brown, "A New Movie-Going Public"), with an extensive canonized array of productions, such as *Little Women* (George Cukor, 1933), *The Wizard of Oz* (Victor Fleming, 1939), *Meet Me in St. Louis* (Vincente Minnelli, 1944) and *The Sound of Music* (Robert Wise, 1965), running parallel with Disney's live-action and animated productions after 1937, with the release of *Snow White and the Seven Dwarfs* (Brown, *The Hollywood Family Film*). However, family entertainment changed radically following the release of George Lucas's *Star Wars* (1977), which not only attracted audiences of all ages and backgrounds, but paved the way for a new orthodoxy in which individual films became inextricably linked with broader multimedia franchises. Moreover, Hollywood family entertainment since the early 1990s—including such recent series as *Harry Potter* (2001–10), *Toy Story* (1995–), *Shrek* (2001–10) and *The Chronicles of Narnia* (2005–)—is coterminous with corporate media strategies of vertical and horizontal expansion. During the early–1990s, several of the newly conglomerated Hollywood studios created "family film" divisions, with the express intention of targeting increasingly-accessible global audiences. The material profitability of the family film has been matched by its potency as a brand. As of early 2013, 27 of the 30 highest-grossing films of all time internationally are family-friendly Hollywood blockbusters (Brown, "Family Entertainment and Contemporary Hollywood Cinema," 3). As I have argued elsewhere, family entertainment is "the *material* manifestation of a broader universalistic agenda; conglomeration, expansionism and synergy are the equivalent *corporate* manifestations. They are two sides of the same coin" (Brown, "'Family Entertainment and Contemporary Hollywood Cinema," 10).

In contrast, European children's and family films have struggled to make their mark. Although several countries in Central and Western Europe (such as Denmark) have vibrant children's film industries, most are heavily dependent on subsidies. Moreover, they generally remain small-scale, poorly distributed, founded predominantly on pedagogic and/or nationalistic impulses, and consequently non-commercial. A 2008 article published in the European Children's Film Association's *EOFA Journal* addressed the issue of the "visibility" of home-grown child-oriented productions in a market dominated by Hollywood blockbusters, noting a "lack of money and a lack of screens," with public broadcasters injecting fewer funds and multiplexes gravitating towards blockbusters (Hermans et al. 1–3). There is comparatively little tradition of children's films in France—a fact attributable, I suspect, to the historical aversion to juvenility in Francophone cinema, and ongoing emphasis on "serious," "auteur" films. Guy Austin has speculated that the *bande dessinée*—the comic book—has provided a "national outlet" for fantasy, with Hergé's *Tintin* (1946–93) and Goscinny's and Uderzo's *Astérix* the most popular subjects (143–44). In fact, there have been a number of animated adaptations of the *Astérix* comics, produced intermittently by Dargaud Films (between 1966 and 1986) and others (since 1989), although none have matched the international appeal, or local profitability, of the presently-discussed films.

Asterix & Obelix vs. Caesar

The Astérix franchise has generated comic book sales of approximately 325 million, a Disneyland-esque amusement park (Parc Astérix, near Paris), and a vast array of ancillary merchandise. Its appeal has been described by Anthea Bell—the comics' English translator—as

> incorrigibly French [...] crammed with French jokes, puns, wordplay and cultural references, ranging from obvious humor for eight-year-olds to parodies of great art and extended cultural gags designed to appeal to older (and well-educated) teenagers and adults [133–34].

Matthew Screech, conversely, while acknowledging that the comics can be multiply interpreted as affirmations of the French national character, ultimately argues for an ineffably universalistic appeal, in which "freed from loyalties, prejudices and other historical baggage, people of all nationalities and all political persuasions read whatever they like into the Gaulish warrior's exploits[...]. Consequently, people the world over, holding radically different opinions, claim that Astérix speaks for them" (86).

Asterix & Obelix vs. Caesar underwent a particularly long incubation—a reflection of the complications of mounting such a lavish, technically-demanding production, as well as the demands of funding and co-production. Most European films (at least, beyond a certain budgetary threshold) are co-productions, with companies usually unable to raise finance from a single source. At the time of its release, average budgets for European films were below U.S. $5 million, against approximately U.S. $75 million in Hollywood (Jäckel, 42–43). It is an indication of the disparity between these markets that *Asterix & Obelix vs. Caesar*—with a budget of U.S. $45 million—constituted the most costly French-language film ever made, whereas in Hollywood it would merely rank as a mid-range production (and unusually low for a fantasy subject). The fact that it was made with production and funding involvement from several companies across France, Germany and Italy underpinned not only the economic realities of co-production, but also the commercial necessity of transcending borders of language, culture and nation. Indeed, *Asterix & Obelix vs. Caesar* qualified for, and received, over €600,000 in financial assistance from Eurimages—a relatively insignificant proportion of the budget, admittedly, but revealing in terms of its perceived cultural and commercial importance. Nevertheless, in terms of production, the film was predominantly French, having been executive produced by the prolific Parisian mini-mogul Claude Berri, directed by acclaimed screenwriter/director Claude Zidi, and with French leads in stars Christian Clavier and Gérard Depardieu.

Whilst appropriating story elements from several Astérix comics, the plot remains purposely straightforward. As with Goscinny's and Uderzo's source material, the film is set during the Roman occupation of Gaul (latter-day France), circa 50 BC. One Gaul village has successfully resisted the invaders, thanks to the efforts of a druid, Getafix (Claude Piéplu), who is capable of brewing a magic potion that confers super-strength. The story centers on two such Gauls: the small, wily Asterix (Clavier) and large, simple-minded Obelix (Depardieu)—who, having fallen into a cauldron of the potion as a child, permanently possesses super-strength. When Caesar (German actor Gottfried John) discovers that the Gauls have successfully held out against the Romans, he orders an attack on their village, but with the aid of the potion, it is easily repelled. Discovering that the magic potion is made by Getafix, Caesar's villainous adjutant Detritus (Italian Roberto Benigni) kidnaps him and extorts the secret, whereupon he stages a coup, and has Caesar imprisoned. Asterix and Obelix infiltrate the Roman encampment, hoping to rescue Getafix (on whom the besieged Gauls rely for fresh supplies of the potion). Asterix, having overcome various perils in the gladiators' arena, including alligators, lions, a Cyclops and a pit of tarantulas, reunites with Obelix (who has unwittingly aided Detritus's usurpation of Caesar), and together they collect Getafix and rescue a masked man from the dungeons— who turns out to be Caesar. Returning to the village, they realize that the Romans' acquisition of the potion tips the balance of power in their favor, and Getafix intuits that a new, super-magic potion will be required to hold out. Having obtained the vital ingredient—a phial of unicorn's milk—Asterix and Obelix are able successfully to defend the village, overthrow Detritus and return a grateful Caesar to power.

Aside from the prestigious talents in front of the cameras and behind the scenes, there are several elaborate studio sets, extensive location filming and a preponderance of extras employed for the battle sequences. There is extensive use of CGI, most notably in the comic battle sequences in which the heroes use their superhuman strength to send hordes of attacking Romans flying through the air; a sequence in which Obelix defeats an elephant in combat by lifting it into the air by the tusks and dropping it to the ground; and the Romans' climactic assault on the Gauls' village, in which an army of Asterix and Obelix replicas are created by the super-magic potion to repel the Roman army. The CGI sequences are rendered convincingly (although there is nothing to rival a top-of-the-line Hollywood blockbuster), but the studio-bound recreation of the Gaul village fails to convince as a genuine location.

Although there are numerous violent exchanges, there is barely any intimation that characters will come to harm, and no deaths occur onscreen. Special effects designer Pitof explains that "Claude [Zidi] wanted to do an adaptation of the comic series without getting a comic book look. He wanted to balance the comic aspect with an element of realism" (Bergery 186). That is to say, the film does not operate purely as spectacle in the vein of "immersive" Hollywood productions like *The Lord of the Rings*, but balances its action-adventure aspects with comedic visual and performative emphases; a semi-ironic tone (emphasized by the English-language dub, scripted by Terry Jones of "Monty Python" fame) which establishes a distancing tone of unreality. The film is largely devoid of tension—which may, depending on perspective, be a laudatory or lamentable quality in a family-oriented production. Everything is played for comedy, which itself operates on several levels. There are several instances of schoolboy toilet humor (and exclamations of "shithead!" "bastards!" and other expletives in the English dub that make a nonsense of the producers' clear attempts to ensure the film's suitability for young children). There are also relatively sophisticated intertextual allusions of the kind routinely employed in Hollywood feature animations for the benefit of adult spectators. But the overriding broadness of the comedy—the fights and pratfalls; the silly voices and accents; the comedy characters—is uncomplicated and non-culturally specific. One need not be French (or German or Italian) to appreciate the film.

Nonetheless, such productions—in which a great number of producers, funders, distributors and others have invested—are, inevitably, compromises. This is doubly so in a blockbuster family film, a format defined by the need to please as many, and offend as few, consumers as possible. Small wonder, perhaps, that there is a whiff of dissatisfaction in critical responses to the film. Having been proclaimed by French newspaper *Le Monde* as "the image of resistance to American cinematographic imperialism" (Riding), *Asterix & Obelix vs. Caesar* received short shrift from French critics, with Andre Bercoff in *France Soir* writing, "Yes, I confess it; I am a traitor to French cinema[...]. After a few minutes full of hope, I ended up bored senseless by Asterix and Obelix" (Riding). And *Libération*'s critic felt that "The move from comic book to film has fatally put an end to a dream[...]. The bubble has burst" (Riding). Most damning was Laurent Marie's assessment that the film "might prove rather poisonous and French independent production could be smothered by Obélix's overweight as small budget films would not be getting the breathing space they need to find their public" (232). North American responses were no better, with *Variety* presciently predicting that "beyond continental Europe, and especially in English-speaking territories, its true market is as a dubbed video for kids" (Elley).

More importantly, from the filmmakers' perspective, the film was a significant commercial success, with international box office grosses in excess of $100 million. With over 300 million copies of the Astérix comic books sold worldwide, one wonders whether the film *could* have flopped; certainly, producer Berri thought that it could not, confidently predicting over 10 million admissions in France alone—in the event, it had only slightly fewer (Riding). Equally revealingly, *Asterix & Obelix vs. Caesar* was not even picked-up by a U.S. distributor. The insularity of the North American movie-going public is a matter of historical record, but there are other factors at play, including aversion to dubbed or subtitled screen entertainment (partially a corollary of its unfamiliarity), and the fact that, like his compatriot Tintin, Astérix himself has made little impact in the United States, having debuted as recently as 1994 (Riding).

Asterix & Obelix vs. Caesar is not a film that rewards close analysis of its formal properties. Points may fruitfully be made concerning its straightforward plotting, linear, transparent narrative structure, broad, universalistic comedic emphases, use of big stars and expensive visual effects, etc.; but in the final analysis it is a production deriving its significance from its cultural-contextual implications, as the loci of European fears regarding loss of cultural heritage, and as the spearhead of (an ultimately abortive) attempt to beat Hollywood at its own game. No doubt its juvenility and cinematic thinness account for its comparative neglect by scholars. To this extent, it contrasts noticeably with its sequel, which utilizes a broader range of formal strategies in the pursuit of a global consumer base.

Asterix & Obelix: Mission Cleopatra

Asterix & Obelix: Mission Cleopatra (2002) was made without Italian participation, but again numerous companies had a hand in its manufacture, led by Berri's Renn Productions and the involvement, as before, of Canal Plus. With a slightly expanded budget (estimated at U.S. $48 million, thereby surpassing its predecessor as the most expensive French-language film ever), a new writer-director in acclaimed actor/comedian Alain Chabat, and lessons seemingly having been learned from the first film, *Asterix & Obelix: Mission Cleopatra* is slicker, and more assured. Christian Clavier and Gérard Depardieu reprise their central roles, joined on this occasion by smoldering Italian actress/model Monica Bellucci (as Cleopatra) and rising French-Moroccan actor Jamel Debbouze. Furthermore, the adult appeal is more pronounced. Although the comparatively lowbrow slapstick and occasional schoolboy vulgarity is still apparent, the humor is more allusive (or "postmodern," as some critics would have it), with a preponderance of anachronistic meta-textual references in the vein of the recently-released DreamWorks global box office hit, *Shrek* (Andrew Adamson and Vicky Jenson, 2001).

Unlike its predecessor, *Mission Cleopatra*'s storyline is lifted directly from one of Goscinny's/Uderzo's comics, *Astérix et Cléopatra* (1963). The story begins with Caesar (Chabat) in the company of his lover (and ruler of Egypt), Cleopatra. Cleopatra becomes enraged at Caesar's contention that her people are racially inferior to Romans, and engages Caesar in a wager that she can build him the most magnificent palace ever designed in a mere three months. Incredulous, Caesar accepts the offer. Reluctant young architect Numerobis (Debbouze) is engaged for the task, to the fury of court architect Amonbofis (Gerard Darmon). Quickly realizing that he has no hope of completing the commission, and with the threat of execution if he fails, Numerobis recalls hearing a legend about a band of Gauls possessing super-human strength. Travelling to Gaul alone, he successfully locates Asterix, Obelix and Getafix (Claude Rich) and persuades them to accompany him and help him complete the palace. With the help of the Gauls, and an army of Egyptian laborers similarly imbued with super-strength, the palace takes shape, despite Amonbofis's attempts to sabotage the project. Eventually, Caesar himself—unable to endure the thought of losing his wager—begins attacking the palace, but Asterix succeeds in getting a message to Cleopatra, who demands that he leave the construction unimpeded, and Numerobis ultimately completes his task.

The film is replete with sly, tongue-in-cheek references to topical sociopolitical currents, such as France's then–35-hour working week, and—in the Egyptian workers' persistent threats of strike action—industrial unrest. The intertextual anachronisms are also more pronounced, as in an early scene, where Numerobis—in the company of his assistant, Otis—attempts to remember Getafix's name:

> NUMEROBIS: When I was little, my daddy told me stories about a druid. Guestlix? Getchakix?
> OTIS: Something "ix"? Lennykravix?
> NUMEROBIS: It begins with "Get" and ends in "ix."
> OTIS: Getupanboogix?

There is a further hint of self-conscious irony when Otis later insists, "Boss, the magic potion's a myth. It's in a comic papyrus for kids. This is reality." Of course, this film is *not* purely for kids. Aside from the cultural references,[1] which assert its playfulness, the film is arguably truer to the spirit of Goscinny's and Uderzo's comics than its predecessor; the meta-textuality is updated and contextualized, but in essence it is not dissimilar to Goscinny's patented brand of ironic allusiveness. Such fidelity in adaptation is a highly desirable attribute in a film trading not only in the comics' global readership, but also cultivating more zealous devotees, for whom bowdlerization or mere deviation are unpardonable failings. Moreover (and initially disorientingly), several hit songs are diegetically worked-in to the narrative, with characters singing and dancing to numbers such as James Brown's "I Got You (I Feel Good)." Even John Williams' Darth Vader theme from *Star Wars* (George Lucas, 1977) and Boots Randolph's "Yakety Sax" (i.e., the Benny Hill theme) find their way on to the soundtrack. *Asterix & Obelix vs. Caesar* could hardly be said to possess a realist framework, but its successor willingly sacrifices internal logic for the sake of its purportedly feel-good emphasis; fun and frolics are clearly the order of the day.

The most flagrant, amusing (and presumably inexpensive) example of its lampooning of narrative convention is a scene where a Roman garrison attacks the palace. Obelix prepares to face them alone, with the incidental music consciously invoking a western shoot-out. At this point, the voice-over narration intones, "The violent scene that follows has been replaced by a documentary on lobsters," whereupon the camera cuts exactly to that; when the prior scene recommences, the attackers have been repelled. As well as circumventing the need for costly CGI, this vignette lightly satirizes both the cartoonish violence characteristic of the Astérix comics and the occasionally hysteric aversion to such aspects in children's entertainment. Shortly thereafter, one centurion remarks to another, "Is all this violence really necessary?" to which his colleague replies, "Doesn't bother me." In actuality, it is hard to imagine the bloodless (and seemingly painless) violence exacted on the attacking hordes offending any but the most puritanical—although the casting of sex siren Bellucci, revealingly outfitted in a variety of flimsy and low-cut costumes, raises a salient point about the seemingly less-contentious role of sex in selling such entertainments to adult consumers.

Far more than its predecessor, *Mission Cleopatra* adopts the broad-appeal strategies of its Hollywood counterparts. Its intertextuality chiefly draws on the collective cultural memory of potential consumers across the world, with few jokes playable solely to Francophone audiences. The impressive location filming (Morocco, standing in for Egypt); the technically-accomplished computer-generated effects; the big international stars; the broad humor, with countless visual gags, knowingly terrible puns and optional (which is to say that their recognition is not necessary to enjoy the film) allusions to cultural and sociopolitical currents; the highly populist soundtrack, drawing on familiar hits and musical motifs. All these aspects belong to a collective cultural consciousness, but for local consumers derive their import from the conditions of production—the fact that they reside within a distinctly European family entertainment franchise. Accordingly, domestic attendances were notably higher for *Mission Cleopatra* than *Asterix & Obelix vs. Caesar*—although globally they were slightly lower—and reviews, while remaining ambivalent in France, were appreciably warmer. Perhaps attracted by strong international response to *Asterix & Obelix vs. Caesar*, and *Mission Cleopatra*'s voguish appropriation of Hollywood family film tropes, Miramax picked up the distribution rights to both films in mid–2001 (James and Dawtrey).

Asterix at the Olympic Games and *Asterix & Obelix: God Save Britannia*

The two most recent live-action Astérix films have been beset by behind-the-scenes wrangles over adaptation rights, personnel changes, and seemingly inexorable artistic decline. Berri was well into advance planning on the third installment in the series when negotiations with rights holders Editions Albert René stalled (Klaussmann). Consequently, *Asterix at the Olympic Games* was delayed by several years, by which point much of the franchise's creative and commercial momentum had dissipated, and Berri had handed over the reins to his son, Thomas Langmann (latterly producer of *The Artist*, Michel Hazanavicius, 2011). Like its predecessors, *Asterix at the Olympic Games* was the most expensive French-language production ever, at a reported U.S. $115 million. The role of Astérix was recast, with Clavier having elected to concentrate on "more serious" roles, but Depardieu reprised his role as Obelix. An increasingly gimmicky approach to casting (cameos by, amongst others, Formula One racer Michael Schumacher, footballer Zinedine Zidane and basketballer Tony Parker) underpinned a broader descent into self-parody. *Asterix at the Olympic Games* had the dubious distinction of being recognized as the worst film of the year by Paris' Gérard du cinéma—roughly equivalent to the American "Razzies." Reviews were similarly scornful, but once again the film proved highly popular (though not profitable, because of its high costs), with nine million admissions in France alone.

Although retaining the services of Gerard Depardieu as Obelix, *God Save Britannia* was made by an entirely different production team, headed by French company Fidélité Films, and without German and Italian involvement. Fidélité overcame competition in the form of Langmann and eminent producer-director Luc Besson. With the adaptation rights to each film having been negotiated on an individual basis, this possibility had always been present. Although fashionably converted to 3-D, the casting is less ostentatious than in *Asterix at the Olympic Games*, with fewer celebrity cameos, an improved Astérix (in Edouard Baer) and prominent appearance by Catherine Deneuve as the titular Queen. Otherwise, the film is dominated by a now-familiar cocktail of sight gags, and predictable reliance on national stereotyping, with the age-old socio-political tensions between France and Britain mined for comic effect (and outrageous pseudo–English accents affected by several Gallic performers). In this case, the critical apathy was apparently shared by audiences, with less than four million admissions domestically.

Conclusion

The dream—perhaps "fantasy" would be more apt—that the Astérix films constitute a legitimate challenge to Hollywood international dominance has long since dissipated. Rather, they demonstrate that populist, non–Hollywood family entertainment *can* succeed at the local levels, but are unable to compete internationally due to the well-established competitive advantages held by the post–Hollywood multimedia giants. Equally, due to the inhibiting factors of finance and distribution in European cinema, the Astérix series has not, as was initially hoped, encouraged further projects of a similar ilk. Local children's film industries remain beset by age-old problems: lack of funding, leading to over-reliance on subsidies; an emphasis on pedagogical, rather than commercial, attributes; and poor circulation. Nevertheless, operating on a multilayered mode of appeal (from slapstick to formal experimentation) the live-action Astérix franchise demonstrates that broadly-appealing family entertainment is not solely Hollywood's province, offering further evidence that home-grown productions drawing on local cultural specificities can thrive. Perhaps unsurprising, then, that to some the notion of a handful of independent European studios and investors grouping together in an heroic attempt to resist Hollywood cultural imperialism appears as romantic as the stories of the beleaguered but stoic and indefatigable Gauls themselves, whose timeless and enduring popular adventures have provided an irresistible avenue through which these issues of culture and commerce can be explored.

Notes

1. Not all of the cultural references translate to English, but the dub substitutes others, such as naming four minor characters John, Paul, George and Ringo, referencing the Beatles.

Works Cited

Austin, Guy. *Contemporary French Cinema: an Introduction*, 2d ed. Manchester: Manchester University Press, 2008.
Bell, Anthea. "Asterix on Screen." *Children's Literature in Performance and the Media*. Fiona M. Collins and Jeremy Ridgman, eds. Bern: Peter Lang, 2006. 133–45.
Bergery, Benjamin. "Virtual Effects—Asterix and Obelix Versus Caesar." *Reflections: Twenty-One Cinematographers at Work*. Hollywood: ASC, 2002. 185–206.
Brown, Noel. "'Family' Entertainment and Contemporary Hollywood Cinema." *Scope: An Online Journal of Film and Television Studies* 25 (February 2013): 1–22. Web.
____. *The Hollywood Family Film: A History, from Shirley Temple to Harry Potter*. London and New York: I.B. Tauris, 2012.
____. "'A New Movie-Going Public': 1930s Hollywood and the Emergence of the 'Family' Film." *The Historical Journal of Film, Radio and Television* 33:1 (2013): 1–23.
Elley, Derek. "Asterix & Obelix vs. Caesar." *Variety* 1 February 1999: 57.
Hermans, Gert, Wendy Koops and Nina Cetinic. "It Is Time for a New Approach." *EOFA Journal* No. 4 (December 2008): 1–3. Web.
Jäckel, Anne. *European Film Industries*. London: BFI, 2003.
James, Alison, and Adam Dawtrey. "Miramax Stamps 'Asterix' Passport." *Variety* 1 June 2001: 3.
Klaussmann, Liza. "'Asterix' Makers in a Fix over Sequel." *Variety* 5 June 2003: 11.
Lanzoni, Rémi Fournier. *French Cinema: From Its Beginnings to the Present*. London: Continuum, 2002. 356–57.
Marie, Laurent. "French Cinema Today." *Contemporary French Cultures and Societies*. Frédéric Royall, ed. Bern: Peter Lang, 2004. 229–44.
Miller, Toby, et al. *Global Hollywood 2*. London: British Film Institute, 2005.

Morrison, Donald. "The Death of French Culture." *Time*, 21 November 2007. Web. 5 March 2013.
Olson, Scott Robert. *Hollywood Planet: Global Media and the Competitive Advantages of Narrative Transparency*. Mahwah, NJ, and London: Lawrence Erlbaum, 1999.
Riding, Alan. "French Comic Book Heroes Battle Hollywood's Hordes." *The New York Times*. 10 February 1999. E5.
Screech, Matthew. *Masters of the Ninth Art: Bandes dessinées and Franco-Belgian Identity*. Liverpool: Liverpool University Press, 2005.

Section Two: Film Adaptation and Transmedia Forms

Re-Mixing The Chronicles of Narnia: *The Reimagining of Lucy Pevensie Through Film Franchise Texts and Digital Fan Cultures*

NAOMI HAMER

Since its original publication, C.S. Lewis's *The Lion, the Witch and the Wardrobe* (1950) has been adapted across media forms including a theatrical production, a radio play, an animated feature, and twice as a BBC television serial. Most recently, the 2005 release of the Disney/Walden Media film remodeled the text within contemporary commercial and cross-media cultures. Lewis's novel is now situated as part of an extensive franchise that includes two feature film sequels (2008; 2010), DVDs with bonus features, video games, and interactive websites. While all adaptations of Lewis's text involve the translation of textual discourse into a new context or format, the recent Disney/Walden Media film exemplifies the translation of discourse across a number of media forms simultaneously in the context of a branded franchise. In addition, the *Narnia* film franchise involves multiple digital fan communities that expand the textual discourse far beyond the limits of the fictional characters and narratives.

This franchise illustrates the concept of "trans-media storytelling" (Jenkins 2003; 2006). Distinct from the adaptation of an isolated narrative from one media form to another (e.g., a film adaptation of a novel), Henry Jenkins defines a "transmedia story" as one that "unfolds across multiple media platforms with each new text making a distinctive and valuable contribution to the whole" (2006: 95–96). The responses to these diverse texts are facilitated by engagement across modes and media, particularly within digital fan cultures. These cross-media practices may be defined as New Literacies. Colin Lankshear and Michele

Knobel define New Literacies as those practices that draw upon new technical affordances but also cultivate a "new ethos" that is often defined as "participatory," "collaborative," and "distributed" (9). As New Literacies, digital fan cultures may function to transform and potentially disrupt dominant discourses of childhood innocence and gendered maturation rooted in the original text.

This essay addresses how franchise texts and digital cultures reveal the continued re-mixing and reimagining of Lewis's *Narnia* texts within contemporary cross-media cultures. This examination utilizes Gunther Kress and Theo van Leeuwen's concept of "multimodal design" (1996; 2001) as a tool to examine how discourses of childhood and girlhood, rooted in the representation of Lucy in Lewis's text, are translated across diverse formats. "Multimodality" is a concept coined by Kress and van Leeuwen to define "any text whose meanings are realized through more than one semiotic code," often integrating several modes of communication in its representation (Kress and van Leeuwen 1996: 183). Kress and van Leeuwen propose that design

> requires the choices of materials and modes which for reasons of cultural history and provenance, or for reasons of the individual's history, are best able to (co-) articulate the discourses in play at the particular moment [...] in relation to the purposes of the producer of the text, expectations about audiences and the kinds of discourses to be articulated [2001: 31].

Following this framework, both franchise and fan producers of the *Narnia* texts select discourses rooted in a cultural history and articulate them through design. The design of franchise and fan texts may function to both reinforce and challenge the dominant discourses of childhood innocence and maturation rooted in Lewis's original text.

Discourses of Childhood Innocence and Maturation in Lewis's Novel

The representation of Lucy Pevensie in Lewis's original novel primarily articulates a discourse of childhood innocence. Lucy is the youngest of the Pevensie siblings and the first to discover and access the fantasy world of Narnia. Of the children, she is also represented as the most faithful believer in Narnia and Aslan. Lucy and Susan are witnesses to Aslan's sacrifice on the Stone Table in order to save Edmund, the most explicit reference to Christian mythology in the text (Lewis 2005: 154–155). Lucy's participation in this event emphasizes her function as a moral symbol of faith and innocence. Her role as the innocent female child is further emphasized through the contrast of her youthful innocence with the representation of the other significant female figure in the narrative: Jadis, the White Witch. Inspired by Hans Christian Andersen's fairytale "The Snow Queen," Circe from Homer's *Odyssey*, Medusa of Greek mythology, as well as other witches in Nordic mythology, Jadis exemplifies the femme fatale qualities of these mythological characters (Kirk 10). The representation of Jadis also may cultivate discursive associations with the powerful witches, evil stepmothers and jealous queens of Disney's fairytale adaptations (Do Rozario 2004). Similar to these popular representations of femme fatale antagonists, Jadis is represented as a seductive, morally flawed, and cruel adult female who is contrasted with an innocent child heroine. Lewis's representation of Lucy reinforces a Romantic discourse that conceptualizes childhood as an innocent sphere, separated from sexuality and other adult corruptions. In addition, Jenkins observes that "[t]he Romantics valued the child's easy access to the world of the imagination and sought to free themselves to engage with the world in a more childlike fashion" (1998:18). Following this discourse, Lucy is represented as an innocent, preadolescent girl whose curiosity, mixed with goodness, gives her special access to magical powers or fantasy spaces. The perceptual and psychological facets of the initial wardrobe experience are represented solely through Lucy's point of view in Lewis's text (Lewis 2005: 8). Her role as a focalizer for the initial entry into the fantasy realm emphasizes her connection to the discourse of Romantic childhood innocence (Genette 1980).

Translating Lucy Discourse in Disney/Walden Media Film Franchise Texts

The Disney/Walden Media film and franchise texts reinforce the discourses from Lewis's text through their multimodal design. In their guidebook for packaging designers, Marianne Rosner Klimchuk and Sandra A. Krasovec outline the development of characters in the design of brand products: "[c]haracters can be developed to support brand communication, promote product attributes, and become the embodiment of the brand's personality" (28). The visual images of the four Pevensie children are integral to the transformation of *The Chronicles of Narnia* into a branded franchise across multiple texts. The brand images of the film franchise (employed on all franchise texts including the DVD cover, film poster, video game case, and *Movie Companion* text) include the representation of the four siblings in stylized poses: the image of Susan in a long green dress posed determinedly with bow and arrow; Peter cloaked in full armour in the midst of a battle; Edmund proceeding towards the White Queen's castle; and the image of Lucy looking out curiously as she stands beside the lamppost. This visual representation of Lucy reinforces her discursive role as an innocent child full of wonder and curiosity. Her small figure in comparison to a vast snowy backdrop emphasizes her youth and vulnerability, while her location by the lamppost holds a semiotic linkage for the viewer to her initial entry into the fantasy realm and her role as focalizer during that episode.

Most of the franchise texts reinforce the discourse of childhood innocence in relation to Lucy. However, *The Chronicles of Narnia: The Lion, the Witch and the Wardrobe* video game, produced as part of the film franchise by Buena Vista Games, exemplifies a potential alternative to the dominant discourses of the film franchise. This video game is classified as an action adventure game with 15 levels of game play, and is geared towards younger players and fans of the film. Video games within the action adventure genre tend to mix the physical challenges from action games (related to reaction times and hand-eye coordination) with the conceptual and problem solving challenges related to the story structure of adventure games. (See Adams 2010) In the *Chronicles of Narnia* video game, players can choose between the four siblings to complete a range of action and conceptual challenges or can team up two of the siblings in a cooperative action for specific challenges. The skills allotted to the siblings within the video game reflect gifts given to the Pevensies from Father Christmas in Lewis's novel. Father Christmas gives gifts of "tools not toys" to Peter, Susan, and Lucy on their quest to find Aslan and save Edmund (Lewis 2005: 108). Peter is given "a shield and a sword"; Susan "a bow and a quiver full of arrows and a little ivory horn" (Lewis 2005: 108). Father Christmas describes Lucy's gifts as follows: "a cordial made of the juice of one of the fire-flowers that grow in the mountains of the sun. If you or any of your friends is hurt, a few drops of this will restore them. And the dagger is to defend yourself at great need. For you also are not to be in the battle" (Lewis 2005: 108). These specialized gifts function to emphasize the specific moral and social qualities associated with each of the child protagonists.

These gifts also highlight the stereotypical gender roles of the siblings for which Lewis has been extensively criticized (See Ezard 2002). Upon receiving the gifts, Lucy asks Father Christmas "I think—I don't know—but I think I could be brave enough [to join the battle]," and his response to her is "That is not the point[...]. But battles are ugly when women fight" (Lewis 2005: 109). In an attempt to update the narrative to more current social conventions, the film omits this explicitly sexist discourse in Lewis's narrative. In addition, articulating the mainstreaming of a popular "Girl Power" discourse (See Harris 2004), the film and video game reemphasize Lucy and Susan's prowess with the dagger and arrow respectively. Nevertheless, while Lucy is visually represented with her dagger in the video game, the salient image across the franchise is of Lucy by the lamppost, reinforcing her Romantic innocence and wonder rather than her bravery.

Players of this video game are required to choose skills provided by each of the four Pevensie siblings. Due to this teamwork component, Lucy is positioned in battle with various ogres, minotaurs, and other creatures from the Narnia fictional universe. These actively aggressive engagements are primarily associated with the representation of Peter in the novel and film and may reflect the need to adapt Lucy's character within the context of an action-adventure video game. Greg Mueller, one reviewer of the videogame on gamespot.com, describes the role of each sibling in the gameplay:

> Peter is the strongest of the bunch, so you can use him for fighting off enemies or breaking through barriers. Susan is your ranged attacker, and she can throw snowballs and tennis balls, as well as use a bow and arrow. Edmund is a decent melee fighter, but he's also light and athletic enough that he can climb trees or posts and walk on delicate surfaces like thin ice or weakened floorboards. *Lucy is small, so she can crawl through small passages to reach arenas that the other children can't. Lucy can also charm animals and use them to attack, and she can use a first-aid skill to heal all the children* [My italicized emphasis. Mueller].

The function of the Lucy avatar in the game play provides consistency with her representation in the novel, film, and other franchise texts. Lucy is small; however, in the context of the game this quality is perceived as a physical asset in the game play as well as its semiotic function to signify innocence, youth, and vulnerability. Similarly, Lucy's ability to charm animals supports her role as a Romantic child close to nature and wonder; however, in the game this may also provide a useful skill. Nevertheless, Lucy's power as healer, a traditionally feminine role, continues to be her most powerful and agentive quality.

In a special behind-the-scenes feature on gamespot.com, Andy Burrows, the associate producer of the video game, describes Lucy's character in the video game as: "the trusting soul [...] who proves to be as fierce and determined as any of the White Witch's minions.... Her hardy spirit gets release through the little dagger and the skill of climbing on top of the wolves (among others) and controlling them while they do their best to shake her off" (Burrows). While continuing to sustain Lucy's innocence through her role as "a trusting soul" with healing powers and closeness to animals, the game re-articulates Lucy as a fiercer version of her character in the film. However, despite these enhanced qualities and skills in the game context, in comparison to her siblings, Lucy continues to be the least active and the most defensive avatar in the gameplay.

Disrupting Discourses of Innocence: Behind-the-Scenes Texts and Fan Cultures

Although Lucy is represented primarily within a discourse of childhood innocence and wonder, a discourse of moral and social maturation also plays an influential role in Lewis's text. Devin Brown proposes that the *Narnia* texts follow the developmental discourse of mythic and quest narratives: "a universal pattern-departure from a familiar home, initiation into a larger unknown world, trial and testing, some form of death and renewal, and then finally return and reinvigoration" (99). However, while the novel as a whole exemplifies elements of the mythological quest narrative, each child protagonist articulates a specific developmental moral trajectory throughout the novel and the *Chronicles of Narnia* as a series. Victor Watson observes that the dominant maturation discourse in British children's literature may be traced specifically to the influence of John Bunyan's allegorical narrative that posits life as a journey towards salvation, *The Pilgrim's Progress* (1678) (Watson 2003). As a canonical text in this tradition, Lewis's novel articulates a discourse of social maturation that is closely linked to moral development for the child protagonists (Trim 1995). As part of an allegorical framework, the maturation of each child protagonist exemplifies a specific moral trajectory rather than an individualized quest narrative.

Lucy Pevensie is often represented in relation to the characterization and developmental trajectories of her siblings. In terms of a discourse of gendered maturation, Lucy is often represented in contrast to her older sister Susan. While in the first *Narnia* text, Susan is presented as a well-behaved role model for her younger siblings, later in the series in *The Last Battle*, Susan's development into a young woman who focuses on "nylons and lipstick and invitations" disconnects her from the fantasy world (Lewis 1986: 128). Susan's movement into adulthood exemplifies a coming-of-age transformation discourse that underpins most novels of maturation about adolescent female characters; however, this transformation discourse contradicts the Romantic childhood of Lewis's *Narnia*. Thus, Susan's coming-of-age narrative works to reinforce Lucy's representation within a discourse of childhood innocence.

Stuart Aitken observes that because in Western culture childhood is conceptually separated from the adult world and its related vices and realities, children are conceptualized as both innocent and wild simultaneously:

> Children are excluded from many moral judgments because they are embodied by discourses that foist a child-centred pedagogy on a socially constructed innocence or wildness. Through their bodies, children are seemingly exempted (or, rather, located differently) from the moral order until they can be marked as other or with appropriate maturation, embraced [67].

In comparison to her siblings, Lewis's Lucy is situated firmly as an idealized, non-sexual body, prior to physical and sexual maturation and thus, distinguished from discourses of maturation and development.

A number of film franchise texts disrupt these discourses related to Lucy from the novel through the representation of a behind-the-scenes narrative for the film production. For example, *The Chronicles of Narnia: The Lion, the Witch and the Wardrobe: The Official Illustrated Movie Companion* further extends the film discourse through a blurring of the experiences and qualities of Lucy with the qualities and experiences of Georgie Henley, the actor who plays the character Lucy in the production of the film. Perry Moore, one of the producers of the film, addresses the fans of the film directly through a first-person narrative that runs through this behind-the-scenes text. The *Movie Companion* articulates a maturation discourse in relation to the child actors including Georgie:

> There are so many ways Georgie has grown over the course of the film.... By the time they reach the coronation scene, you can see that Lucy the girl is showing signs of becoming Lucy the young woman. I think it choked up her mom to see Georgie in that Queen's dress for the first time [Moore 86].

Moore's representation of Georgie further blurs the identities of Lucy and the child actor through his references to Georgie's physical transformation exemplified by the observation that "Lucy the girl is showing signs of becoming Lucy the young woman" (86). Moreover, the coronation of Queen Lucy is represented as an emotional moment for Georgie's mother who is depicted as responding to the coronation scene as the experience of her daughter Georgie, not the fictional character Lucy. This coronation scene is further emphasized in the *Movie Companion* through the inclusion of film stills of Lucy in her coronation dress as well as design sketches for the costume. The coronation scene is a common feature of Disney films and coming-of-age maturation narratives (similar to graduation, the prom, marriage or coronation in the case of the film *Princess Diaries* 2). The emphasis on this significant element in maturation narratives articulates a maturation discourse rather than the primary discourse of childhood innocence in Lewis's text.

A number of fan videos that may be found on YouTube (and other fan venues) integrate elements of the *Narnia* film with the narratives, characters, and themes of other texts including the coming-of-age narratives of *Princess Diaries*. Henry Jenkins notes that "while some fans remain exclusively committed to a single show or star[,] many others use individual series as points of entry into a broader fan community linking to an intertextual network composed of many programs, films, books, comics, and other popular materials" (1992: 40). Drawing on Michel de Certeau's work on popular reading, Jenkins defines these fan practices as forms of "textual poaching" characterized by "a type of cultural bricolage through which readers fragment texts and reassemble the broken shards according to their own blueprints, salvaging bits and pieces of the found material in making sense of their own social experience" (1992: 26). In the digital cultures of young people, the emphasis on production is often through this act of "re-mixing." Lankshear and Knobel define "re-mixing" as a new literacy practice "where a range of original materials are copied, cut, spliced, edited, reworked, and mixed into a new creation" (8). A popular fan culture activity is the creation of montage music videos that edit and remix clips from favorite films or still images of specific characters and actors.

A popular trend in the production of *Narnia* film fandom is the use of songs from the soundtracks of popular film franchises aimed at preadolescent and adolescent viewers. A number of *Narnia* fan videos re-mix scenes of Lucy set to the song "Breakaway" by Kelly Clarkson, from the soundtrack of the popular coming-of-age film *Princess Diaries 2: Royal Engagement* (2004). (For examples of this trend see: mogi93 2006; keionna 2006; and LiviaEvans 2006). A transformative coming-of-age discourse is central to *The Princess Diaries* books and film adaptations. The quirky outsider Mia discovers that she is a princess of a small (fictional) country called Genovia, and under the tutelage of her grandmother, the Queen, she struggles first against and then towards the development of the social, physical, and emotional qualities required of a princess. Thus, the re-mixing of elements from *Princess Diaries 2* with those from *The Chronicles of Narnia* results in the production of a coming-of-age transformative discourse of maturation for Lucy Pevensie.

The use of the song "Breakaway" in this fanvideo draws upon multiple levels of intertextual meaning associated with tween girlhood and specific contemporary tween girl texts. Performed by *American Idol* winner Kelly Clarkson, the song was released on *The Princess Diaries 2* soundtrack (2004). Significantly for the Lucy fanvideos, the music video for "Breakaway," is included as one of the film's DVD bonus features. The music video interweaves a visual narrative of the young Kelly Clarkson dreaming of becoming a pop star with scenes from the film of Princess Mia's transformation from awkward young teenager to adult princess. The fan video "Lucy-Breakaway" by user mogi93 (2006) is specifically modeled on Mia's transformation in the *Princess Diaries* film narratives (2001; 2004) and Kelly Clarkson's coming-of-age visual and textual narrative in the music video for the song "Breakaway." This fan video matches the song "Breakaway" with edited clips of Lucy throughout the Narnia film that include early scenes of Lucy full of wonder, Lucy discovering Narnia, and concludes with filmic images of Queen Lucy in royal costume in the coronation scene (mogi93 2006). Other fan videos that re-mix images of Lucy with this song follow a comparable structure with individual emphases on Lucy's relationships with her siblings or Mr. Tumnus (keionna 2006; LiviaEvans 2006). Through multiple levels of intertextuality, these fan producers have resituated Lucy within a maturation discourse outside of Lucy's original articulation as an innocent child. This type of play with discourses through fan video production exemplifies the possibility for a disruption of the discourse of Romantic innocence by young consumers of the film and novel; however, in disrupting the childhood discourse, the representation instead articulates a normative adolescent discourse of maturation.

Unlike the majority of narratives of girlhood maturation on current film and television, Lucy and Susan are not represented in Lewis's *Narnia* texts in relation to potential heterosexual romance. Notably, in the Disney/Walden Media film sequel *The Chronicles of Narnia: Prince Caspian*, a romantic relationship is represented between Susan and Caspian that does not exist in Lewis's novel *Prince Caspian: Return to Narnia*. While Lucy is not explicitly situated within a heterosexual romance narrative in the film sequels, in *The Chronicles of Narnia:* The *Voyage of the Dawn Treader*, a number of episodes are included in the film that allude to Lucy's physical and emotional maturation from child to adolescent. In these segments, Lucy is represented as secretly envious of Susan's beauty, and in one key scene, Lucy finds a book of incantations and transforms herself through a beauty spell into her older sister. However, the message that underscores this narrative is that Lucy must have faith in herself as she is closest to Narnia and Aslan of the Pevensie siblings (*The Chronicles* 2010). Thus, the film franchise expands upon Lucy's maturation while sustaining the dominant discourse of innocence through the absence of a heterosexual romance narrative. Nevertheless, there are multiple examples of digital fan cultures around Lucy Pevensie that cultivate relationships and potential romances that are not explicitly represented in the novel or film franchise. These include fan communities around the relationship between Lucy and Mr. Tumnus.

In Lewis's novel, Lucy's interaction with the faun Mr. Tumnus primarily emphasizes her curiosity and openness to experiences of magic and wonder. In addition, as a faun, a half-goat, half-human creature from Roman mythology, Mr. Tumnus has a range of mythical associations. Fauns are spirits, followers of Bacchus that are often compared to the satyrs of Greek mythology and the god Pan as well as pastoral and rustic elements (i.e., shepherds, flocks, nymphs, harps). These qualities of Tumnus as a mythical creature further emphasize Lucy's role as a Romantic heroine. However, fauns also have semiotic associations to drunken revelry, sexuality, and fertility (Kirk 10). Notably, Lewis's description of Tumnus accentuates his human characteristics as well as his mannered and civilized qualities ("pleasant little face" as well as "umbrella" and "red woolen muffler") (Lewis 2005: 10). Nevertheless, as a signifier of sexuality and animalistic tendencies, he connotes various elements that create conflict with Lucy's otherwise innocent character.

Pauline Baynes's illustration represents Mr. Tumnus and Lucy walking arm and arm in the snowy woods (Lewis 2005: 13). Lucy is represented as a small, thin girl, about a head shorter than the faun, wearing a short-sleeved dress with a bow at the back and knee socks. This stylized depiction of Lucy reflects the idealized and often stereotypical childhood figures characteristic of children's picture books of the 1950s and supports the salient discourse of Lucy as a Romantic child. In this particular image, the representation alludes to her innocent connection to elements of wonder, nature, and fantasy, in this case exemplified in her closeness to the mythological character of the faun. It is significant that this visual representation does not share the undertones of violence (sexual or otherwise) or seduction often represented by an unknown, male adult animal in the woods, particularly within the moral development discourse exemplified by the Grimms' and Perrault's versions of Little Red Riding Hood (Zipes 55–57). This discourse of moral or social pedagogy aimed at young females is not explicitly represented in Baynes's illustration of Mr. Tumnus and Lucy walking together through the woods. Nevertheless, the visual allusion to the Little Red Riding Hood tale and its associated discourses of preadolescent sexuality, moral development, and danger complicate the representation of Lucy's idealized innocent nature in her relationship with Mr. Tumnus. These intertextual associations are negotiated in diverse manners by readers, viewers, and producers in their adaptations of the text.

In an article on *Harry Potter* fandom, Catherine Tosenberger observes that fans may be interested to differing degrees in the presence of their favored slash (same-gender) pairings in the source texts. Moreover, she discusses how these relationships may be cultivated or acknowledged by the authors (in the case of J.K. Rowling) or film producers (See Tosenberger 196). Similarly, while the Disney/Walden Media film franchise sustains Lewis's representation of Lucy as an innocent child, the filmic adaptation and behind-the-scenes franchise texts may cultivate the possibility of a close relationship between Tumnus and Lucy. Lewis's original text describes Lucy's meeting with Mr. Tumnus in terms of an immediate close connection: "And so Lucy found herself walking through the wood arm in arm with this strange creature as if they had known one another all their lives" (2005: 14). The film adaptation expands upon Lewis's written text through the representation of a visually explicit kindred and close relationship between these two characters and the actors who play them. The closeness of this relationship is articulated through the physical closeness of their first meeting as depicted through close camera shots on the faces of the two figures, and a candid awkwardness of the encounter as cultivated through the adapted script of the scene and the interactions of the actors. For example, the faun slouches slightly to speak with Lucy, creating a physically close encounter. Her interaction with a young Mr. Tumnus is not unlike the meeting scene in a teen romance novel, including the gift of her handkerchief. Moreover, the casting of James McAvoy, a young, attractive actor who was listed in the celebrity magazine *People* as one of the "Sexiest Men Alive" (2008), offers a possibility for viewers to identify Mr. Tumnus as a normalized object of heterosexual affection for preadolescent and adolescent female viewers.

The *Movie Companion* elaborates the relationship between Lucy and Mr. Tumnus in the film through the representation of the relationship between Georgie Henley and James McAvoy (who plays Mr. Tumnus) in the behind-the-scenes of the film production. Moore describes the believability of their relationship on screen as a result of their off-screen friendship: "What charges their scenes with so much emotion and depth is the magical friendship that Georgie and James McAvoy enjoy in real life" (81). Moreover, he observes that "[t]heir chemistry is palpable; you can see two people who enjoyed hanging around each other, and it makes such a difference to the movie" (83). The director Andrew Adamson also confirms this "magical relationship" in his written section of the *Movie Companion* text:

> the thing that I could never have hoped for or anticipated was how much he [McAvoy] developed a kinship with Georgie—they genuinely liked each other. They would goof around between takes. That's so important to the role. And they would do Posh and Beckham. You would hear them between takes doing their little skits [Moore 129].

The relationship is represented as silly and fun (i.e., "they would goof around") as well as drawing on popular culture terms that would address young readers such as the allusion to the two actors pretending that that they were the celebrity couple Victoria (Posh Spice) and David Beckham (i.e., "they would do Posh and Beckham"). Furthermore, Georgie describes her first meeting with McAvoy in the language of physical attributes and fashion or style signifiers that are often used in magazines and adolescent fiction: "He had piercing blue eyes, lovely eyes, nice curly chestnut hair.... And he was wearing this cool vintage jumper and trainers" (Moore 83). Through this description, Georgie Henley represents James McAvoy as a potential heterosexual object of romantic interest. The result is the cultivation of a high modality for a close relationship between Lucy and Mr. Tumnus developed through the blurring of information about the interactions between the actors Georgie Henley and James McAvoy.

The examples of Mr. Tumnus/Lucy fandom are numerous from fan sites dedicated to their relationship in the book and feature film. Similar to the remix fan video of "Lucy Breakaway," the writer of the fanfiction text "Everywhere"

(2007) provides an example of fantasy fan fiction around the Lucy Pevensie and Tumnus relationship (BlackMoonWhiteSun). This fan fiction text integrates the lyrics of a Michelle Branch song about lost love "Everywhere" (Branch) within a fictional narrative about Mr. Tumnus and Lucy that follows the style and narrative conventions of an adolescent romance novel.

This fictional story exemplifies anarchic and intertextual play with the discourses around Lucy Pevensie. The narrative expands upon the potential maturation and sexuality of Lucy in conflict with the Romantic child discourse in the written text and the Disney/Walden Media film franchise. The tag line for this story reads, "It's been nine years since Lucy's seen her beloved Mr. Tumnus[,] but everywhere she turns, she sees curly locks and red mufflers. It's time they were reunited, don't you think?" (BlackMoonWhiteSun). This introductory tag-line situates this narrative as both a sequel (nine years ahead in the future of *The Lion, the Witch and the Wardrobe* narrative) and an expanded story that focuses on a relationship that is not fleshed out in the primary text. Moreover, the tone of the tag line (everywhere she turns, she sees curly locks and red mufflers) and the imperative voice (Don't you think?) situates the story in the realm of adolescent fiction and particularly teen romance narratives (BlackMoonWhiteSun). The description of "curly locks" also humanizes the faun character, placing him as the romantic protagonist of adolescent fiction rather than a mythological creature. Thus, while the intrinsic fantasy content at the crux of this story—a romantic and potentially sexual relationship between an adult half-human/half-animal mythological creature and a preadolescent girl—is phantasmagoric in nature, the other discourses drawn upon in the story, such as the setting and plot conventions of an adolescent romance novel, function to minimize the anarchic elements.

In order to produce this romantic narrative within the normative conventions of coming-of-age discourses, Lucy is represented as an adolescent female protagonist, beyond the discourses of tween girlhood, particularly the discourse of Romantic innocence that is articulated in both Lewis's novel and the Disney/Walden Media film. This adolescent Lucy is exuberant as she races towards an individual she believes to be Mr. Tumnus wearing a red muffler: "She flung her arms around the person's waist and exclaimed, 'Oh, it's so good to see you again'" (BlackMoonWhiteSun). In the story, Lucy dreams that she is with Mr. Tumnus in Narnia at a Valentine's Day ball. In this dream sequence, she is "Queen Lucy," an older incarnation of the child Lucy with "Her long golden hair [...] tied into a knot on top of her head" and a "mocking scornful look" (BlackMoonWhiteSun). The narrative primarily follows the conventional narrative from adolescent romance fiction of a burgeoning romance between a bashful male revealing his love to a mocking and exuberant royal female.

In this revision of the final narrative of Narnia, the Christian utopia created by Lewis in *The Last Battle* (1956) is subverted by this fan writer's vision of Narnia as an idealized image of inter-species and inter-generational coupling. The narrator describes how "couples of different ages and species danced, holding each other tightly. The Faun looked over to her" (BlackMoonWhiteSun). Moreover, despite the conventions of courtship that allude to Victorian and Edwardian novels of maturation, within this fantasy space, Tumnus is a "stammering" and insecure male suitor, and Lucy is an active sexual agent who "stood on tip-toe and kissed him firmly on the lips" while later in the story she "kissed his lips and mounted her horse" as well as "pulled her hand away from the Faun's and wrapped both of her arms around his shoulders" (BlackMoonWhiteSun). In this story, the return to Narnia through death allows her to return to Mr. Tumnus. The fantasy space of Narnia in this text not only allows Lucy to live forever in Narnia, as she does in Lewis's original narrative, but also allows for her to engage in a romantic relationship with an adult male faun. Thus, this representation of Lucy and Mr. Tumnus challenges the socio-cultural norms around relationships between adults and children as well as humans and animals.

This examination reveals the continued engagement and reimagining of Lewis's *Narnia* texts within contemporary cross-media cultures. Moreover, this analysis demonstrates how discourse articulated in a canonical children's literature text may be transformed across media and cultural contexts. The act of tracing the articulation of discourse across franchised texts highlights how historically rooted discourses are reaffirmed through a contemporary film franchise. In the case of Lucy Pevensie, discourses of childhood innocence and maturation from the original novel are rearticulated through distinct design choices that address and engage with viewers, consumers, and readers directly. Although the representation of Lucy by film franchise producers continues to reinforce discourse from the original novel, digital fan cultures distinctly apply discourse from outside the original text and film franchise. Behind-the-scenes discourses may expand upon the film discourse through the blurring of the real and fictional identities of Georgie Henley and Lucy Pevensie. However, it is the designers of fan videos and fan fiction who illustrate the production of alternative and disruptive narratives that continue to challenge, transform, and re-imagine Lewis's original *Narnia* texts.

Works Cited

Adams, Ernest. *Fundamentals of Game Design*, 2d ed. Berkeley, CA: Pearson, 2010. Print.
Aitken, Stuart C. *Geographies of Young People: The Morally Contested Spaces of Identity*. London: Routledge, 2001. Print.
BlackMoonWhiteSun. "Everywhere." *Fanfiction.net*, April 2007. Web. 5 March 2010.

Branch, Michelle. "Everywhere." *The Spirit Room*. Writers: Michelle Branch and John Shanks. Maverick. 2001. CD.

Brown, Devin. "The Ongoing Appeal of *The Chronicles of Narnia*: A Partial Explanation." *New Review of Children's Literature and Librarianship* 9.1 (2003): 99–112. Web. 28 June 2010.

Bunyan, John. *The Pilgrim's Progress*. 1678. Oxford World's Classics edition. W.R. Owens, ed. Oxford: Oxford University Press, 2003. Print.

Burn, Andrew. "Potterliteracy: Cross-Media Narratives, Cultures and Grammars." *Papers: Explorations in Children's Literature* 14.2 (2004): 5–17.

Burrows, Andy. "Developing the Characters for *The Chronicles of Narnia* Videogame." Gamespot.com, 2005 December. Web. 10 May 2010.

Cabot, Meg. *The Princess Diaries*. New York: HarperCollins, 2000. Print.

The Chronicles of Narnia: The Lion, The Witch and The Wardrobe. Dir. Andrew Adamson. Perf. Georgie Henley, Skandar Keynes, William Moseley, Anna Popplewell, Tilda Swinton, James McAvoy. Walt Disney Pictures, Walden Media, 2005. DVD release: 2006. DVD.

The Chronicles of Narnia: The Lion, The Witch and The Wardrobe. Buena Vista Games, Traveller's Tales, November 14, 2005. ESRB: Teen. Videogame.

The Chronicles of Narnia: The Voyage of the Dawn Treader. Dir. Michael Apted. Perf. Ben Barnes, Skandar Keynes, and Georgie Henley. Fox 2000 Pictures, Walden Media, 2010. Film.

The Chronicles of Narnia: Prince Caspian. Dir. Andrew Adamson. Perf. Ben Barnes, Skandar Keynes and Georgie Henley. Walt Disney Pictures, Walden Media, 2008. Film.

Clarkson, Kelly. "Breakaway." *The Princess Diaries 2: Royal Engagement Soundtrack*. Writer: Avril Lavigne, Bridget Benenate and Matthew Gerrard. Walt Disney Pictures, 2004. CD.

De Certeau, Michel. *The Practice of Everyday Life*. Berkeley: University of California, 1984. Print.

Do Rozario, Rebecca-Anne. "The Princess and the Magic Kingdom: Beyond Nostalgia, the Function of the Disney Princess." *Women's Studies in Communication* 27.1 (2004): 34–59. Print.

Ezard, John. "Narnia Books Attacked as Racist and Sexist." *The Guardian*, Guardian.co.uk, 3 June 2002. Web. 8 March 2010.

Genette, Gerard. *Narrative Discourse*. Ithaca, NY: Cornell University Press, 1980. Print.

Harris, Anita, *Future Girl: Young Women in the Twenty-First Century*. New York: Routledge, 2004. Print.

Jenkins, H. *Convergence Culture: Where Old and New Media Collide*. New York: New York University Press, 2006. Print.

____. *Textual Poachers: Television Fans and Participatory Culture*. New York: Routledge, 1992. Print.

____. "Transmedia Storytelling: Moving Characters from Books to Films to Video Games to Make Them Stronger and More Compelling." *Technology Review* 15 January 2003. Web. 10 December 2008.

Keionna. "The Chronicles of Narnia—Breakaway." *YouTube*, 25 June 2006. Web. 28 June 2011.

Kirk, E.J. *Beyond the Wardrobe: The Official Guide to Narnia*. New York: Harper Collins, 2005. Print.

Klimchuk, Marianne Rosner and Sandra A. Krasovec. *Packaging Design: Successful Product Branding from Concept to Shelf*. Hoboken: John Wiley & Sons, 2006. Print.

Kress, Gunther and Theo van Leeuwen. *Multimodal Discourse: The Modes and Media of Contemporary Communication*. London: Oxford University Press, 2001.

____. *Reading Images: The Grammar of Visual Design*. London: Routledge, 1996. Print.

Lankshear, Colin and Michele Knobel. *A New Literacies Sampler (New Literacies and Digital Epistemologies)*. New York: Peter Lang, 2007.

Lewis, C.S. *The Last Battle*. 1956. Illus. Pauline Baynes. London: Fontana Lions, 1986. Print.
____. *The Lion, the Witch and the Wardrobe*. Illus. (and cover art) Pauline Baynes. London: Geoffrey Bles, 1950. Print.
____. *The Lion, the Witch and the Wardrobe*. 1950. Illus. Pauline Baynes. New York: HarperCollins, 2005. Print.
LiviaEvans. "Breakaway." *YouTube*, 22 June 2006. Web. 28 June 2011.
mogi93. "Lucy-Breakaway." *YouTube*, 20 November 2006. Web. 2 December 2007. This video is no longer accessible.
Mueller, Greg. "Review of *Chronicles of Narnia: The Lion, the Witch and the Wardrobe*." Gamespot.com, 9 December 2005. Web. 20 May 2010.
The Princess Diaries. Dir. Garry Marshall. Perf. Anne Hathaway, Julie Andrews. Walt Disney Pictures, BrownHouse Productions, 2001. Film.
The Princess Diaries 2: Royal Engagement. Dir. Garry Marshall. Perf. Anne Hathaway, Julie Andrews. BrownHouse Productions, Walt Disney Pictures, 2004. Film.
"Sexiest Men Alive 2008." *People*. November 14, 2007. Print.
Tosenberger, Catherine. "Homosexuality at the Online Hogwarts: Harry Potter Slash Fanfiction." *Children's Literature* 36 (2008): 185–207. Web. Accessed 10 March 2010.
Trim, Mary. "The Pilgrim's Progress: Literary and Psychological Echoes in *The Chronicles of Narnia*." *The New Review of Children's Literature and Librarianship* 1.1. (1995): 119–133. Print.
Watson, Victor. "Introduction." *Coming of Age in Children's Literature*. Victor Watson and Margaret Meek, eds. London: Continuum, 2003. 1–44. Print.
Zipes, Jack. *The Trials and Tribulations of Little Red Riding Hood: Versions of The Tale in Sociocultural Context*. South Hadley, MA: Bergin and Garvey, 1983. Print.

An Evolutionary Journey: Pokémon, *Mythic Quests* and the Culture of Challenge

Lincoln Geraghty

Pokémon, the Japanese trading card craze turned computer game and merchandising phenomenon, has captivated millions of children across the globe for more than 15 years. Although loved by its young fans it has also attracted plenty of criticism from parents and cultural commentators who have focused their attention on the hyper-commercialism of the Nintendo brand and the supposed commodification of childhood that having to "catch 'em all" encourages. As well as the toys, cards, and popular television series based on the games there have been 16 feature length films (to date and with the majority made for television and released on DVD) that introduce new characters, creatures and extend the Pokémon narrative universe.[1] In many ways Pokémon is the prime example of a contemporary "commercial supersystem of transmedia intertextuality," as defined by Marsha Kinder (3), where the children's brand spreads out across multiple media platforms and commodities, driven by the central story-arc of Ash Ketchum's ongoing journey to become a Pokémon Master. Within this narrative, Ash's physical journey to new regions (catching new Pokémon) plays out in conjunction with his more emotional and personal journey, learning life lessons and making new friends (never separated from his best friend, Pikachu).

While a consideration of transmedia aspects of the Pokémon brand is important, I want to focus more on the relationship between transmediality, the collecting ethos (catching and training Pokémon) and how this informs a culture of challenge as seen in the various films that depict Ash, Pikachu, and friends continuing their travels around the fictional world.[2] The challenges they face are numerous and range from the physically dangerous to the morally uplifting, from preventing the destruction of Earth to reuniting family members. While the games and TV series might be seen to encourage a culture of consumption, reflected in the need to collect and trade Pokémon in order to progress to the next level, the films offer a more didactic narrative where the notion of challenge is central. As intermediate points in the overarching series narrative depicted in the television series, the films do not focus on the collecting aspects of the franchise (battling trainers and catching new pokémon). Rather, their narratives center on the continuing personal journey of Ash and his associates; their encounters with other trainers and enemies emphasize the heroism of the quest, the mythic nature of the story, and the utopian elements of the regions through which they travel. So, building on David Buckingham and Julian Sefton-Green's argument that the "catch 'em all" ethos mediated through watching, trading and playing helps children develop new media skills and allows them to participate in modern society, I argue that the films encourage their audiences to learn the value of personal achievement in the face of moral and physical adversity; that simply collecting Pokémon and acquiring more is not enough to offer happiness and emotional fulfillment. Instead of teaching children to be lazy—staying indoors or simply buying everything they can to be the most popular kid in the playground—the activities of watching, collecting, trading, and playing with the cards, toys and related merchandise converge to make children active participants in the fictional world of *Pokémon*. They are challenged to watch and play, create and achieve, question and learn.

The following analysis of two films in the series will focus on Ash's mythic quest through the utopian world of *Pokémon*. Examining the quest itself, Ash's journey and role as hero, the first section provides an interrogation of *Pokémon: The First Movie* (1998). Released with much fanfare following the immediate success of the television series, the first movie took a much darker turn. Ash's role as trainer is relegated as he must broker peace between two powerful pokémon: the mythical Mew and the legendary Mewtwo.[3] With the fate of the world at stake Ash puts his personal ambitions aside and takes on the role of savior. Mirroring Vladimir Propp's structuralist approach to narrative, Ash's challenge is to bring order to chaos—undergoing a metaphorical transformation as he battles evil. The second film I discuss, *Pokémon: 4Ever* (2002), draws more on the utopian elements of the fictional world. When a forest is threatened and the pokémon Celebi, spirit of the forest, is captured by an evil hunter, Ash is called upon to provide balance between nature and science, the modern world and the utopian paradise which provides a home for humans and pokémon. The Pokémon universe is a utopia and the narrative of this film provides a social critique of contemporary issues such as environmentalism and animal rights when that utopia is threatened. Ash's challenge to protect utopia reflects the moralistic tone of the entire Pokémon franchise and again underscores the importance of self-sacrifice and the individual's role in a just and equal society.

The Mythic Quest

Despite the dubious nature of commercialized merchandise and syndicated animated television David Buckingham and Julian Sefton-Green see the more recent *Pokémon* phenomenon in a more positive light than most critics. They feel that the "catch 'em all" mantra that inspires children to buy also encourages children to create and learn the value of friendship, important in the formation and development of adult relationships in the future. For Buckingham and Sefton-Green the mythical world where kids must collect and train "pocket monsters" is transformative, where children are encouraged to embark on a "hero's quest" (386): "The narrative tropes and themes" of this quest, most obviously located in the associated cartoon series and video games, "are characteristic of the role-playing games and fantasy literature favored by boys slightly older than the average Pokémon fan," yet, as Buckingham and Sefton-Green point out, this only serves to indicate how sophisticated the toy range actually is.

Using Henry Jenkins' work on the virtual spaces of the computer game, the authors see *Pokémon* as providing children with "a very extensive space ... a self contained universe [informed by the fictional narrative of the main characters and the signature Pokémon, Pikachu] with its own unique geography and cosmology, that can only be mastered through active exploration" (Buckingham and Sefton-Green 387; see also Jenkins). As well as being a form of "'consumer training—a means of inducting children into" our commercially driven culture, it can also be seen as "partial training ... as a means of developing in children the 'multiliteracies' that are now essential for democratic participation" (394). This idea of training can also be linked to the specificity of the medium itself, as John Hartley (218–219) sees television as a "paedocratic regime" that not only tells the viewer how to watch television but also how to enjoy it.

The notion of quest is not unfamiliar to children's media and literary culture. For Deborah O'Keefe, "The most basic story pattern shows a human or animal child leaving home to find adventure in a puzzling world, finding it, then returning home wiser" (30). Further, according to Bruno Bettelheim, the journey and return teach "the child that permitting one's fantasy to take hold of oneself for a while is not detrimental.... The hero returns to reality—a happy reality, but one devoid of magic" (63). For Ash, his homecoming to Pallet Town in the Kanto Region after every trip to enter a Pokémon tournament represents this return to reality. His mother welcomes him back and he takes stock of his travels, adding newly captured pokémon to his collection and sharing stories with his mentor Professor Oak who heads up the laboratory in Pallet Town. Adventure rarely comes calling at home—Ash's adventures start as he sets out to the next tournament.[4] Indeed, part of the challenge that is presented to Ash is the requirement to wait, to be patient, before he can head off on his next journey. Once he does then his exuberance takes over and his role of hero becomes more apparent.

Of course, as a Japanese text transplanted across the globe and translated through an American lens, *Pokémon* inevitably changes meaning as it crosses international borders and is received in the contexts of local audiences. The central premise of the story, Ash's journey to become a Pokémon Master, might seem the one thing that is universally translatable but even the quest changes depending on the national contexts of reception. In Japan Ash is called Satoshi and his role as protagonist is very much on a par with the ensemble cast of characters. The Americanized Ash is more heroic, his quest is more individual, and as an audience we are meant to see his enemies and challengers as obstacles to his eventual goal:

> The Japanese narrative focuses less on heroism and more on the complex relationships that develop among characters. The good/bad guy dichotomy is more clearly defined in the U.S. version of the series in which Ash is clearly marked as the hero [Katsuno and Maret 84].

Using Propp to deconstruct the *Pokémon* narrative further we might understand Ash's hero role and quest as part of a larger structure of storytelling that includes certain elements and characters. In *Pokémon: The First Movie* Ash is called upon to stop the villainous Giovanni, head of Team Rocket,[5] who has created a group of super-clone pokémon including a genetically enhanced version of Mew he calls Mewtwo. With psychic powers that threaten the peace in Kanto Mewtwo is corrupted and rebels against his creator and other pokémon. Driven by hatred for humans and the pursuit of revenge against Giovanni Mewtwo almost accomplishes its plans. However, Ash and Pikachu stand up to Mewtwo and through their battling, bravery and obvious compassion for each other show it that violence is not the answer and won't bring it any peace or closure. For John Fiske, "Mythic approaches to narrative are essentially paradigmatic in that they emphasize the cultural-ideological system that underlies the syntagmatic flow of the narrative" (135). Using Propp's work on Russian folk tales he argues that popular entertainment narratives, as *Pokémon* clearly is, follow a similar structure. This structure emphasizes that the individual is propelled to act by a number of functions and aided or hindered by certain characters that perform specific roles. The following breakdown of *Pokémon: The First Movie* is based on Propp's model as outlined in Fiske (135–137).

Ash's call to defeat Giovanni and save Mewtwo and those he threatens to hurt comes when he is encouraged to battle Giovanni's super-clones, under the guise of an invitation to a pokémon competition. The preparation stage sees Ash leave home (Pallet Town) and be deceived by Giovanni. When Ash learns of his plan, of the super-clones and sees Mewtwo being made to fight he decides to help and free all the captured pokémon. Planning action against Team Rocket is part of Propp's complication stage. In the transference stage the hero is typically aided by a magical helper given by a donor and transferred to the scene of the action against the villain. In the film we can see these roles shifting across different characters. The donor is Professor Oak, who has already given Ash Pikachu to accompany him on his original journey.[6] Pikachu, an electric mouse pokémon and highly attractive to Team Rocket, is akin to the magical helper and as such uses its powers to fight for and with Ash. It is this bond that eventually convinces Mewtwo that humans and pokémon can live in peace with each other and therefore ends his quest for vengeance. So, although Mewtwo does perform the villain role initially, it is Giovanni who remains the villain as he leaves to continue his mission to capture all pokémon and use them to conquer the world. Mewtwo is redeemed, becoming the victim of Giovanni during and after the struggle stage when it battles Ash and Pikachu. The last two stages of Propp's narrative functions are the return and recognition, and we can see these clearly in the film. However, Ash does not return home to the safety of his family. Instead he returns to the road as he eagerly continues his journey to be a Pokémon Master. His heroism is recognized by his friends, Brock and Misty, and Mewtwo who shows mercy and acknowledges Ash's bravery and sacrifice.

Pokémon uses myth intelligently; it adapts its stories to incorporate familiar mythical narrative paradigms that figure centrally within our own society, history, and culture. These stories may be centuries old and have been resigned to the past, but *Pokémon* breathes life back into them by retelling them through the eyes of a young person always eager to learn and ever enthusiastic to carry on. Jack Zipes argues that fairy tales are myths that set "examples for human beings that enable them to codify and order their lives" (*Fairy Tale as Myth* 1) and as the fairy tales became an increasingly popular form of storytelling for children the genre "formed a multi-vocal network of discourses through which writers used familiar motifs, topoi, protagonists, and plots symbolically to comment on the civilizing process and socialization in the respective countries" (15). In *Pokémon*, where the main protagonists are children, this process is made all the more relevant and particular to young viewers because they can see themselves in the children on screen. Myth is an important mode through which stories can be written and told. Richard Slotkin describes myth as "the primary language of historical memory: a body of traditional stories that have, over time, been used to summarize the course of our collective history." Myths not only make up these stories they also "assign ideological meanings to that history" (Slotkin 70). Thus, if the *Pokémon* films use myth to tell a tale then they also carry meaning.

Myth serves as a mode of national identity-making; a shared history common to those who have the power becomes myth when used to create a sense of collective cultural capital. Countries thrive on myths to create, substantiate, and preserve their national identity. Jeffrey Richards describes them as "episodes from [a shared] history that are removed from their context, shorn of complications and qualifications, stripped down to their essentials and endlessly repeated as manifestations of the nation's character, worth and values" (26). Therefore they are imbued with what Slotkin calls "ideological meaning" because myths are created to represent nations and peoples who themselves have their own political and social agendas. The Americanized version of *Pokémon* as depicted in the first feature film projects the image of the hero Ash as savior of the people and pokémon within his fictional world. As a form of storytelling *The First Movie* combines elements of the Japanese trading card game and TV series (1997–present) but its mythic narrative and structure are symbolic. The form of the quest and the challenges that face Ash are more culturally familiar to the western audiences that watch and inform a narrative that teaches children the value of self-sacrifice, heroism and individuality.

Utopia

As a utopia, originally imagined as a trading card game and then spread across multiple media platforms, *Pokémon* shares similar ground with the utopian world imagined by children's author L. Frank Baum in *The Wonderful Wizard of Oz* (1900) and its thirteen sequels.[7] Baum created what has been described as a "'socialist' utopia" which saw Dorothy and Toto transported from a barren Kansas to Oz, a world of plenty and magical characters (Zipes, *Fairy Tales and the Art of Subversion* 129). In Oz everyone is equal, there is no poverty or hunger and (almost) everyone lives in peace and harmony—if there is trouble, such as the Wicked Witch of the West, then by the end of the story Dorothy and her friends easily triumph. Jack Zipes sees Oz as "a specific American utopia ... a place and space in the American imagination," and because Dorothy Gale and her family eventually come to live in Oz rather than continue farming in Kansas "it embodies that which is missing, lacking, absent in America" (*Fairy Tale as Myth* 138). America, at the time Baum wrote his first book, was going through a national crisis: Farmers were struggling to make a living, depression and strikes characterized the 1890s, and war with Spain was testing the country's mettle (Zipes, *Fairy Tales and the Art of Subversion* 126). To his readers, children in particular, Baum's utopia offered something different. Oz's popularity in the early part of the century continues to this day, according to Zipes it "stems from deep social and personal desires that many Americans feel are not being met in this rich and powerful country" (*When Dreams Come True* 182).

Pokémon then, like Oz, is a utopia that many children find attractive. Its vision of the simple life allows for escapism and wish-fulfillment. There is also an element of American self-help which characterizes Ash's quest, a quest characterized by heroism and sacrifice as discussed above, and his transformation as hero along his journey is very much part of the attraction for children. Throughout the Pokémon world humans and pokémon live in harmony. Humans use them to battle and attain status while pokémon benefit from human care, love and affection. The more they battle and train the better they become; many evolve the more they battle, thereby giving more status to their trainers. Indeed, the union between Ash and Pikachu is underscored by the fact that Pikachu resists evolution so that it can remain by Ash's side on his journey. As he travels across the regions, entering contests and collecting pokémon, Ash wants for nothing. Society in the Pokémon world is structured so that trainers on their journey receive support, food and accommodation in the towns and cities they visit. This indicates that the fictional society supports the utopian principle that there is nothing stronger or more important than the bond between trainer and pokémon.

Pokémon represent the natural world and thus in the trainer's bond with their pokémon they also have a duty to protect the environment in which they live, train and travel. Since Ash's bond with Pikachu is so strong we might understand his response to people that threaten the forests, seas, skies and the other pokémon within as equally intense. When the utopian world is under attack by forces seeking to do harm, Ash is again challenged to protect nature and pokémon. We see this overt environmental message clearly in *Pokémon: 4Ever* where Ash, Brock and Misty attempt to save a magical forest and the time-travelling pokémon, Celebi, from Team Rocket's Iron Masked Marauder. With a dark ball that can turn pokémon into evil versions of themselves, the Marauder captures Celebi and uses it to destroy the forest and attack its inhabitants. Ash, as ever, is determined to restore peace and save those pokémon under threat. With the aid of Sam, a boy from the past who had originally saved Celebi from a pokémon hunter, they battle the giant tree monster brought to life with Celebi's dark powers.[8] As the forest is contaminated, with lakes and trees dying from the evil power of the dark ball, Suicune (a legendary pokémon who travels on the north wind and with the power to purify polluted water) uses its magic to cure the environment and bring Celebi back to life. Ash could only do so much, in defeating the Marauder, but he could not repair the damage to the forest. The magic of Suicune and Celebi, along with Ash's determination, combine to bring order to utopia.

Pokémon: 4Ever's attention to issues of environmental protection and the threat posed to nature by unscrupulous organizations like Team Rocket no doubt reflect contemporary concerns reported in the world's media every day. Yet, the fact a children's film should use these issues as the basis for its story is not unusual considering the history of children's literary culture. Alison Lurie argues that many of the well-known and loved children's novels from around the turn of the nineteenth century indicate a fascination for tales set in natural settings such as forests and gardens. As child protagonists enter these enchanted realms they are transformed and become sympathetic to the vulnerable ecosystem contained within. Religion is replaced by nature in these stories, which is "full of power to inspire and heal" (Lurie 183). We can clearly see this in *Pokémon: 4Ever* as the forest contains magical pokémon with the ability to travel through time and bring creatures back to life. So, as the story that preaches an environmental message to children (utopia under threat requires sacrifice and cooperation to save it), it also presents a fantastical and neo-religious view of how humans and pokémon can coexist and maintain nature's balance. I would argue, therefore, this film fits within a tradition of children's literature as outlined by Lurie:

> Many children's classics of the late nineteenth and early twentieth centuries present nature as divine, naturally good, and full of inspiration and healing properties. There is a pagan tone to some of these books: the Christian god is replaced by spirits of another order, sometimes associated with natural features of the landscape, or with water or wind [176].

Similarly, Deborah O'Keefe argues that the place marked as special within children's stories is "somehow out of the world it nestles in but ultimately subject to its laws; it is a moment both in and out of the natural cycle of time" (77). The forest in the film is literally in and out of time as Celebi moves between different generations, pulling Sam and Ash together to help defeat the Marauder. Further, the sheltered space is "sacred" and only attainable if participants enter through a threshold and undergo a transitional experience (O'Keefe 79). As liminal characters these participants are renewed through ritual, both spiritual and physical. Thus, we can see Ash and Sam moving between time and the boundaries of the forest to save Celebi as liminal characters, going through a challenging but necessary transformation to protect nature and maintain the utopia. As I have argued about the first film, Ash is on a mythical quest to be a Pokémon Master and must endure hardship on his journey to attain his goal. In this film Ash's quest becomes a spiritual one as he temporarily ascends from his human state (on the road to mastering his talents) to join Sam, Celebi and Suicune in the utopia of the magical forest (putting his ambitions and desires aside) and assumes a more divine role.

Conclusion

Both films discussed in this chapter explore notions of challenge through the lens of myth and in doing so they both depict a utopia that is under threat. Ash's quests in both revolve around the need to protect and stand up against those who would do harm to the world of *Pokémon*. Therefore, as well as using myth to tell entertaining stories to children, the creators of this multinational and global media brand use myth to teach children important life lessons about friendship, adversity, responsibility and compassion. These lessons may not necessarily be ones adults would think come from a simple trading card game, but nonetheless these are lessons deeply embedded in the cultural framework of the mythic quest motif. It crosses transnational borders and is clearly translatable to both Japanese and western audiences.

Pokémon's culture of challenge is clearly aimed at a youthful audience, using myth and metaphor to tell didactic stories that inform, educate and entertain. The fact that the franchise continues to make new films, TV episodes and computer games signals that there is always going to be an audience eager to consume its messages. However, we should not ignore the fact that *Pokémon* is part of a long tradition of children's literature and media which has communicated important social and cultural messages to its readership and audience over many decades. The narrative framework of the films suggests that Ash's physical and emotional journey to becoming a Pokémon Master (at least in the U.S. version) is a model for children to follow in their lives. Using the card and computer games in conjunction with watching the characters go through trials and ordeals on screen, children are able to play at being the hero—making those sacrifices to win and learning how to be a socially aware citizen within a global media society.

Child play is not unique to the twenty-first century and the *Pokémon* films are not the first to suggest to children how to behave and act. Throughout the history of childhood and children's media play has been an important component of the developmental process, of managing the transition between child and adult. Constructions of childhood in the media therefore play an important part in representing that transition and communicating to child audiences the process and how to manage it sensibly. However, that the films combine fantasy, magic, adult themes and humor suggests the franchise is not treating its audience as children. In this multimedia age, the use of traditional children's narratives as seen in the films discussed in this chapter highlights the continuation of certain values and pedagogies within popular culture. They are able to cross international borders and remain youthful even as children grow up faster and faster as new media technologies open them up to the adult world sooner than in past generations. Perhaps the challenges presented in the *Pokémon* films might seem simple in terms of real world scenarios, but the fact children's film still uses the mythic quest as a narrative trope suggests we are all still fascinated by the hero's journey and what it might prove to show us.

Notes

1. The films are (U.S. release date): *Pokémon: The First Movie* (1998), *Pokémon: The Movie 2000* (2000), *Pokémon 3: The Movie* (2001), *Pokémon: 4Ever* (2002), *Pokémon: Heroes* (2003), *Pokémon: Jurachi Wish Maker* (2004), *Pokémon: Destiny Deoxys* (2005), *Pokémon: Lucario and the Mystery of Mew* (2006), *Pokémon and Ranger and the Temple of the Sea* (2007), *Pokémon: The Rise of Darkrai* (2008), *Pokémon: Giratina and the Sky Warrior* (2009), *Pokémon: Arceus and the Jewel of Life* (2010), *Pokémon: Zoroark, Master of Illusions* (2011), *Pokémon: Black—Victini and Reshiram* (2011), *Pokémon: White—Victini and Zekrom* (2012), *Pokémon the Movie: Kyurem vs. the Sword of Justice* (2012), *Pokémon the Movie: Genesect and the Legend Awakened* (2013). Several of the films were released alongside special shorts, featuring Pikachu and a group of cute pokémon going on an adventure. The television series started in 1998 in the USA and has lasted 16 seasons, with more on the horizon.

2. The Pokémon world is not officially named yet it is split into regions which are named and do differ in terms of geography, types of pokémon, and local customs and beliefs. Each region also holds its own tournament, which provides the impetus for Ash and Pikachu to continue their journey and encourages him to become a Pokémon Master. The regions charted so far are: Kanto (where Ash lives), Johto, Hoenn, Sinnoh, and Unova.

3. Pokémon are categorized by type—there are 17 types in total—with many pokémon combining characteristics and abilities of two or more. The types are: bug, flying, normal, dragon, ghost, poison, electric, grass, psychic, fighting, ground, rock, fire, ice, water, dark, and steel. While most pokémon are plentiful in number across regions some are rare (emphasizing the collecting nature of the franchise) and are described as either legendary or mythical, having inspired stories and tales amongst the people who live in the different regions (see Silvestri).

4. New trainers can start their first journey to enter a tournament at age 10. Each receives one of three training pokémon (particular to the region) which they train to learn new moves and enter battles. Ash's first adventure in the television series and game sees him set out to enter the Pokémon League in his own Kanto Region.

5. Team Rocket is the name of the villainous organization bent on capturing the entire world's pokémon. Two of its agents, Jessie and James (Musashi and Kojirō in Japan), are regular adversaries of Ash and aim to kidnap Pikachu for their master, Giovanni. Jessie and James are accompanied by Meowth (Nyarth), the only talking pokémon.

6. In the first episode of the television series Oak supplies Ash with his first training pokémon, in addition to Pikachu whom Ash saved and brought to Oak for medical treatment.

7. See L. Frank Baum, *The Wonderful Wizard of Oz* (Chicago: Reilly and Lee, 1900). The sequels are listed with original publication date only: *The Marvelous Land of Oz* (1904), *Ozma of Oz* (1907), *Dorothy and the Wizard in Oz* (1908), *The Road to Oz* (1909), *The Emerald City of Oz* (1910), *The Patchwork Girl of Oz* (1913), *Tik-Tok of Oz* (1914), *The Scarecrow*

of Oz (1915), *Rinkitink in Oz* (1916), *The Lost Princess of Oz* (1917), *The Tin Woodman of Oz* (1918), *The Magic of Oz* (1919), *Glinda of Oz* (1920).

8. It turns out that Sam, the boy from the past, is actually Professor Oak as a child; his experience helping to save Celebi and the forest inspired him to become a scientist and expert on all types of pokémon.

Works Cited

Bettelheim, Bruno. *The Uses of Enchantment: The Meaning and Importance of Fairy Tales*. New York: Vintage, 1977. Print.
Buckingham, David, and Julian Sefton-Green. "Gotta Catch 'em All: Structure, Agency and Pedagogy in Children's Media Culture." *Media, Culture, Society* 25.3 (2003): 379–399. Print.
Fiske, John. *Television Culture*. London: Routledge, 1987. Print.
Hartley, John. *The Uses of Television*. London: Routledge, 1999. Print.
Jenkins, Henry. "'Complete Freedom of Movement': Video Games as Gendered Play Spaces." *From Barbie to Mortal Kombat: Gender and Computer Games*. Justine Cassell and Henry Jenkins, eds. Cambridge, MA: MIT Press, 1998. 262–297. Print.
Katsuno, Hirofumi, and Jeffrey Maret. "Localizing the Pokémon TV Series for the American Market." *Pikachu's Global Adventure: The Rise and Fall of Pokémon*. Joseph Tobin, ed. Durham, NC: Duke University Press, 2004. 80–107. Print.
Kinder, Marsha. *Playing with Power in Movies, Television and Video Games: From Muppet Babies to Teenage Mutant Ninja Turtles*. Berkeley: University of California Press, 1991. Print.
Lurie, Alison. *Boys and Girls Forever: Reflections on Children's Classics from Cinderella to Harry Potter*. London: Chatto and Windus, 2003. Print.
O'Keefe, Deborah. Readers in Wonderland: The Liberating Worlds of Fantasy Fiction. New York: Continuum, 2003. Print.
Pokémon: The First Movie, directed by Kunihiko Yuyama, Japan: OLM/Toho, 1998. Film.
Pokémon: 4Ever, directed by Kunihiko Yuyama, Japan: OLM/Toho, 2002. Film.
Richards, Jeffrey. "Fires Were Started." The Movies as History: Visions of the Twentieth Century. David Ellwood, ed. Stroud: Sutton, 2000. 26–35. Print.
Slotkin, Richard. "Myth and the Production of History." *Ideology and Classic American Literature*. Sacvan Bercovitch and Myra Jehlen, eds. Cambridge: Cambridge University Press, 1986. 70–90. Print.
Silvestri, Chris. *Pokémon: Essential Handbook*. New York: Scholastic, 2012. Print.
Zipes, Jack. *Fairy Tales and the Art of Subversion: The Classical Genre for Children and the Process of Civilization*. New York: Routledge, 1983. Print.
____. *Fairy Tale as Myth/Myth as Fairy Tale*. Lexington: University Press of Kentucky, 1994. Print.
____. *When Dreams Come True: Classical Fairy Tales and Their Tradition*. New York: Routledge, 1999. Print.

Diary of a Wimpy Kid:
Film Adaptation and Media Convergence for Children

Karin Beeler

Until relatively recently, the study of film has largely been based on the centrality of the theatrical release. With the appearance of films on DVDs or Blu-ray and the "media convergence" (Henry Jenkins) of other kinds of digital entertainment, however, the film experience has expanded into other avenues (e.g., games on DVDs, Blu-ray, iPods, Nintendo and online environments, and books that tie in with movies). This re-configuration of the film experience is particularly apparent in children's entertainment like the recent *Diary of a Wimpy Kid* films based on Jeff Kinney's cartoon novels of the same name. The building of a multi-faceted context for viewing film is not only evident in the way digital discs and games are marketed for animated films (e.g., Disney's Pixar and DreamWorks Animation) but this kind of interconnectedness is also the case for live action/animation combination films. *Diary of a Wimpy Kid* (2010), *Diary of a Wimpy Kid: Rodrick Rules* (2011) and *Diary of a Wimpy Kid: Dog Days* (2012) have been made into DVDs/Blu-ray versions with special features including deleted "diary pages" or deleted scenes, and in the case of the second film *Rodrick Rules*, bonus shorts not seen in theaters (http://www.diaryofa wimpykidmovie.com/). The availability of digital copies of these films in Digital Rights Management formats such as Ultraviolet or in home-made copies ensures that the films will adapt to the transitional media culture of multiple devices (iPhones, tablets, etc.) that characterize the households of many North American families. Furthermore, the combined live action/animation format of *The Wimpy Kid* films exists in an intervisual and intertextual path to the books on which they are based. These children's films and their special DVD features can foster further interest in Jeff Kinney's books. Interest in the books in turn generates renewed/further interest in the films. Kinney's companion book *The Wimpy Kid Movie Diary: How Greg Heffley Went Hollywood* (2011) also serves as a particularly innovative way of teaching children about the unique characteristics of the film medium and industry. It is therefore not surprising that the transformation of the film viewing experience for children has also opened up possibilities for the ways in which film adaptation can be discussed.

As Henry Jenkins, Barbara Klinger and Francesco Casetti have argued,[1] the filmic experience has undergone some significant changes with the shift from the theatrical release of films to other modes or sites of delivery. This move from the uni-directional consumption of film in the context of the cinema/movie theater to the more user friendly/user driven experience of enabling the user to control access to film on various media devices (DVDs, videogames, Internet movie clips) has altered the way many of us experience film.[2] This is perhaps most obvious in the way media products have been created, marketed or reconfigured for younger viewers. DVDs offer a multi-faceted experience for the child viewer since they come bundled with bonus features, games, or bloopers that build upon or act as a precursor to a child's viewing of and interactive play with a feature film.[3] One does need to be aware that for those who still want to access films without the accompanying features, there are other modes of delivery (Netflix, etc.) but for children, DVDs in the context of home entertainment still offer a portable/condensed network of media experiences even though the kind of convergence of film and games in a DVD/Blu-ray environment is already slowly being replaced by other technology such as video on demand or streaming options. It is important to note that the convergence of film and other features on DVDs can provide a similar, although not identical, "film experience" for children viewing movies downloaded onto a personal media player, game console, or smartphone. (limited screen size is one obvious difference). While these devices may not have the bonus features of a DVD/Blu-ray setup, they can allow a child/parent to add applications (apps) or online games featuring characters from films. For example, Disney has a website with downloadable games such as *Pirates of the Caribbean* games (http://games.disney.com/). Children may access these online games through various devices depending on their home or personal media environment.

However, even with DVD technology slowly being supplanted by other media,[4] it is worth noting that convergence culture continues to thrive, especially in the context of films for children. The live action/animated films *Diary of a Wimpy Kid* (2010), *Diary of a Wimpy Kid: Rodrick Rules* (2011), and *Diary of a Wimpy Kid: Dog Days* (2012) focus on the character of Greg Heffley and his experiences in an American middle school *Diary of a Wimpy Kid* and *Diary of a Wimpy Kid: Rodrick Rules* reflect several aspects of the usual adaptation process from literature to film. These films still offer some "fidelity to the adapted text" (Hutcheon 6) while also including the "change" that viewers apparently desire along with the repetition of a familiar narrative (9). The film *Dog Days* is based on the fourth book in the series, *Diary of a Wimpy Kid: Dog Days*, and also includes elements from the third book, *Diary of a Wimpy Kid: The Last Straw* As Hutcheon argues, fidelity criticism was once the "critical orthodoxy of adaptation studies" (7); she prefers to view a film adaptation as "an extended intertextual engagement with the adapted work" (8). The *Diary of a Wimpy Kid* films distinguish themselves from more traditional film adaptations by presenting multiple media including animated drawings of the characters based on the cartoon drawing in Kinney's books. The adaptations preserve some of the textual "content" and the illustrations of the cartoon novel while adding live action characters as well as animated cartoon drawings. In a sense, these shared drawings appear to be part of the shared "content" but they have been transformed into animation, thus reinforcing the fact that the medium in film is the message; form and content merge. In other words, the film versions of the *Wimpy Kid* novels are not only the products of adaptation into a different medium, but they also showcase the multi-faceted convergence of various media. Another, pertinent example of this principle may be found in a scene in the first film which opens with a shot of Rowley's (Robert Capron) videogame Twisted Wizard; then the camera cuts to a shot of Greg (Zachary Gordon) and Rowley playing the game. The physical incorporation of videogame scenes in the film goes beyond the necessarily static references to game playing that are present in the print media form.

Indeed, Thor Freudenthal's film *Diary of a Wimpy Kid* (2010) involves an interesting case of intermediality that foregrounds the convergence of image and text in a variety of ways. One of the key examples of adaptation involves the shift from cartoon drawings in the novel to the live action characters depicted in the film . However, the film does not remain a purely live action production. It borrows/embeds the cartoons found in Kinney's novel and uses them to reinforce the action of the live action characters; just as the drawings in the book reinforce the text. Thus, rather than providing a complete transformation of the cartoon novel into a live action context, the film also adapts the static graphic elements to the moving medium of film. The embedded images in the novel appear as moving animated images in the film that sometimes appear on screen alone and sometimes interact with and even transform into their live action versions. This transformation of animated cartoon drawing to live action character occurs with Zach's younger brother Manny (Connor Fielding) in the second film. Similarly, in the first scene of the third film, the members of Zach's family appear as animated drawings in an otherwise live action scene, and then change into their live action identities. Text from Kinney's novel also appears alongside the cartoon images in several introductory scenes of the first *Diary of a Wimpy Kid* film but later in the same film, text is supplanted by voiceover narration as a way of engaging with the animated drawings. This is in keeping with general principles of film adaptation as sound and image rather than text (except for subtitles) are the dominant tools for transmitting a film's message.

Narrative Point of View

In any adaptation, narrative voice or point of view may also be presented differently than in the "adapted text."[5] It can be difficult to sustain a first person narration throughout the course of a film since films are often more about showing than telling; but it is worth noting that this kind of attention to variation of the medium by means of a mixture of showing and telling is already present in Kinney's novel through the use of cartoon drawing and bubble dialogue text. Thus, when we see the shift from live action to an animated drawing in the film, the shift in "form" is not completely unexpected or as unsettling as one might expect. The film also repeats the idea of resistance to genre that is already present in the novel, but it also offers a bit of a twist. For example, in the cartoon novel, Kinney's character Greg begins his narrative by resisting a particular genre or form—the use of the term "diary" for his narrative—thus trying to construct an image of himself as a serious, masculine writer: "First of all, let me get something straight: this is a JOURNAL, not a diary" (Kinney *Diary of a Wimpy Kid,* 1). He addresses his audience/reader directly to communicate a sense of authority, but also reveals his anxiety about some "jerk" calling him a "sissy" (1) because he has found Greg with a diary. He thus equates the genre of the diary with a feminine gender and by extension with a less "serious" form of writing. The fact that the word JOURNAL is in all capital letters visually reinforces this preference for the term journal. In the film, Greg repeats the same phrase, "this is a JOURNAL, not a diary," thus demonstrating how the film repeats a key component of Kinney's novel. However, on the DVD cover of *Diary of a Wimpy Kid*, this resistance to the diary genre is developed further and transformed into a change in *medium*, "It's Not a Diary, It's a Movie!" Moreover the film highlights the first person and screen-centric aspects of film by portraying Greg's image of himself on giant videoscreens/billboards as he envisions his parents looking up at these images in awe of their son's fame.

The adaptation of the first person narrative in the *Diary of a Wimpy Kid* films is achieved in two key ways: first, through voiceover narration, which reinforces the interaction between live action characters/settings and animated images while also highlighting the importance of sound in film, and second, through the direct form of address. The first technique enables the film to engage in the art of "compression" (Hutcheon 47) by showing animated images from the cartoon novel without also having to show Greg on screen at the same time. The visual presentation of the animated images at the same time as text transcribed into voice-over takes advantage of film's two channels of information to compress what may take more time or space to accomplish in the purely visual medium of the novel. The second technique, direct form of address, involves Greg facing and directly addressing the camera/audience, thus breaking the fourth wall.[6] This technique introduces a level of self-reflexivity that highlights the convergence of the film and the (implied) adapted text by Kinney. One of the developments of transmitting narrative content across various media has been heightened self-reflexivity within these narratives. Tom Brown has already commented on this phenomenon in the animated film *The Lion King 1½* in which Timon the Meerkat (Nathan Lane) and Pumbaa the Warthog (Ernie Sabella) watch the first Lion King film while controlling the remote and by extension, the process of viewing a film in which they appeared. The *Diary of a Wimpy Kid* films break the fourth wall by not only having the character address the audience but by also including a veiled reference to the adaptation process: "I always figured they'd make a movie about my life, but I didn't think they'd start the movie here. But seriously, who wants to see a movie about a kid who's stuck in middle school with a bunch of morons" (*Diary of a Wimpy Kid*). This convention of breaking the fourth wall has become more common in both animated (*The Lion King 1½*) and live action film. For example according to Steve Weintraub, *The Muppets* (2011) (initially called *The Muppet Movie*) apparently broke "the fourth wall every five minutes" ("Nicholas Stoller on the Muppet Movie"). The increasing exposure of children to this technique suggests that children of this generation will become familiar with how various media forms draw attention to themselves as art forms or narrative conventions.

There are many examples of the convergence of media culture as a theme in the second and third *Diary of a Wimpy Kid* books and films, although they still share similarities with the first film in the co-existence of animated drawings with live action characters. In Kinney's book *Diary of a Wimpy Kid: Rodrick Rules* there is a reference to an embarrassing video of Greg's mother dancing at his brother's rock concert performance and how this video ended up on the Internet (216). This reference incorporates images of a cartoon character in front of a computer, thus embedding an image of the computer into a novel and highlighting the transference of the image of Greg's mother dancing into the video medium. In the film the focus of this media transmission has shifted to the possibility of Rodrick posting a video on YouTube; the video was a film of Greg accidentally running around in his underwear in a women's washroom. However, Rodrick eventually returns the videotape to Greg after he does a favor for Rodrick so that his older brother can perform with his rock band. *Dog Days*, the third *Diary of a Wimpy Kid* movie, like the first film, includes shots of Greg playing his Twisted Wizard videogame; in *Dog Days*, he plays the game on his Xbox all day long during his summer vacation. These references to other kinds of media in the films reinforce the interconnectedness of the screen cultures embedded in all three film adaptations.

The Book on the Making of the *Diary of a Wimpy Kid* Films and Self-reflexivity

The narrative example of self-reflexivity in the first *Diary of a Wimpy Kid* film creates a sense of book/film convergence through Greg's reference to someone making a movie about him: "I always figured they'd make a movie about my life." However, the existence of Kinney's companion book *The Wimpy Kid Movie Diary: How Greg Heffley Went Hollywood* (2011) also serves as an educational tool to make children even more media savvy and aware of the "medium" as the message. The book is described by the author-persona as "the story of how a little idea got turned into a major motion picture, and how a fictional cartoon character became a real boy" (1). This text is a particularly innovative way of teaching children about the unique characteristics of the film medium. It incorporates information about the kinds of props and special effects that were used in the films as well as a discussion of the challenges of shooting in Vancouver, Canada, which is known as Hollywood North because of the large number of American films shot in this city. Kinney's "movie diary" indicates that Vancouver was used as the location to serve as the image of a "typical American town" (27). However, there were a number of issues: apparently this city had few houses with finished basements (148); the chilly and rainy October weather made it imperative to get the shots right in one take (154) and, in the case of the second film *Diary of a Wimpy Kid: Rodrick Rules*, there is no roller rink in Vancouver, "so one had to be built from scratch" (198).

Jeff Kinney's companion "movie diary" is informative yet the film-making details are presented in an engaging fashion, suitable for a younger readership. The narrative voice of the "diary" could be the voice of Jeff Kinney, but he never inserts himself into the narrative by referring to "his" books or "his" characters; instead the voice appears more objective while still managing to connect with his audience by addressing them more informally as "you" ("As you can see" 2).

The book provides some key commentary on the adaptation process through the inclusion of sections called "Page to Screen" (152). These sections employ parallel photographs from the first movies and the books, thereby highlighting both the repetition and change involved in the adaptation process (Hutcheon 9). Kinney's companion text engages in a unique intertextual and intervisual play with the film, thus encouraging media convergence. Parents who may have feared that the so-called passive viewing of films has displaced the reading of books can take heart in the prominent place of a book which can also be used to provide children with the critical skills to study films. Linda Hutcheon points out that film adaptations of books "are often considered educationally important for children" (118) and can motivate children to read the books upon which they are based. The Wimpy kid multi-media/convergence phenomenon clearly shows how text and film converge in an interconnected way, allowing multiple entry points to different media and in a different order whether one accesses the characters/storylines through the cartoon novel, the film, its bonus features, through the movie diary/book or even through Jeff Kinney's official website: wimpykid.com. In fact, the novel series started as a web-based publication in 2004.

Conclusion

The *Diary of a Wimpy Kid* films and texts offer the child viewer/reader an intense intervisual or intertextual play with media form and content. Image and text converge in these children's books and computer based products; the films offer live action and animated images while also adding sounds to this interplay. They even go so far as to seamlessly transform animated images into live action images in the middle of performances (e.g., the transformation of Greg's brother Manny in the first film). Moreover, *The Wimpy Kid Movie Diary* enhances the media convergence by discussing the adaptation process. I would like to conclude with the observation that the very process of writing this chapter has been an example of media convergence for me as a film studies scholar. I have searched for material online, including Jeff Kinney's online site, watched DVDs and their bonus features, accessed videofiles, read books, and consulted with my pre-teen daughter who has engaged with the different forms of the *Diary of a Wimpy Kid* material. By examining these kinds of film adaptations for children and the associated texts or media that highlight film as process and product, film studies scholars can reconceptualize the way we talk about how film is experienced today.

Notes

1. See Henry Jenkins' *Convergence Culture: Where Old and New Media Collide*, Barbara Klinger's *Beyond the Multiplex: Cinema, New Technologies and the Home* and Francesco Casetti's "Back to the Motherland: The Film Theatre in the Postmedia Age" as well as his article on the "Filmic Experience."

2. Casetti argues that even the cinematic experience is potentially a multifaceted/complex interaction for the viewer who may bring other experiences/technologies (cell phones) into the movie viewing experience. "Back to the Motherland" (Web).

3. For a discussion of how play theory can inform a study of children's film, see Karin Beeler's "DVD Screen Culture for Children: Theories of Play and Young Viewers" (December 2011) in *Screening the Past* (Web).

4. Molly McHugh mentions the displacement of DVDs by other forms of technology such as streaming or video on demand in "The Death of DVD" *Digital Trends* (March 8, 2011) and "Disney Studio All Access Offers Video on Demand" *Digital Trends* (February 21, 2011).

5. Linda Hutcheon uses the term "adapted text" as a substitution for the term "original" to negate the primacy of the literary text (*A Theory of Adaptation* 7).

6. The fourth wall stems from a term in stage drama to describe "that part of the traditional proscenium set that allows the audience to see the action, since only three of the four walls are present. This invisible 'fourth wall' is also what separates the audience from the *characters*, until of course a character addresses the audience directly" (*The Complete A–Z Media and Film Studies Handbook* Eds. Vivienne Clark, et al., 82) The breaking of the fourth wall can also occur when characters discuss a film in a self-reflexive manner.

Works Cited

Beeler, Karin. "DVD Screen Culture for Children: Theories of Play and Young Viewers." *Screening the Past* (December 2011). Web. 2 May 2014.

Brown, Tom. "'The DVD of Attractions'? The *Lion King* and the Digital Theme Park." *Film and Television After DVD*. Tom Brown and James Bennett, eds. New York: Routledge, 2008. 81–100. Print.

Casetti, Francesco. "Back to the Motherland: The Film Theatre in the Postmedia Age." *Screen* 52:1 (Spring 2011). http://francescocasetti.files.wordpress.com/2011/03/back-to-the-motherland.pdf. Web. 3 June 2011.

____. "Filmic Experience." *Screen* 50.1 (Spring 2009): 56–66. Print.

Clark, Vivienne et al., eds. *The Complete A–Z Media and Film Studies Handbook*. London: Hodder Arnold, 2007. Print.

Diary of a Wimpy Kid. Dir. Thor Freudenthal. 20th Century–Fox, 2010. Film.

Diary of a Wimpy Kid: Dog Days. Dir. David Bowers. 20th Century–Fox, 2012. Film.

Diary of a Wimpy Kid: Rodrick Rules. Dir. David Bowers. 20th Century–Fox, 2011. Film.

Hutcheon, Linda. *A Theory of Adaptation*. New York: Routledge, 2006. Print.

Jenkins, Henry. *Convergence Culture: Where Old and New Media Collide*. New York and London: New York University Press, 2006. Print.

Kinney, Jeff. *Diary of a Wimpy Kid*. New York: Amulet, 2007. Print.

____. *Diary of a Wimpy Kid: Dog Days*. New York: Amulet, 2009. Print.

____. *Diary of a Wimpy Kid: The Last Straw*. New York: Amulet, 2009. Print.

____. *Diary of a Wimpy Kid: Rodrick Rules*. New York: Amulet, 2008. Print.

Klinger, Barbara. *Beyond the Multiplex: Cinema, New Technologies, and the Home*. Berkeley: University of California Press, 2006. Print.

McHugh, Molly. "The Death of DVD." *Digital Trends* March 8, 2011, http://www.digitaltrends.com/computing/the-death-of-dvd/. Web. Accessed 2 May 2014.

___. "Disney Studio All Access Offers Video on Demand." *Digital Trends* February 21, 2011, http://www.digitaltrends.com/computing/disney-studio-all-access-offers-video-on-demand/Web. Accessed 2 May 2014.

Weintraub, Steve "Frosty." "Nicholas Stoller on The Muppet Movie, Gulliver's Travels, Stretch Armstrong, and Five-Year Engagement." http://collider.com, May 19, 2010. Web. Accessed 15 January 2013.

Nurturing Young Cinephiles: Martin Scorsese's Hugo

Dan North

Brian Selznick's book *The Invention of Hugo Cabret* tells the story of an orphaned boy who lives in hiding in the Gare Montparnasse, Paris, in 1931. While he secretly keeps the station's clocks running, Hugo has also been attempting to mend the automaton draftsman left to him by his late father, a skilled horologist; the boy believes that the machine contains a personal message that may explain his feelings of isolation, and reveal his place in the world. He crosses paths with Papa Georges, a taciturn old man who runs a toyshop in the station. Aided in his quest by Georges' goddaughter Isabelle, Hugo discovers that Papa Georges is actually the film pioneer Georges Méliès, forgotten by history, and traumatized by the collapse of his career many years earlier.

A film adaptation of a book aimed at young readers might have seemed like a strange assignment for director Martin Scorsese, who is still best known for violent adult crime dramas about flailing, masculine protagonists. However, as this essay will demonstrate, the film develops Scorsese's advocacy work for film preservation and cineliteracy, narrativizing his passion for the history of cinema. What is interesting about *Hugo* is the way it uses modern imaging technologies to aggrandize an earlier model of spectatorship. Even as it extols the virtues of early cinema (Méliès produced films from 1896 to 1913), Scorsese's film proudly exhibits the capacities of digital image-making, mixing elaborate visual effects with virtual camerawork and stereoscopic digital 3D. *Hugo* mobilizes discourses concerning the preservation of cinema's celluloid heritage, even as it embraces the new media technologies that are superseding it, but it is through appeals to a sense of child-like wonder in the face of visual spectacle that Scorsese makes a case for film preservation: adult and child spectators are addressed at the same level by *Hugo*'s conflation of new and old modes of spectacular address.

The Kid in the Window

In April 2013, Martin Scorsese delivered the National Endowment for the Humanities' prestigious Jefferson Lecture in Washington, D.C. He was the first filmmaker to be invited to lead this event, following in the footsteps of a long list of novelists and historians, and spoke passionately about the need to promote visual literacy and an awareness of cinema history in order to safeguard cinema's heritage as both a physically preserved medium and as a culturally understood art form.

Scorsese began by showing a scene from John Boulting's *The Magic Box* (1951), a biopic of William Friese-Greene (1855–1921), who may have been the first person to make and patent a motion-picture camera. The film was one of more than twenty produced for the 1951 Festival of Britain, a national science, technology, arts and culture exhibition intended to foster a sense of cohesion and recovery following the Second World War (Easen 1). A film that situated a British inventor as the creator of the cinema might, it was supposed, help to assert Britain's cultural relevance, but this was not a triumphal or nationalistic film: Friese-Greene dies during a meeting of industry professionals, where he stands up to implore them not to forget the origins of the medium in their rush to capitalize on the commercial applications of film. In this film, which Scorsese sometimes cites as "the film that created the biggest impression on me about films and filmmaking—the one that prompted me to say 'maybe you could do this yourself'" (Carnevale), and in *Hugo*, an early pioneer is forgotten when the burgeoning film industry forgets his foundational contributions to the primitive art of the cinema. Both assert the pre-industrial purity of early film as an important historical key to understanding and sustaining a contemporary film culture. If his lecture was primarily targeted at adults, Scorsese's *Hugo* is made to continue his advocacy work in a format that is intelligible to young filmgoers.

Scorsese has frequently used his childhood viewing experiences to explain how he developed his love and knowledge of the cinema. The favorites that he references most often (*Duel in the Sun*, *The Searchers*, *The Red Shoes*, *The Magic Box* and *The Life and Death of Colonel Blimp*) are invariably those films he saw as a child with one or both of his parents. He was a sickly, asthmatic child, he tells us, and his parents didn't read books. As a result, they would take him to the movies.

The gangster films for which he remains famous were drawn from observations of his childhood growing up in the Bronx, New York. But, as Roger Ebert noted, "Scorsese's protagonists are not the guys with the shiny cars, although they are common enough in his movies. His identification is with the kid in the window" (5). This is a reference to the early scenes of *Goodfellas* (1990), where the young Henry Higgins observes the comings and goings of the local mobsters (whose ranks he will grow up to join) from inside his parents' house. Hugo Cabret is another isolated child, an observer of his environment who longs to take up his place in the systems of adult business.

Embedded in *Hugo* is an injunction to watch films like a child, to reinvest the moving picture with some of its original novelty value. The film never directly impels young viewers to study film, though the narrative's secrets are unlocked through the *reading* of certain clues including instructive visits to the library and the cinema. Primarily though, the film's advocacy theme comes through the alignment of films with dreaming. As a child, Hugo's father visits Méliès's film studio at Montreuil. "If you've ever wondered where your dreams come from," Méliès tells him, "you look around. This is where they are made." Hugo's father (Jude Law) later tells him that watching films was like "seeing your dreams in the middle of the day." This is the most clichéd way in which the film metaphorizes film as a pre-rational function of imagination, but it does chime with statements Scorsese has made about the rapturous and ritualistic engagement he recalls from his childhood cinemagoing:

> The posters outside sell you dreams, you know. And you go in there, and the dream is real, almost. And then if you're sharing these very strong emotions with your father, whom you don't really talk to very much, this became the main line of communication between us [Scorsese quoted in Schickel 6].

It seems significant that both Hugo and Scorsese recall watching films with their fathers. Scorsese has often worked his parents and his upbringing into his interviews and his work; his profile as an auteur is cemented by his personal story, and his energy as a consumer of cinema as much as a maker of it.[1] This point is picked up in Katy Marriner's "*Hugo* Study Guide," published in the journal *Screen Education*; the guide, designed to help educators to use the film for class discussions and coursework assignments makes explicit the fact that Scorsese grew up watching films with his father, and that this must therefore have some bearing on the film's reception by young viewers, but also that *Hugo* was intended to be the first of Scorsese's films he was able to show to his daughter, Francesca (who has appeared in small roles in *The Aviator* [2004], *The Departed* [2006], and can be seen in a café scene of *Hugo*) (Marriner 23).

Scorsese also advocates a visual literacy program, partly through his *Story of Movies* teaching resources. His Film Foundation aims to promote the teaching of film in a medium-specific manner that fosters "a critical way of looking at these images and what they mean and how to interpret imagery" (quoted in *Edutopia*). His promotion of film preservation, then, is tied to an engagement with film literacy, since an appreciation of the importance and aesthetics of film is a key part of any future-proof archival scheme. As Scott Higgins notes, Hugo's filmic references "prime viewers to attend to film form" (206). Therefore, even in scenes that are not directly *about* film history, there is an encoded discourse about the indebtedness of contemporary cinema to its past stylistic history.

Scorsese simplifies and romanticizes Méliès story to posit him as a maker of films for children, thus diluting the spiky, satirical bent of much of his work, not to mention its diversity of genre and technique. As Davidson puts it, the film "takes pains to make Méliès's products seem like dreams, cultivated in a greenhouse of industrial activity to become larger-than-life projections obscuring modern industry" (879). Furthermore, he argues that "*Hugo* assures the viewer that the technological wonder of future filmmaking is rooted in a romanticized image of a thoroughly bourgeois past" (879). For Davidson, the film is really about *work*, even though it obscures the factory labor that makes capitalist society run (this is not entirely true, since we do see the mechanics of Méliès's filmmaking operations; it is the role of the industry in proscribing certain *kinds* of filmmaking, such as the creative fantasies that made Méliès famous, that is obscured). Early film was "part of a bodily training through technology for the thought and perceptual habits that would become part of but not determine our future" (885). Scorsese is not *really* interested in the biographical actuality of Méliès's story (this is not a *reconstruction* of events), but in the way he represents a missing value from contemporary cinema.

A Technologized Adaptation

According to its author, *The Invention of Hugo Cabret* is "not exactly a novel, and it's not quite a picture book, and it's not really a graphic novel, or a flip book, or a movie, but a combination of all these things" (Selznick, "A Letter from Brian Selznick"). It consists mostly of monochromatic pencil drawings to illustrate a tale that is supported rather than led by text. The coarse grain of the images gives the story a handmade, human quality. Occasionally, Selznick incorporates photographs, most of them production stills from Méliès's films, and their sudden sharpness has a comparative intensity that makes them feel stronger, more vivid than fiction. The drawings frequently subordinate detail and spectacle to minute focus on individual moments of time from a sequential event, rather than the more traditional "comic art" style of presenting key moments in a story's development. For instance, the first chapter begins with a "close-up" of the moon, before revealing an "extreme long shot" of Paris. Subsequent pages show closer and closer views of the city, moving the reader's perspective towards the Gare Montparnasse, past the crowds of morning commuters to single out Hugo himself, following him through his secret passageways to the interior of the clock tower from where he spies on Papa Georges in his shop. The sense of motion in these illustrations, achieved by following a clear progression and direction from one to the next is clearly intended to be cinematic, simulating the flight of a disembodied camera through space.

Scorsese's film does not imitate the graphic appearance of the book, but instead blows it up into a full-color, technofilmic extravaganza. *Hugo* draws upon almost every available form of filmic special and visual effects: a computer-generated simulation of the Paris cityscape and virtual actors for crowd scenes, large studio sets, miniature model work (including a recreation, for a dream sequence, of the famous Montparnasse train derailment of 1895), digital color correction, etc. The figure of the automaton, achieved using complex mechanics, motion-controlled by computers and occasionally replaced by a digital double for a few full-body shots, is an ideal summary of how the film blends arcane and modern ways of visualizing the body and the machine. It is both an impressive technical sight that mixes analogue and electronic technologies, but also a special effect that embodies the film's central metaphor of the world as machine.

One could suggest that, by working the film over so thoroughly with digital processes, Scorsese has made *Hugo* as much a *drawn* work as Selznick's book, subjected to what Aylish Wood has called the micromanipulation of the image (75). It is clear that Scorsese has cinematized the book rather than attempted to adapt its appearance directly for the screen; the effect is to break film's usual allegiance to literary texts and to foreground the film's distinctly filmic textures, just as Selznick's book makes a feature of the author's grainy draftsmanship.

According to Sabine Haenni, even in the pre-digital stages of his career, Scorsese's films were "populated by fetishizing close-ups that move in on particular objects in space, making them objects of desire, relishing in their materiality, but also isolating them from the urban fabric to which they belong. Such close-ups translate urban fragmentation into a cinematic language" (76). *Hugo* is *driven* by objects, a cluster of McGuffins that move the plot forward (Hugo's notebook, the automaton, the locket that activates it, or the book that reveals the origins of Papa Georges). But if Scorsese's earlier city films were about dislocation, and isolation, the protagonists' failure to adapt to a changing urban landscape (Haenni refers to them as "a negotiation of the crisis, of the breakdown in communication and exchange, that characterized New York City in the early 1970s" [77]), *Hugo* is more optimistic about the city's capacity for fluidity and connection. It is finally the screening of Méliès's films that unites all the characters.

What gives those objects enhanced clarity and significance, and validates the extreme digitality of the film's construction, is the film's use of 3D at the stages of both shooting and exhibition. According to David Bordwell, 3D has been the "killer app" that persuaded exhibitors to convert to digital projection, consolidating the digital turn that dominated the production of images over the last three decades (65). Whether it will prove to be a permanent fixture of cinema for many years to come, or will turn out to have been a passing fad (as it proved to be in the 1950s, the '70s, and, briefly, the '80s), at the time of *Hugo*'s production, 3D was still a contested, but widely used novelty technique, primarily associated with blockbuster action films and animated children's fare. Sandifer dismisses 3-D as a short-lived curiosity, "a medium of demos and, as a result, of gimmicks" that sacrifices narrative for the sake of spectacle (78).

Scorsese was touted as the first big-name auteur to adopt 3D for a new film and perhaps lend it some artistic credibility apart from its reputation as a gimmicky pop-up conceit with limited applications. The Scorsese connection led Andrew O'Hehir to brand *Hugo* "the future of 3D moviemaking," while the BBC's Mark Savage used it as an excuse to ask the question "can Martin Scorsese's *Hugo* save 3D?" It was expected that Scorsese would find other uses for 3D beyond eye-prodding shock tactics (though these are in evidence in *Hugo*, as when the station inspector's Doberman dog thrusts its menacing muzzle out towards the audience), but what is interesting about *Hugo*'s use of 3D is that it is tied up with the film's attempts to re-fresh the spectator's sense of the novelty of cinema, and of the position of the spectator in relation to the image. The most striking 3D effects are those that emphasize space for emotional effects, as when the image is suddenly flattened when Isabelle falls at the station and is nearly trampled by the crowd, conveying the distress of the tight space with an empathetic compression of the image field. When Hugo and Isabelle retreat into the secret passageways of the station, "space expands around the characters to express the exhilaration of their escape" (Higgins 207). Aside from these expressive and subjective uses of the 3D tools, most notable about *Hugo* is the way it foregrounds the work of Georges Méliès and other film pioneers, through elaborate reconstructions of their sets and costumes, and by the inclusion of 3D-rendered replays of their original works.

Noël Burch contrasted Méliès's "affirmation of the surface," with the Lumière Brothers' "affirmation of depth," evidenced by their preferences for theatrical flats with lateral compositions, or for deep perspectival framing respectively (173).[2] We see examples of both in *Hugo*. When Méliès retells the story of his first encounter with the Lumières' Cinématographe shows (which, in reality, happened at the Lumières' invitation to the Grand Café in Paris, December 1895, but in the film occurs when Méliès chances upon the show at a fairground), we see a replay of the primal scene of public cinema, the famed, but possibly apocryphal, moment when the audience flees from the train approaching the camera in *L'arrivée d'un train en gare de La Ciotat* (1895). Scorsese reports that they originally converted the film to 3D for use in *Hugo*, but found that it didn't have the same effect, since the Lumières had already composed the image to *simulate* the illusion of depth in a 2D image. Scorsese had therefore to embed the Lumières' film inside a 3D scene of a watching audience. Méliès's films were more amenable to 3D conversion, since most of them use layers of flat dioramic scenery, so it was clear where the areas of depth should be added to imitate Méliès's fantastically fabricated artifices. In the final scene of the Méliès gala to celebrate the rediscovery of a cache of his films in *Hugo*, we see a montage of 3D-converted films culminating in the famous Man-in-the-Moon shot from *Le voyage dans la lune* (1902).[3] The moon appears to emerge from the screen towards the audience as a rocketship lands suddenly in its eye.

For its inclusion in *Hugo*, Scorsese was able to draw upon the only known surviving hand-colored print of *Le voyage dans la lune*, which had been discovered among a batch of films donated to the Filmoteca de Catalunya in Barcelona in 1993 and recently restored. Before it could be screened, it had to be painstakingly restored by an alliance of archives led by Lobster Films. As part of the restoration process, every frame of the footage had to be digitally scanned, the image stabilized, and in some cases reconstituted and recolored from existing monochrome prints. Such extensive cosmetic work might not have been remotely possible without many of the digital editing and effects technologies available today, raising the question of how far preservation of old films should go before it becomes reconstruction rather than restoration.

Hugo navigates the history of visual effects spectacle by constructing an aesthetic of wonderment that is both diegetic (characters in the film are motivated and inspired by the spectacle of Méliès' films) and external (the film's spectators are invited to marvel at Scorsese's marshaling of the technical resources of contemporary cinema). Also at stake is a competition for the attention of young spectators who will ultimately be the ones who, in later life, decide how cinema history is to be remembered. This competition plays out in Scorsese's efforts to reconcile the analogue cinematic archive with the digital tools he needs to adopt in order to preserve it. In order to make the film more than a lecture, but an emotive appeal for the imaginative sustainability of cinema history, there needs to be a story, and a protagonist to whom potential young cinephiles can relate.

The Perspective of a Child

Children have often served important discursive uses in cinema as in so many other fields, and were particularly important to several of the first Lumière films. Vicky Lebeau points out that at least four of the ten films shown at the first public exhibition of the Lumière Cinématographe featured babies or children (*Repas de bébé, La pêche aux poisons rouges, L'arroseur arrosé, La Mer*) (23). The use of children in early cinema such as the Lumière movies "vitaliz[es] the claims of the moving pictures to document the spontaneity and immediacy of 'life' itself" (13). That unpredictable vitality also makes children subjects for concern, as Dimitris Eleftheriotis notes:

> [T]he child's agency is framed by a multiplicity of anxious custodians and interpreted within a number of legal, ethical, psychoanalytical and political (to mention but a few) frameworks. ... Romanticized for its anarchic freedom, innocence, and ability to see the world with fresh eyes, childhood is at the same time the object of the most incessant discursive and institutional attempts to contain and control it. What is most treasured and celebrated about human life must also succumb to discursive control" [Eleftheriotis 328].

We can read Hugo's run-ins with the station inspector as a reconstruction and escalation of the Lumières' *L'arroseur arrosé*, in which a young boy is punished for a prank he plays on a gardener with a hose. We also see Hugo stealing a bottle of milk as he walks through the station, which might bring to mind Antoine doing the same in *Les quatre cents coups* (1958). These replays of a kind of nested series of references to the history of film (which later give way to direct quotations) comprise a discourse about the relationship between life and film. These film references are not only aimed at the audience for the cinephilic pleasure of remarking them; they also situate Hugo himself in a filmic environment, where echoes and premonitions of movies gone and to come are imprinted on his actions and appearances. It is only when he comes to understand the significance of film, and its relationship to modernity and the city (film is the machine that regulates, links and shapes the disparate mechanisms and people of the plot that Hugo has sought to connect and "fix"), can he find peace and connection. He finally escapes the stationmaster by replaying the clock-hanging scene from *Safety Last!* (1923) that he and Isabelle watched on a clandestine visit to the cinema earlier in the film. Cinema has taught him survival skills.

Timothy Shary reminds us that, since children have little choice in which films they will pay to go and see, American studios have targeted *family* audiences, focusing narratives on the interactions between young people and adults, creating "a tension between representing children from adult perspectives for adult interests, and representing children for their own enjoyment, whether or not such depictions are realistic or profitable" (Shary 7). Being an orphan compounds Hugo's status as an observer-protagonist: he has learned to develop his own perspective, and the film invites us to follow his example.

The figure of the orphan is often used in literature and film to signify freedom (of movement, and from responsibility), a test case of what life would be like without parental guidance. Hugo is archetypal enough of a figure that he can serve as an intertextual compatriot to texts as diverse as Peter Pan, *The Hunchback of Notre Dame*, with Hugo hiding unloved inside the cogs and public facades of the bustling Paris, or literary orphans like Pippi Longstocking, Harry Potter, James Trotter (and *the Giant Peach*). As Melanie Kimball puts it, orphan characters "symbolize our isolation from one another and from society.... Orphans are at once pitiable and noble. They are a manifestation of loneliness, but they also represent the possibility for humans to reinvent themselves" (559). And according to Philip Nel, literary orphans might offer young readers "a sneak preview of the excitement and anxiety of growing up and leaving home" (quoted in Donahue). For Hugo, however, the loss of his father is deeply felt rather than liberating, and he only feels complete again once he has located a surrogate father figure in Méliès.

Hugo does not behave in a traditionally or hegemonically masculine way (after R.W. Connell's phrase, "defined as the configuration of gender practice which embodies the currently accepted answer to the question to the problem of the legitimacy of patriarchy, which guarantees (or is taken to guarantee) the dominant position of men and the subordination of women" [Connell 77]). He cries frequently, flees rather than stands up to physical confrontation, and his goals are achieved with assistance from a series of gatekeeping assistants (Isabelle, Papa Georges, the bookseller, etc.). He is thus *part of* a network of people rather than the hero of, or master over, those people. That is his purpose, his place: he fixes other things to help them work—he does not create or control them; he is an analogue for the work of preservation, shown to be as important as the work of artistic creation. Moreover, he becomes a good observer/spectator. When we first meet him, he is hidden inside the station's main clock face, peering out through one of the numbers, exercising his scopic mastery of the station and the city. The film's central metaphor of the city as a machine is conveyed in visuospatial terms in the opening shot, with Hugo's place as a component at its heart is established through an unbroken tracking motion. A contrast is set up between Isabelle's literary sensibility, where her reference points are heroic narratives and adventurous structure, and Hugo's visual and spatial sense of the city. Hugo says that he would "imagine the world was one big machine," and the film correspondingly bends the diegesis to fulfill his imaginative construction of his environment. Hugo's perceptual framework for viewing the world becomes how the spectator is invited to view it, too, and thus is established a sympathetic link between Hugo and spectator. Hugo's attentive watching, not just of his environment, but of material clues, texts, and films, completes a circuit of artistic creation and consumption, uniting Méliès with his restored audience and bringing together the lovelorn and the wounded to tie up their respective subplots at the film's conclusion.

As he looks out over the city from his privileged vantage point, it is Hugo's gaze of wonderment that allows him to imagine the city as a machine and thus see how it must be made to run. But this simulacrum of the machine-city is also a technologized visual effects shot that visualizes Hugo's imaginings and, furthermore, it is Scorsese's editorial view *through* Hugo at the city, and at the cinematic machine that displays it. The director has found an elegantly efficient way of communicating to young viewers the potentialities that were theorized for cinema in its early years, its links to modernity, motion, and the city, the way it stands in for or articulates something of the psychological state of the modern subject, and Hugo's in making sense of it through observation. In a sinuous meshing of *Hugo*'s narrative, Scorsese's autobiography, and his public advocacy work, we can see how the film operates as an intermediary between the filmic diegesis and the broader issue of film preservation and education.

Notes

1. This interplay of the personal, the historical, and the cinematic is evident in his 225-minute documentary *A Personal Journey with Martin Scorsese Through American Movies* (1995), produced by the British Film Institute (custodians of the United Kingdom's National Film Archive) to coincide with the "Centenary of Cinema" celebrations, and *Italianamerican* (1974), a film in which he interviews his parents about their early years as second generation immigrants to the United States from Italy. Both parents, Catherine (1912–1997) and Charles (1913–1993), also played small roles in many of their son's films.

2. The Mélièsian conception of space is not reducible to flatness, however—it is fascinating for how it depicts a cohesive space (a room, a theatrical stage) with magical spatial potential; things and people can disappear or be transformed *between* the frames; they can disappear into or materialize from the dark zones in the composition where multiple exposures can be effected.

3. In the film, Rene Tabard is a fictional film historian. In reality, this role was performed by Léon Druhot, the editor of *Cine-Journal*, who chanced upon Méliès at the station kiosk in 1926. In 1929, Jean-Paul Mauclair discovered a store of old Méliès films, which were compiled into a program of films shown alongside a screening of Cecil B. De Mille's *The Cheat* (1915). Méliès's daughter died in 1930, and Georges Méliès's granddaughter Georgette came to live with the Méliès' family (possibly inspiring the character of Isabelle).

Works Cited

The Aviator. Dir. Martin Scorsese. Perf. Leonardo DiCaprio, Cate Blanchett, Kate Beckinsale. Warner Bros./Miramax Films, 2004. Film.

Bordwell, David. *Pandora's Digital Box: Films, Files, and the Future of Movies*. Irvington Way Institute: Madison, WI, 2012. E-book.

Burch, Noël. *Life to Those Shadows*. Berkeley: University of California Press, 1990.

Carnavale, Rob. "*Hugo*—Martin Scorsese Interview." *Indie London*. n.d. http://www.indielondon.co.uk/Film-Review/hugo-martin-scorsese-interview. Accessed 4 June 2013.

Connell, R.W. *Masculinities, 2d ed*. Berkeley and Los Angeles: University of California Press, 2005.

Davidson, John E. "Industry in Idealized Form: The Work of Movies in Film's First One Hundred Years." *PMLA* 127.4 (2012): 879–89. Print.

The Departed. Dir. Martin Scorsese. Perf. Leonardo DiCaprio, Matt Damon, Jack Nicholson. Warner Bros./Plan B Entertainment, 2006. Film.

Donahue, Deirdre. "Orphans in Literature Empower Children." *USA Today* 2 July 2003. http://usatoday30.usatoday.com/life/books/2003-07-02-bchat_x.htm. Accessed 4 August 2013.

Easen, Sarah. "Film and the Festival of Britain 1951." *BUFVC* n.d. http://bufvc.ac.uk/oldwebsite/publications/articles/festofbritain.pdf. Accessed 4 June 2013.

Ebert, Roger. *Scorsese by Ebert*. Chicago and London: University of Chicago Press, 2008.

Eleftheriotis, Dimitris. "Early Cinema as Child: Historical Metaphor and European Cinephilia in *Lumière & Company*." *Screen* 46:3 (Autumn 2005): 315–28.

Goodfellas. Dir. Martin Scorsese. Perf. Ray Liotta, Robert De Niro, Joe Pesci, Lorraine Bracco. Warner Bros., 1990. Film.

Haenni, Sabine. "Geographies of Desire: Postsocial Urban Space and Historical Revision in the Films of Martin Scorsese." *Journal of Film and Video* 62.1-2 (Spring/Summer 2000): 67–85.

Hugo. Dir. Martin Scorsese. Perf. Asa Butterfield, Ben Kingsley, Chloe Grace Moretz, Sacha Baron Cohen, Jude Law, Helen McCrory. Infinitum Nihil/GK Films, 2011. Film.

Italianamerican. Dir. Martin Scorsese. Perf. Catherine Scorsese, Charles Scorsese. National Communications Foundation, 1974. Film.

Kimball, Melanie A. "From Folktales to Fiction: Orphan Characters in Children's Literature." *Library Trends* 47.3 (1999): 558–578.

LeBeau, Vicky. *Childhood and Cinema*. London: Reaktion, 2008.

The Magic Box. Dir. John Boulting. Perf. Robert Donat, Margaret Johnston, Maria Schell. Festival Film Productions/British Lion Film Corporation, 1951. Film.

Marriner, Katy. "Mechanical Magic: A *Hugo* Study Guide." *Screen Education* 65 (Autumn 2012): 18–29. Print.

"Martin Scorsese on the Importance of Visual Literacy." *Edutopia* 10 October 2006. http://www.edutopia.org/martin-scorsese-teaching-visual-literacy-video. Accessed 4 June 2013.

O'Hehir, Andrew. "Scorsese's Spectacular 3D *Hugo*," *Salon.com* 24 November 2011, http://www.salon.com/2011/11/24/scorseses_spectacular_3_d_hugo/singleton/.

Les quatre cent coups. Dir. Francois Truffaut. Perf. Jean-Pierre Leaud, Claire Maurier, Albert Remy. Les Films du Carrosse, Sedif Productions, 1959. Film.

Safety Last! Dir. Fred C. Newmeyer and Sam Taylor. Perf. Harold Lloyd, Mildred Davis. Hal Roach Studios, 1923. Film.

Sandifer, Philip. "Out of the Screen and Into the Theater: 3-D Film as Demo." *Cinema Journal* 50.3 (Spring 2011): 62–78.

Savage, Mark. "Can Martin Scorsese's *Hugo* Save 3D?" *BBC* 2 December 2011 http://www.bbc.co.uk/news/entertainment-arts-15967276.

Schickel, Richard. *Conversations with Scorsese*. New York: Alfred A. Knopf, 2011.

Scorsese, Martin. "Persistence of Vision: Reading the Language of Cinema." *National Endowment for the Humanities*. 1 April 2013. http://www.neh.gov/about/awards/jefferson-lecture/2013-jefferson-lecture-live-stream. Accessed 4 June 2013.

Selznick, Brian. *The Invention of Hugo Cabret*. New York: Scholastic, 2007.

Selznick, Brian. "A Letter from Brian Selznick." http://www.amazon.ca/Invention-Hugo-Cabret-Brian-Selznick/dp/0439813786. Web. 9 August 2014.

Shary, Timothy. "Oppositions of Aging: Stories About Children in Movies." *Interdisciplinary Humanities* 29.1 (2012): 7–20.

Stephen, John. *Ways of Being Male: Representing Masculinities in Children's Literature and Film*. London: Routledge, 2002. Print.

Wood, Aylish. "Pixel Visions: Digital Intermediates and Micromanipulations of the Image." *Film Criticism* 32.1 (2007): 72–94. Print.

Young, Paul. *The Cinema Dreams Its Rivals: Media Fantasy Films from Radio to the Internet*. Minneapolis: Minnesota University Press, 2006.

Section Three: Cultural and Consumer Contexts for Children

Russian Animated Films and Nationalism of the New Millennium: The Phoenix Rising from the Ashes

MICHEL BOUCHARD *and*
TATIANA PODYAKOVA

Awed by Mickey Mouse and the animation of Walt Disney in the 1930s, the Soviet Union quickly became a world leader in the field of animated films. At its apogee, thousands of illustrators toiled to produce a myriad of films, but after the collapse of the Soviet Union, the industry fell into disarray. In the 1990s, the animated film industry came close to extinction as the market was flooded with pirated, often poorly dubbed films sold in corner kiosks, while Mexican and Brazilian soap operas became the staple of television. As oil prices soared and as a burgeoning petro-state Russia recovered from the chaotic '90s, the Russian state encouraged and promoted the revival of an indigenous film industry. Under President Vladimir Putin, a new generation of children's animated films was produced, a generation drawing upon older themes while integrating new foreign influences. One such influence was the "dual voice," whereby films possessed parallel narratives that appealed to adults as well as children. Too banal for most researchers studying nationalism in the social sciences, animated films are often ignored in the analysis of nationalism. Yet, animated films aimed—either in part or in whole—at children contribute to the defining of nation, national ideals, and gender-based national identities. This essay will provide a short history of animated films in both the Soviet Union and Russia and will analyze the ways in which concepts of nation, nationality, and gender are both caricatured and reaffirmed in the (pseudo-)history presented in contemporary Russian animated films set in ancient Rus. In spite of the clichés that predominate, children's films can occasionally—using caution and subtlety—

parody contemporary Russian politics, thus promoting a potential rethinking of political norms among adults and providing new cultural and social models for the coming generations.

DVDs and the Russian Market

Unlike their predecessors in the closed-market Soviet Union, Russian films must compete with foreign (read: American) productions, continually having to play catch-up, whether in the shift to computer animation, Blu-ray, and now 3-D animated films. Moreover, Russian production companies could not generate revenues from the sale of DVDs comparable to foreign companies; lax copyright laws and the wide-scale distribution of pirated films minimized potential revenues once the film was released and no longer being shown on-screen in the dwindling number of movie theaters. Alternate sources of funding were necessary, and in the case of Russia, this revenue came from the state, whether directly or indirectly. Now, with new funding, Russian animated children's movies are once again being produced, but the DVD market remains shackled by the weak enforcement of copyright laws in Russia. Whereas Disney and other companies will pursue any violations of copyright laws to ensure that full-length feature films are not pirated and posted to YouTube, it is still relatively easy to watch full-length Russian films online, often released within months. With newer DVD players, it is possible to stream these films directly from the internet to a television, as high-speed internet has become quite widespread across Russia. As such, existing Russian DVDs are quite rudimentary, containing only the film and a few trailers to advertise upcoming films, as market forces limit the profitability of investing in the production of DVDs. Nonetheless, for the state this is a moot point as it matters little if the film is watched in the theater, on DVD, or online, as what is important is that there exists an indigenous film industry, preferably one that reinforces allegiance to the state through the promotion of a revived Russian patriotism.

Nationalism, Children and Popular Culture

In the 1980s, there was a shift in the study of nationalism, a domain that had traditionally been the preserve of political scientists, macro-sociologists, and national historians (Stephens "Editorial Introduction" 7) who focused on nationalism through the prism of the political, as anthropologists and others began to study nationalism as a social and symbolic phenomenon rooted in cultural practices. The focus of the work that came out in the '80s was on the constructed nature of nation and national traditions, whether imagined, invented, or otherwise constructed.[1] The main preoccupation of research was to demonstrate that nations were not primordial, but were in fact modern and, quite often, the state was the agent constructing the nation. The one author providing a dissenting voice was Anthony D. Smith, who examined nations as developing out of existing communities—perennial as opposed to either modern constructs or primordial unchanging artifacts, and quite often tied to larger cultural forces, notably religion. Elsewhere, I have put forward the metaphor of nations being curated, whereby new narratives are created out of older discourses (Bouchard). We will be applying this concept of curation to the analysis of Russian animated films as an act not solely of invention, but rather a reworking of older narratives that are then integrated into the worldview of both children and adults.

While interest in the study of nationalism as a cultural and not purely political phenomenon grew quickly with the published works of Benedict Anderson, Eric Hobsbawm and Terence Ranger, Ernest Gellner and Anthony D. Smith, and while numerous scholars have studied the phenomenon, the study of children and nationalism has received little attention in the emerging field of the study of ethnicity and nationalism. The relationship between nationalism and popular animated films, which will be examined in this essay, has received even less scholarly focus. One scholar who did guide the fledgling field of children and nationalism is Sharon Stephens, editor of *Children and the Politics of Culture* as well as the special issue "Children and Nationalism" for the journal *Childhood*. These two publications marked the beginning of the study of how children negotiate questions of identity, both ethnic and national. This line of study hinges on the premise of seeing children as social actors who participate actively in the negotiation of national identities in their daily lives. The research that is only now coming of age quite often uses ethnographic methods, both observing and interviewing children, to better understand how they understand their social universe and understand, negotiate, and integrate ethnic and national narratives into their daily lives.

Though the literature on children and nationalism is limited, the analysis of popular culture, animated films, children's movies, and nationalism is even more restrained. Tim Edensor builds upon the work of Michael Billig in his seminal work *National Identity, Popular Culture and Everyday Life* to study the nexus of popular culture, national identity and everyday life. As he writes, "Curiously, despite the rise of Cultural Studies as an academic discipline, few have attempted to address the more dynamic, ephemeral and grounded ways in which nation is experienced and understood through popular culture" (Edensor vi). Yet, even in this groundbreaking work, Edensor pointedly ignores children's movies and popular culture. This is certainly a serious oversight, as popular children's television and movies truly "constitute a shared referential resource, and shared discursive formations" defining a national community (139). A Canadian of a given generation can easily identify a fellow national by referring to a "tickle trunk," a prop that was central to one of Canada's longest-running children's television show, *Mr. Dressup,* which ran from 1967 to 1996 on the Canadian Broadcasting Corporation.

Scholars may have been slow to examine the relationship between children's popular culture and nationalism, but states have quickly understood the power of popular culture. Indonesia used children's literature to promote a national culture and language while at the same time buttressing the centralized, paternalistic, and dictatorial power of its president. In recent years, South Korea and China have sought to limit the diffusion of foreign animated films in their respective countries (Ishii 225–6; 229–30). During the Cultural Revolution, China quickly came to understand the power of animated films. The children's film *Sparkling Red Star* provides a telling example of how the agency of children is directly linked to nationalism. Xu Xu describes the hero as the ideal child who "is neither a passive receptacle of adult indoctrination nor an exact copy of the adult" and identifies how this film has become a classic, being shown to a new generation of children by the parents who themselves watched it and loved it as children (403). In doing so, these parents are inculcating national ideals to help prepare their offspring for the new post–Mao China. Over the past decade, China has invested heavily in forming a new generation of animators. Since 2006, it has also sought to block the importation of foreign animated films—notably the very popular Japanese anime films—into the Chinese market. The goal remains the same: to promote a form of Chinese nationalism as the state seeks to satisfy the "spiritual and cultural requirements of the Chinese people, promoting the advanced culture of socialism, providing morality and ethics education for children" (Ishii 227). These moral and cultural aims are tied to the economic ambitions of the state, promoting the development of local industry while striving to produce cultural content that could be exported globally. Given such considerations, it should come as no surprise that the Russian state would seek to promote the revival of its own animated film industry following its virtual collapse in the 1990s.

Russian Nationalism and Animated Films

Natalie Kononenko builds upon Henry Giroux's work to analyze the ideology lurking behind Soviet animated films. In her writing, she highlights that researchers too often overlook the propaganda behind children's films, cloaked as they are under the soft covering of "innocence." Giroux was critical of the works of Walt Disney and others, remarking that, "Under the rubric of fun, entertainment, and escape, massive public spheres are being produced which appear too 'innocent' to be worthy of analysis" (*Disturbing Pleasures* 24). As Kononenko points out, American animated films taught or teach children to disparage people of color. This includes, as Giroux argues in "Breaking into the Movies: Film and the Culture of Politics," those whose English is not standard, while presenting the housewife-in-the-making role model to young girls (qtd. in Kononerko 275–6). At the same time, the Disney model encourages unbridled consumerism, encouraging children and their parents to buy a panoply of film-related goods, including the DVD version of the films. Kononenko's analysis covers the Soviet history of animated film, specifically the use of folklore in films, and she also examines the transition of the industry in the contemporary Russian state. Her research largely ends, where this chapter begins, with the first of the *Tri Bogatyria* or *Three Warrior-Heroes* films released in 2004. Though there are some shifts that have occurred in the meantime, there is nonetheless continuity in the national discourse that is evident in the history of Russian and Soviet animated films.

Though post–Soviet Russian animated films have become more violent, the depiction of non–Russian nationalities follows the Soviet pattern of creating ethnic hierarchies. Kononenko examines how Ukrainians were invariably depicted as "quaint and folksy" (289). She rightfully notes that the Asian-looking Tatars are depicted as "fat, buck-toothed, dark-skinned and greedy" in the first of the *Tri Bogatyria* films (Kononenko 291). Finally, she remarks that Putin's policies are reflected in Russian animated films, as the choice of larger-than-life epic heroes tying Russia to the distant past makes Russia seem ancient, the heir of a thousand-year history. The idealization of the warrior-heroes, it should be noted, also serves to emphasize military prowess. The new films are undeniably hip—Putin's answer to *Shrek*, perhaps—in that they exude an air of contemporary cool. That said, these new films are nonetheless as ideological as what the Soviet Union had produced. "Hidden behind the references to heroic epic," Kononenko writes, "the bright colors, the modern music, and the wisecracking horse are cultural and political messages worthy of Soviet ideology" (290–91). Indeed, our aim is to deconstruct this ideology in order to examine how banal children films are laying the foundation for a revived and invigorated Russian nationalism.

Stephen Norris documents the rise of the Russian blockbuster, an event tied to the creation and spread of the modern multiplex. These multiplexes rely on cutting-edge technology to draw in viewers while mass-producing Russian movies that fill seats in the revived business of making and marketing movies. The ascension of the Russian blockbuster is also linked to Russian politics and the growth of nationalism. "The birth of blockbuster history—or the way American cultural practices could be adapted to make Russian historical epics—parallels the rise of Putin and the resurgence of Russian political nationalism" (Norris 5). The film *Prince Vladimir* [*Kniaz' Vladimir*] (2004) is emblematic of the marriage of nationalism and animation in Putin's Russia; the project was blessed by the Russian Orthodox Patriarch in 1998, and production was started at the end of 1999. The film was funded by the Russian state in 2000 after the project was given the status of "national film," somewhat symbolically bringing together Church and State just as Vladimir Putin rose to power as the new president of the Russian Federation (Norris 220). Russian animation rose out of the ashes like the Phoenix; as Stephen Norris chronicles, chaos reigned in the 1990s for the Soviet Animated Film Studio. The studio not only lost 90 percent of its staff during that decade, its new director (who would eventually be arrested) pillaged the studios and granted DVD rights to an American company in exchange for restoring the Soviet animated films, with none of the profits returning to the studio (Norris 217–18). The Soviet tradition was effectively dead by the end of the 1990s. The subsequent and surprising revival of the industry in the 2000s was due in large part to "new techniques and new heroes," though heavily supported by the Russian state's growing coffers due to rising global prices in oil and commodities (Norris 219).

Russian Perspectives on National Consciousness and Children's Films

The revival of the animated film industry in Russia brought with it a radically new tradition of children's animated films, a tradition that is now beginning to raise flags in Russia as to how these films will shape and influence the development of children in Russia. Scholars, journalists, and activists of all stripes are now beginning to question what children are learning from the new generation of Russian animated films. The analysis of nationalism and children's animated film is shaped by the dominant ideologies of what nationalism is and what it means. Stanislav Samarin, as a case in point, defines nationalism as the marriage of national consciousness or self-awareness with the practical defense of the conditions of life, the territory, the economic resources, as well as the spiritual integrity of the population. However, he regrets that contemporary Russians equate nationalism with "chauvinism" (Samarin). In Russia, chauvinism is understood as an extreme form of ethnocentric patriotism or nationalism. In this chapter, we concentrate on how animated films shape national consciousness and covertly define nation through words and imagery. Samarin identifies how cinematography and popular culture are a powerful means of inculcating national consciousness in children; he even recommends that the export and import of films between Slavic countries—films that would highlight village folk traditions—would help to return the populace to their ethnic roots, unlike films from the West which, according to Samarin, represent a propaganda tool used to promote Western lifestyles in an era of globalization.

This new generation of animated films in Russia has garnered criticism by more conservative commentators. Elena Nikolaeva highlights in her piece "Beware of Animated Films!" that animated films for children must help children understand how to become a person. In her opinion, fairy tales are the ideal medium for shaping the development of children, as they teach children that a "real man" should be "masculine, strong and just" while the "ideal Russian girl" should be "kind, thrifty/domestic, and tender" (Nikolaeva). She is nostalgic for the Soviet-era animated fairy tales, critical of the American ones that too often prevail on the "electronic nanny," and remarks how the expression "if you want to destroy your enemy, raise their children" is very appropriate for the current times. She then goes through a series of films, critical of the lessons being taught, noting that the male ideal in American children's films is to be a successful thief or magical manipulator (Nikolaeva).

The ideas of Elena Nikolaeva were influenced by Soviet ideals, which were in turn shaped by the work of the nineteenth century academic Konstantin Dimitrievich Ushinskii on "anthropological pedagogy" or "educational anthropology" (Ushinskii 16). In one of his most cited works, *On Nationality in Public Education*, he argues that each nation is unique and that education must be tailored to meet the needs of the nation. In recent years, the works and ideas of Ushinskii have been taken up by a new generation of scholars and teachers who are turning to his ideas of the importance of teaching nationality to children. His works have been compiled, edited, and republished in recent years in Russia, and his thoughts on children, education, and nationality are clearly finding a new audience in contemporary Russia. Ushinskii's philosophy is essentially that "A people without nationality [national consciousness] is like a body without a soul; it is subject to the laws of decay and destruction in other [national] bodies that were capable of preserving their identity" (16). Russians thus have a long tradition of expecting children's educational materials, including animated films, to be central in instilling national ideals. This article analyzes how this is being done in contemporary Russian children's animated films, though many adult Russians would certainly cringe at modern content that is much closer to *Shrek* than to the Soviet classics—content that bears little resemblance to the Russian folktales of yore.

The Three Warrior-Heroes

The *bogatyri*,[2] warrior-heroes, were important figures in traditional Russian folklore, heroes with superhuman strength. There were both the older and the younger warrior-heroes, and the ancient died to make way for the younger heroes. The Russian folk tales had two distinct sets of warrior-heroes: the Kievan and the Novgorod. The Kievan featured three warrior-heroes—Ilia Murometc, Dobrynia Nikitich and Alesha Popovich—whereas there were five Novgorod warrior-heroes. The Kievan warrior-heroes are the best known, as they were depicted in Viktor Vasnetsov's 1898 iconic painting *Bogatyrs* of the three warrior-heroes. The films under study do borrow certain superficial features of the traditional tales: the heroes perform great deeds, and they do serve Prince Vladimir; however, as we will examine, they are to Russian traditional folk epics what the tales of Walt Disney were to Grimm's Fairy Tales.

The Double Audience and the Rebirth of Russian Animated Films

In Russia, children's animation had a slow start. At an animation festival held in Moscow in 1934, Walt Disney had sent some short films featuring Mickey Mouse. Impressed by Disney's animations, Soviet officials decided that the Soviet Union must have its own Mickey Mouse—though naturally stripped of his bourgeois trappings (Welkos). In 1935 the Soviet Union established the Union of Children Animated Films (Soiuzdetmultfilm initially before the name was changed to Soiuzmultfilm), and this institution would reign until the collapse of the Soviet Union. The early years of children's animation were marked by Socialist realism, whereby animation was used as a dry teaching tool to properly educate children about the essentials of Socialist life, or to depict traditional folk tales. The real break from Socialist realism would come in the 1950s with the production of *The Snow Queen* [*Snezhnaia koroleva*] (1957), a Soviet animated film directed by Lev Atamanov. A global classic based on the work of Hans Christian Andersen, the film was dubbed into English and enjoyed considerable success in the West. *The Snow Queen* was intended for both children and adults; at the surface, it was a drama meant to be viewed by the entire family.

As was the case in the West, the animated classic films were invariably written for a uniform audience. *The Snow Queen* was a dramatic animated film able to appeal to both children and adults, as were the Walt Disney animations popular in the United States in the 1950s. Family films were generally in the form of dramas mixed with some comedy, which could appeal to all ages; animated slapstick comedies that were also easily understood by a wider audience; or animated films that were meant solely for children. In the Soviet Union, we see a variety of films able to appeal to different ages. As noted, films such as *The Snow Queen* were meant for a broad audience and were film classics in their own right. *The Snow Queen*, however, was much closer to a classic folklore, such as the works of the Grimm Brothers, than the animated movies being made by Walt Disney in the same era. There was also the animated series such as *Nu, pogodi*, an animated slapstick comedy featuring a wolf and a hare. Finally, there were also children's programming involving stop-motion animated figures, including a crocodile and a mysterious creature, *Cheburashka*. The latter was clearly intended for children, though it became popular with contemporary adults as it satisfied nostalgic yearnings for a return to childhood.

The recent history of the film *The Snow Queen* is emblematic of the evolving film and DVD industry in Russia. The American company *Films by Jove* restored the film digitally as they had bought the exclusive international distribution rights to this film and all others in the Soiuzmultfilm animation library after the collapse of the Soviet Union. *Films by Jove* was founded by a Soviet film star, Oleg Vidov, who defected to the United States in 1985, and having bought the international distribution right to the library, gave most of the library back in 1994 and set to work on restoring and marketing the rest including the *Snow Queen* (BBC). The animated film, restored and its soundtrack replaced with a new English version, was first released on television in the series *Mikhail Baryshnikov's Stories from My Childhood* before being released on DVD in 1999. A new release of *The Snow Queen* packaged along with four other Soviet animated films on DVD (*Fairy Tales from Far Off Lands*, 2006) featured its original Russian soundtrack and was subtitled in English. Having faced years of litigation as the new Russian state animation company sought to invalidate the 1992 contract, Films by Jove sold the rights of its remaining films to the Russian billionaire Alisher Usmanov in 2007 who then handed over the rights to the Russian children's television channel Bibigon (RIA Novosti). A new updated remake of the tale was released in Russian in 2012 and is now available on DVD with both a 3D and 2D version. This shift to 3D animated films may help to promote DVD sales in Russia, at least temporarily, as they cannot yet be easily pirated and distributed via YouTube and other online sources.

The significant change in animated films in recent years has been the shift from a single-audience animated film to a double-audience film—a film where different levels of humor are aimed at distinctly different audiences. Such films are now standard fare to North American moviegoers, as films like *Shrek* draw large audiences consisting of both children and adults. The humor includes veiled sexual innuendo that will titillate adult audiences while remaining unnoticed by the children in attendance. Such films target a dual audience by providing a level of content that will appeal to and be understood only by adults, while at the same time providing humor that can be understood and appreciated by both adults and children. After a somewhat fitful start, Russian animated movies are beginning to borrow the practice of appealing to two audiences. The wholesale adoption of identifiably American cinematic practices signals a resistance to American cultural hegemony while adopting the forms of the American consumer culture being resisted (Norris 15). In the current age of computer-generated animation, Russian animated films are making a comeback in Russian movie theaters more than a decade after the collapse of the industry in the 1990s. The film that marked the onset of the resurgence of Russian popular animated films destined for the mass market was *Prince Vladimir* (2004) the first truly successful mass-audience Russian animated film of the new millennium. Not only did it speak to both adults and children, it also heralded a revival of the historical animated film as a venue for promoting a reinvigorated Russian patriotism. Filmmakers would adopt styles reminiscent of the iconic *Shrek*, while still conforming to "the cultural obsessions with patriotism and the past" (Norris 16).

The Russian film *Prince Vladimir* was premiered at the Cannes Film Festival in 2004 and released in Russia in 2006. It became a box office success, grossing over 150 million rubles (approximately $5.3 million). Though a paltry revenue figure by Disney standards, it was a princely sum for a Russian domestic film. Financed by the Russian state, the sums collected at the box office allowed the film to effectively break even, as the production cost roughly $5 million, leaving a profit of a few hundred thousand dollars. What is striking about the film is the apparent mixing of genres in order to appeal to both older and younger audiences. The protagonist of the film, though animated, is depicted as a very lifelike—though larger-than-life—human. Vladimir participates in animated battle scenes that feature rather realistic depictions of warriors being maimed and killed. Indeed, one of his warriors is tricked by a cunning sorcerer, Krivzha a name derived from the Russian word for crooked, unable to stay his sword, kills the prince's brother right in front of Vladimir. Scenes like this are clearly not intended for children. Indeed, there are other scenes which refer to the Perun's sorcerer and allude to the ancient Slavic gods using images and vocabulary that would be understood only with great difficulty by children. Interspersed between the moments of high drama, however, are scenes that could best be described as comic relief aimed at a younger audience. Two brothers who play the role of buffoons, for example, are animated in classic cartoonish style. The brothers are seen fighting off hundreds of Pechenegs, the brothers each grabbing a tree trunk to use as a club against their enemies. The violence in these scenes is not realistic, and would be much better suited to young children. Thus, the film can be considered a dual-audience film, one in which the animation shifts between animated realism and cartoon surrealism. The film *Prince Vladimir* does feature one child, Aleksha, a boy from Novgorod, as one of the heroes of the film, who is instrumental in guiding the Prince to Christianity, having carried with him from Constantinople a "holy book" that will be used to convert Vladimir to Christianity. A child is thus necessary to reconcile a pre- and post–Christian Rus where both can be presented as a "harmonious paradise lost" both populated by "good and noble" people (Norris 224). The more recent films do not feature any children or even adolescents in the animated cast.

The level of violence depicted in the film Prince Vladimir clearly breaks with older tradition. As Kononenko identifies, Soviet films were largely devoid of violence, and even effaced the violence that was in the original folk tales when presenting the animated versions. In the film *Prince Vladimir*, the prince even takes pleasure in killing women and children before their husbands and fathers, and the violence is drawn with careful detail. Though this is used to emphasize Vladimir's barbarity before converting to Christianity, it is nonetheless a radical departure from earlier Soviet traditions. Though Vladimir may be presented as a masculine ideal, he is certainly a much darker and tortured hero than was normally the case in Soviet animated films.

In the film *The Three Warrior Heroes and the Shamanic Czarina* (2010) there are two telling scenes that target an adult audience—and a relatively well-educated audience, at that. In one scene, we see one of the warrior-heroes wearing his reading glasses, sitting at a desk surrounded by piles of papers and typing away as his wife, a chronicler, dictates an account that could easily have been taken from *The Primary Chronicle*, one of the foundational documents of Kyivan[3] or Kievan Rus. To fully understand the humor, it is necessary to understand a bit of the history of Kievan Rus as well as the true nature of the anachronism being presented. Adults will recognize the typewriter as a trope, yet children watching the film may have never seen one. Russia, like North America, has moved to the use of computers for word processing. The adult viewing this scene will also understand that as the typewriter would be an anachronism in the present, as it would also have been an anachronism in medieval Rus. The humor thus rests on understanding the double anachronism. In another scene, the Prince is beset by boredom and decides to go inspect Kiev's library. A crow sent by the Shamanic czarina drops a feather that magically transforms into a book entitled *Generation "X"* [*Pokolenie "Kh"*]. The Prince asks, "why Generation 'Kh,'" naturally pronouncing the "X" as the equivalent Russian letter (*Three Warrior Heroes*). His talking horse, who is also Kiev's librarian, answers that it is because they live in the tenth century. The humor of the scene is quite multi-layered, and to fully understand the joke it would be necessary for a Russian speaker to have heard of the book Generation X, necessitating a relatively high level of literacy and knowledge of foreign literature. This is not something a child would be expected to know and understand. At this point in the film, a photograph drops out of the book. A short note on the back of the photograph mocks what would normally be found on a dating website, or in the older print-based classified ads. Once again, the humor is aimed not at children, but rather at adults who will have the knowledge to be able to fully understand all its nuances.

Where the dual audience is most evident is when humor is presented that deals with issues of gender and nationality. Here, the humor subtly makes light of entrenched Russian expectations and ideals regarding gender and gender roles—while still cementing those same gendered divisions of labor. Defending the homeland, these films show us, is the true nature of men. These films use existing gender inequalities to appeal to adult audiences without challenging the legitimacy of those inequalities *per se*. Likewise, the films also present highly stereotyped images of other peoples (notably Africans and Asians) while subtly poking fun at the contemporary Russian tendency to blindly and slavishly follow European and American trends. Quite often, this humor relies upon a subtle understanding of history and language, an understanding that would be beyond the normal comprehension of children, thus clearly targeting the adult viewers. The lesson that the makers of the *Tri Bogatyria* films have obviously learned is that it is best to appeal to a dual audience to ensure profitability while avoiding the appearance of openly challenging cultural expectations when it comes to issues of gender and nation.

Kiev and the One Thousand Year History of Russia (and Certainly Not Ukraine)

Contemporary Russian children's animated movies serve to enculturate children into a Russian nation, affirming a very nationalist vision of history whereby Kievan Rus was populated by Russians and is considered ancestral to Russia. This narrative is certainly not new, being merely an extension of older Russian national narratives that affirm Russia's one thousand year history and view Kievan Rus as the ancestral state to modern Russia. In the first film of the series, *Alesha Popovich and the Turagin Snake* [*Alesha Popovich i Turagin Zmei*] (2004), the film starts with the writing of a chronicle. In the film, the existence of a Russian land [*russkaia zemlia*] and a Russian people [*russkii narod*] are affirmed on a number of occasions; it is even shown that they all speak contemporary Russian. The lesson being taught to children is quite clear: the history of Kievan Rus belongs to Russia, the true heritors of the glory of Kievan Rus, and contemporary Russians are the legitimate descendants of the warrior-heroes of Kievan Rus. We see a Russian Land, one besieged from the very beginning, as Alesha's home city of Rostov is attacked by a horde of Muslims. These invaders exact tribute, taking all the gold in the city down to the grandmother's last gold tooth. To prove his warrior mettle, Alesha must devise a plan to safeguard the gold; when that fails, he must battle the horde and bring back the riches of the city. To do this, he is required to outwit the Prince of Kiev, who is intent on keeping the gold left in his safekeeping.

The contours of Russian history are thus defined for a new generation in the *Tri Bogatyria* films, using a narrative quite common to the Russian national discourse. In a highly nationalistic and patriotic song entitled "We are Russians," Zhanna Bichevskaia sings of Russia, Ukraine, and Belarus as the "tri bogatyria," the warrior-heroes of the Slavic tribes. She affirms that Russia will rise from its knees in spite of death, starvation, and prison camps, horrors beset upon the nation by foreign enemies, then concludes the song by stating that Saintly Rus will once again rise up with the grace of God.[4]

In addition to affirming the Russian national identity as one of inheritance, the films present stereotypes of other peoples and nations. Muslims and Asians are of course depicted as the enemies of Rus, but they are no match for the warrior-heroes who stand tall above the enemy, capable of defeating hundreds, even thousands in battle. The only challenge is the one monstrous Turagin, who is ultimately defeated and put on display in Kiev. Then there are the "Tcygane"—a term equivalent to the English "Gypsy"—who are seen as capable dancers, but are even better at tricking an old grandfather out of his sword, money and clothes, leaving a somewhat scrawny talking horse in exchange (*Alesha Popovich*). This depiction plays upon the prevalent Russian stereotypes of the Roma as exotic, dancing beauties when young, somewhat repulsive when older, but at all times deceitful. Asian peoples are depicted with exaggerated features, notably the eyes, while Africans are represented in the final film with thick lips and childlike mannerisms. Indeed, the films are far from subtle when it comes to generating humor relating to the Other; rather, they play upon extremely stereotypical images: sometimes exotic, occasionally dangerous, but always inferior to the Russians of Rus.

The film, in its presentation of other ethnic groups, could arguably be presenting a "Russian for [ethnic] Russians" worldview. Though Soviet animated films did possess subtle biases—notably in presenting non-ethnic-Russians as folksy, somewhat backwards, and in need of the guidance of their "brother" nation, the ethnic Russians—the Soviet-era stereotypes pale in comparison to those in more contemporary films (Kononenko 287–91). Given that the Russian Federation is a multinational/multiethnic federal state, the stereotyped and negative portrayal of the ethnic Other that inhabits contemporary Russia is worrying. Questions can be raised as to what the goal of the state is in financing and supporting the new generation of animated films being produced. Though it could ostensibly be written off as simply "children's entertainment," the films nonetheless personify a certain understanding of what it means to be Russian, thus shaping the ways in which children will view and understand other ethnic communities. The films promote a new vision of nation that is ethnically Russian and Orthodox in faith, with all others being represented as enemies.

While stereotyping the Other, the films at the same time appeal to the stereotypes that others have of Russians. In one scene, the shamanic Czarina comments that Rus is known for its balalaikas and nesting dolls. This is a prime example of the dual audience discussed earlier, as the humor is certainly aimed at adults and their perception of what it means to be Russian. Later in the film, at his wedding, the Prince of Kiev observes that it is not a true Russian wedding without a fight. The films are thus gently making light of the stereotypes of Russians, while also gingerly highlighting some of the contemporary traits associated with modern Russians. In short, the films are helping to define the nation.

While Africans and Asians are depicted crudely using base stereotypes, the problematic Other in the films is the European. In the film *Three Heroes on a Distant Shore* (2012), one of the antagonists, a man who presents himself as a German, encounters the Prince of Kiev. The Prince falls too easily for the man's fabricated European traditions, a bucket of water dumped on the sleeping prince in the morning as a greeting being a case in point. Here, the film addresses the adult audience by parodying the Russian propensity to slavishly follow the fashions of Europe and the West. The humor works well, as the Prince of Kiev is portrayed as having a childlike intellect, shown to the audience as a bit of a fool who is too easily manipulated. Unlike the earlier film *Prince Vladimir* in which the prince is noble, the prince of the *Tri Bogatyria* films is seen as a somewhat irrelevant dupe who must be continually saved by the warrior-heroes. This depiction of the Prince conforms more closely to older Soviet standards. As Natalie Kononenko remarks, the tsar, a figure representing pre-revolutionary society and/or the capitalist threat, was often depicted in animated folktales as "capricious, demanding, prone to poor judgment, and often diminutive in stature" which is precisely how the Prince of Kiev is portrayed in the *Tri Bogatyria* (276).

Unlike the Soviet films, it is not clear who the Prince is meant to represent: the current President of Russia, Vladimir Putin; Boris Yeltsin,[5] who presided over the chaotic 1990s; or someone else altogether.

The subtle subtext that runs throughout the films is that foreigners are after the riches of the land of Rus, but they can only succeed if they divide the population. In one film, the witch separates the prince from the people; in another, the people are made to believe that the prince is crazy and a traitor. Redemption occurs when the population realizes that they have been duped and must work together against the foreigners who are trying to cheat them. The same motif is also present in the earlier film *Prince Vladimir*. Here, too, the Pechenegs are not a true threat to the Rus; rather, the threat is internal, with Perun's sorcerer using magic to turn Vladimir against his brother. The sorcerer is paid by the Pechenegs, but his true goal is the destruction of Rus. He intercepts a messenger, kills him, then changes the content of a letter from Vladimir's brother, causing Vladimir to attack Kiev and commit fratricide. In all the films, the threat is external, but the true danger is betrayal from the inside. Again, this is the narrative that is driving a revived contemporary Russian nationalism, one in which the modern dissidents—the protestors and liberals—are portrayed as having sold themselves to the West.

Enemy at the Gates

The series of films surrounding the *Three Warrior Heroes of Ancient Rus* serve to reinforce contemporary fears that are propagated by the Russian national discourse. The narrative is summarized in one telling scene in the film *Dobrynia Nikitich and the Dragon* [*Dobrynia Nikitich i Zmei Gorynych*] (2006). In the early scenes of the animated film, a signpost demonstrates the clear national distinction: to the left "Rus," to the right "Enemies" (*Dobrynia Nikitich*). This is the centerpiece of the films and of the national narrative: the land is surrounded by enemies seeking to invade and plunder the wealth of Rus/Russia, and it is the duty of patriotic men to defend the land against all enemies. In this narrative, any foreigner is by definition a potential foe. This is not necessarily a new narrative, as it harkens back to the Soviet period, notably to the animated films on the same topic created in the 1970s as well as to earlier Soviet films such as *Alexander Nevsky* from the 1930s. The contemporary films, as discussed, are quite normative in following the standard storyline that cuts across both Russian and Soviet cultural history. What is intriguing is the discussion of democracy that is evident in one, and only one, of the modern Three Warrior Hero animated movies. This was a discussion directed not at children, but rather at adults in the audience, making use of the dual-audience approach as described *a priori*.

Unlike the other films in the series, the film *Ilia Murometc and the Nightingale Robber* [*Ilia Murometc i Solovei Razboinik*] (2007) openly parodies Russian politics. The production integrates into its narrative questions of freedom of the press, democracy, and censorship under the guise of an animated children's film. The release date of the film is perhaps telling: December 2007, a time when President Vladimir Putin's first presidency was coming to an end and a few months before Dmitri Medvedev would be inaugurated. It is likely not an accident that the filmmakers of the series, through allegory, presented a biting critique of power and freedom in this period of political transition under the non-threatening auspices of children's animated entertainment.

One of the central characters of the film is the chronicler Alenushka, the future wife of the warrior Ilia Murometc. The chronicler is presented as an investigative reporter, and mention is made of freedom of the press. The Prince of Kiev often hampers her efforts; indeed, at the end of the film her work is censored. When the new chronicler arrives, the Prince does not want to let her in. Before her arrival, the Prince is seen railing that it has comes to this, that in the past they would not have been tolerated, but now "the people want to know the truth" [pause] "what they say in the West" (*Ilia Murometc*). In other words, now he has to tolerate journalists, because he must grudgingly conform, at least superficially, to the opinions voiced in the West. The toady boyar agrees with the actions of the prince and says that it is better not to let the chroniclers/journalists in as they will once again scribble some filth.

Old History, New Freedoms Transposed

When the chronicler arrives, the boyar throws out "*baba*" and she answers: "I am not a broad, but a chronicler." She states that she is with the publication New Birchbark [*Novaia Beresta*], an allusion to contemporary newspapers that are critical of the state, specifically *Novaia Gazeta*. The internationally acclaimed journalist Anna Politkovskaia worked for this newspaper. Politkovskaia is best known for her work examining the war in Chechnya, where she was critical of Vladimir Putin. On October 7, 2006—Putin's birthday, as coincidence would have it—she was shot and killed in her apartment building's elevator. Politkovskaia's alleged murderers were arrested and tried, but later acquitted. The journalist/chronicler in the animated film takes the role of Politkovskaia in the film, though without a tragic end. This is an interesting turn of events: she is a chronicler, but effectively a journalist. She is accompanied in the film by an artist who is the projected medieval equivalent of a photojournalist. This is another clear example of the dual audience being used in the film to interest adults: it is unlikely that young children would be fully capable of understanding the subtle references to freedom of the press, the need for journalists, and the ways in which the Russian state hinders the work of journalists in an effort to muzzle the truth.

As the power of journalists is limited, Alenushka must convince the Prince to take her with him on the expedition. She explains that all the other chronicles will tell the story of the horse that was stolen and the treasury that was emptied, and that Ilia will know the truth. The Prince cynically says, "That is freedom of speech for you." She tells him to take her with them as she will be able to fix things; "I will write about your bravery in the chronicle," she tells the Prince, explaining that she will get material to write and the Prince will get respect. Note that she mentions, "and what will the people think" (*Ilia Murometc*). The Prince likes the idea of his bravery being recorded. Hearing that that Nightingale Robber has sacked the land and stolen the gold, the Prince must convince Ilia to help him. Alesha asks to join him, as she is writing a chronicle entitled "The Daily Life of Russian Heroes" and shows him a manuscript with Ilia's image on the cover. He then orders that Alesha be thrown out. The Prince has no interest in having a journalist who will promote the work being done by the warrior-heroes. As she is being carried out, she yells out that "This is an outrage, the suppression of the press," and she screams out that the Prince is not respecting her freedom of speech (*Ilia Murometc*). The film thus presents a veiled critique of the policies of the contemporary Russian state, through a critique embedded in the dual-audience discourse of an animated children's film.

De-Mo-Cra-Cy: Political Parody and Pushing the Animation Envelope

Not only does this one animated film present issues of freedom versus the state, it also wrestles with the topic of democracy and the will of the people. Central to the storyline is the Prince having to convince the warrior, Ilia, to help him regain the treasury's gold. The one motif that cuts across all of the contemporary *bogatyria* films is the portrayal of the Prince of Kiev as a greedy, foolish, and largely incompetent Prince who makes bad decisions and must continually be saved by the warrior-heroes. It is in the 2007 film that the Prince's failings and disdain for democracy are most evident, while it is the wisdom of the folk and the bravery of the warrior-heroes that saves Kievan Rus from destruction.

Absolute power is critiqued in the 2007 film, and once again the humor is tied to the dual-audience presentation of the film. Obviously, the subtle discussion of democracy is not intended for young children, as the humor is certainly intended for the adults. However, such humor is usually extremely subtle, and though sometimes aimed at contemporary politicians, the allusion is typically so indirect that it is hidden deep within the narrative of the film. Given that these animated films are funded by the state, it would be foolhardy of the producers and creators to overtly criticize the leadership of the Russian state. However, in this particular film, the envelope is clearly being pushed and the limits of parody being tested as contemporary politics are being quite obviously mocked.

One telling moment occurs in the first minutes of the *Ilia Murometc and the Nightingale Robber* film, as the Prince and his bookkeeper are counting pieces of gold and the Prince concludes that they do not have enough money to cover the expenses of the principality. The Prince suggests raising taxes, while the bookkeeper replies that perhaps it would be better to cut expenses. The Prince then asks condescendingly whether the bookkeeper would happen to be a democrat. The old grizzled accountant answers "God help me," the epithet of democrat somehow being equated to being cursed (*Ilia Murometc*). However, it is the Prince's greed and obstinacy that are the cause of much grief. When Ilia goes to the Prince to complain that the Nightingale Robber was released for 100 coins, the Prince answers that he is the Prince; as such, he will run the show and act as he wants. Ilia then announces that he refuses to do the Prince's bidding, and the Prince retaliates by taking away Ilia's beloved and mighty horse. The robber then steals the gold and the horse, and both the Prince and Ilia must set out to Constantinople to recover what they have lost. Alenushka plays the part of the investigative reporter, secretly following both parties in order to get her scoop.

The Prince and Ilia share little in common in terms of their political beliefs. The Prince mocks Ilia because of his proverbs. Ilia answers that the proverbs are based on centuries old popular wisdom, and that they always tell the truth. During the trip, Ilia seeks to impose a form of equality. When they are hiking through the forest, Ilia informs the Prince that he will have the first shift to keep watch. When the Prince objects, Ilia states: "Here, we are all equal. Understood." He then sounds out the word democracy "De-mo-kra-ti-ia." The Prince answers, "Your democracy will bring turmoil!" (*Ilia Murometc*). After a few minutes, the Prince throws away the lance/spear and lies down to sleep, and Ilia grudgingly gets up to keep guard. In the morning the Prince is captured, but this was Ilia's strategy all along: to observe and then arrive in the nick of time to save the Prince. Nonetheless, he orders the bandits to respect the Prince. Here again, we have the film wrestling with issues of equality and democracy, as Ilia seeks to gain a certain degree of respect and equality from the Prince, but nonetheless sides with the Prince when facing the foreigner, the Nightingale Robber and his clearly Asian forces. Loyalty to the Prince in the face of a foreign threat trumps individual grievances. Ilia also liberates Alenushka, who had been taken prisoner by the band, but he does not want to take her along. The Prince counsels Ilia that they should take her, noting that it would be useful to bring a *baba* or "broad" along as she will be able to cook and wash their clothes. When Ilia discovers that the Prince has tricked him in order to recover the treasury's gold, he sets off on his own. The Prince then blurts out to Alenushka, "I am the Prince and it is his [Ilia's] duty to serve me!" (*Ilia Murometc*). Again, the film mocks the authoritarian tendencies of the Prince while at the same time underscoring that the Prince is incapable of doing anything on his own without his warrior-heroes. Yet, he vainly believes himself to be the true hero, becoming frustrated when Alenushka questions him about Ilia. He asks her about whom she is writing the Chronicle, and then tells her, "You have a hero next to you and you have a deserter [Ilia] on your mind" (*Ilia Murometc*).

Medieval Tourists, Contemporary Stereotypes

Once the Prince and Alenushka all reach Constantinople, the film plays upon existing stereotypes of the foreign Other. In Constantinople, Alenushka encounters a man who looks like Elvis who tries to recruit her to work in "show business." In the previous scene, he was shown with a number of women imprisoned on his ship, sipping a cocktail as he slides the wooden shutter closed over a small window, hiding the faces of the women weeping, trapped behind bars. Again we see an example of dual-audience humor, as there is a fear/belief that women can fall into sex slavery if they venture overseas. Some of the occurrences while the Prince is in Constantinople are reminiscent of cautionary tales told by Russian travellers: the Prince is told to sit in a chair and relax, and then he is obliged to pay. Likewise, the Arab-looking man tells the Prince that it is free to ride the elephant, but once he is up, he must pay to come down. Alenushka warns the Prince, but the Prince refuses to listen to her, reinforcing once again his depiction as a fool. "You are like a child, that is the honest truth," Alenushka tells the Prince when he gets on the elephant in spite of her admonitions (*Ilia Murometc*). Similar warnings are given to Russian tourists in contemporary Egypt or Turkey; Russian travelers must not get on a camel if told the ride is "free," as they will be invariably forced to pay an exorbitant price to be given the privilege of disembarking (*Ilia Murometc*). Clearly, the film is playing upon the experience and fears of modern Russians traveling overseas, while mocking the pretensions of leaders past and possibly present. The film also serves up a helping of slapstick humor to please the children, with adult humor interspersed along with the occasional dash of masked satire.

In the end, the film requires Ilia, the warrior-hero, to defeat a band of villains that are portrayed as very "Arab" in clothing and look. They tie him up and throw him down a well, berating him as a "damn Rus." The elephant that he had been kind to pulls Ilia out of the well, at which point Ilia discovers a horseshoe with traces of his native soil. As he believes it is the soil of his homeland that he gives him strength, he now has the power to defeat the band of villains, claiming they are "girls" before heading off to defeat the entire Byzantine army (*Ilia Murometc*).

Upon the group's return to Rus, Alenushka completes her account of the bravery and heroic acts of Ilia, but the Prince orders that his name replace Ilia's in the written account, censoring her work for his own glory. This is a very cynical ending, one where the Prince does as he wishes, and the film concludes with a very jaded view of power whereby the powerful use the efforts of others for their ends. As noted, this particular film features a number of satirical moments that seem to be making a political comment on contemporary politics in the Russian Federation. As the filmmakers are funded partially by the state, such parody is certainly very indirect, but it does indicate a contribution to the larger political and national discourse being communicated through the unlikely medium of a children's animated movie. The film still promotes a national consciousness, still promotes a certain fear of dangerous foreign forces, all the while affirming the power of the people and the real men, the Russian warrior-heroes, to overcome them; however, it does not present an uncritical view of the power of the Prince. Instead, the film delivers a critique of the dangers of giving the Prince unfettered power, especially when taking into consideration that the Prince is nothing but a fool.

Conclusion

Traditionally, the study of nationalism has focused on the grand narratives of politicians and the outcomes of clashing armies fueled by nationalistic fervor. As a cursory analysis of the banal nationalism evident in animated movies intended for children highlights, national narratives appear in mundane animated films intended to amuse children and hopefully lure adults into the theaters as well. The particularities of the Russian DVD market mean that film producers cannot expect to garner a profit on DVD sales, as the market is constrained by black market sales and digital uploading of DVDs. Though copyright laws are being tightened, most Russian films find themselves quickly becoming available via YouTube. Given the economics of the industry, Russian filmmakers have turned to the Russian state to fund their endeavors, while at the same time adopting wholesale the tools of Hollywood in order to capture the Russian market. Thus, contemporary Russian producers must strive to out–Disney Walt Disney Pictures—American films dubbed in Russian are readily available to the public—while creating a patriotic film that appeals to the national narratives being promoted by the state.

The film *Prince Vladimir* brought the Russian state and the Russian Orthodox Church together in supporting the production of a Russian animation blockbuster that drew upon a mythic past. Though the film grossed modest amounts compared to Disney blockbusters, it announced the rebirth of a new Russian animation industry that drew upon new technology, computer animation, to produce a film that was both patriotic and sufficiently religious to promote a strong sense of nation. This film featured elements that would appeal both to children and adults, borrowing the dual voice that defines contemporary animated films both in Russia and the United States. Following the success of *Prince Vladimir*, new animated films were quickly made in succession, including an entire series based on the traditional warrior-heroes, the *tri bogatyria* or three warrior-heroes. Unlike traditional Soviet animated films, it clearly draws upon elements from popular American animated films to produce films that feature, for example, a talking horse as a librarian and medieval characters dancing hip-hop, which would have been unthinkable in the more conservation Soviet animated films. Though, superficially, Russian animated films increasingly resemble their American counterparts, the discourse is still Russian, in that the cultural ideals of masculinity and valor that define the ideal Russian warrior-hero still mirror the values being promoted in Russia by the state and society at large. These new Russian animated films were funded by the state, which helps to compensate for the relatively limited revenue that can be gathered from the sale of DVD's given the history of pirated DVD's and now the uploading of full films onto YouTube which can then be watched on internet enabled televisions. Further analysis of children's movies and how they help to both articulate and inculcate national narratives is certainly warranted, whether in Russia, the United States, or elsewhere. Along the same line of thought, other forms of banal nationalism would merit study—from Facebook posts to viral internet memes—in an effort to better understand how nations are affirmed and animated in this technologically connected era.

Notes

1. Examples of concepts of nationhood as "imagined," "invented," or otherwise "constructed" are highlighted by the works of the following authors, in order: Anderson; Hobsbawm, "Introduction"; Hobsbawm, *Nations and Nationalism Since 1780: Programme, Myth,*

Reality; Hobsbawm and Ranger; and Gellner.

2. The Russian language has case endings and treats plurals differently than the English language: one and all numbers ending in one are treated as singular, while numbers in ending in 2, 3 or 4 have the plural ending while all other numbers will have a genitive plural ending. Thus, it is one bogatyr, 2, 3 or 4 bogatyria and 5 or many bogatyri.

3. Kiev is based on the Russian-language designation of the city, while Kyiv is the spelling that conforms to the transliteration of the Ukrainian name of the city. Rus is often written with an apostrophe that is used to designate the soft sign letter in Russian, but for the sake of simplicity, Kievan Rus will be used in this chapter instead of Kyivan Rus' that could be used if following strict linguistic standards.

4. Lyrics: http://lyricstranslate.com/en/my-russkie-my-russkie-we-are-russians.html and one version of the song on YouTube http://www.youtube.com/watch?v=BklGiMK3-M8.

5. Here, it would have been preferable to write Eltcin to conform to the transliteration being used in this chapter, however Yeltsin is the spelling best known in North America. The transliteration used follows the guidelines set by the Russian state in the transliteration of Russian names written in the Cyrillic alphabet using Latin letters and put into place since 2010.

Works Cited

Alesha Popovich and the Turagin Snake [Alesha Popovich i Turagin Zmei]. Dir. Konstantin Bronzit. Russia, 2004. Film.
Anderson, Benedict. *Imagined Communities: Reflections on the Origin and Spread of Nationalism*. London: Verso, 1983.
BBC. "Battle over Classic Russian Cartoons." 16 June 2003. Web. 25 August 2013.
____. "Sale of Soviet Films Disputed." 5 June 2003. Web. 25 August 2013.
Billig, Michael. *Banal Nationalism*. London, Thousand Oaks and New Delhi: Sage, 1995.
Bouchard, Michel. "La Grande Guerre patriotique: narrations sociales et monuments de guerre." *Anthropologica* 55.1 (2013): 113–126.
Brubaker, Rogers. *Nationalism Reframed: Nationhood and the National Question in the New Europe*. Cambridge, New York: Cambridge University Press, 1996.
Cangià, Flavia. "'Children of Kinegawa'and the Transformation of the 'Buraku Identity'in Japan." *Childhood* 19.3 (2012): 360–74.
Christou, Miranda, and Spyros Spyrou. "Border Encounters: How Children Navigate Space and Otherness in an Ethnically Divided Society." *Childhood* 19.3 (2012): 302–16.
Dobrynia Nikitich and the Dragon. [*Dobrynia Nikitich i Zmei Gorynych*]. Dir. Ilia Maksimov. Russia, 2006. Film.
Edensor, Tim. *National Identity, Popular Culture and Everyday Life*. New York: Berg, 2002.
Fairy Tales from Far Off Lands: Classic Animation Collection. Collection of 5 Films: Snow Queen [Snezhnaya Koroleva], Golden Antilope [Zolotaya Antilopa], Bench [Skameika], Cyclist [Velosipedist] and Fence [Zabor]. DVD Producer Izabella Khanoukova. USA, 2006. Film.
Gellner, Ernest. *Nations and Nationalism*. Ithaca, NY: Cornell University Press, 1983.
Giroux, Henry A. *Breaking into the Movies: Film and the Culture of Politics*. Malden, MA: Blackwell, (2002).
____. *Disturbing Pleasures: Learning Popular Culture*. Routledge, 1994.
Greenfeld, Liah. *Nationalism: Five Roads to Modernity*. Cambridge, MA, and London: Harvard University Press, 1992.
Hart, Jason. "Children and Nationalism in a Palestinian Refugee Camp in Jordan." *Childhood* 9.1 (2002): 35–47.
Hecht, Ana Carolina. "The Struggle of Being Toba in Contemporary Argentina: Processes

of Ethnic Identification of Indigenous Children in Contexts of Language Shift." *Childhood* 19.3 (2012): 346–59.

Hobsbawm, Eric J. "Introduction." *The Invention of Tradition*. Eric J. Hobsbawm and Terence Ranger, eds. Cambridge: Canto, 1983. 1–14.

———. *Nations and Nationalism Since 1780: Programme, Myth, Reality*. The Wiles Lectures. Cambridge [England] and New York: Cambridge University Press, 1990.

———, and Terence Ranger, eds. *The Invention of Tradition*. Cambridge: Canto, 1983.

Huber, Véronique Pache, and Spyros Spyrou. "Introduction: Children's Interethnic Relations in Everyday Life—Beyond Institutional Contexts." *Childhood* 19.3 (2012): 291–301.

Ilia Murometc and the Nightingale Robber [*Il'ya Murometc i Solovei Razboinik*]. Dir. Vladimir Toropchin. Russia, 2007. Film.

Ishii, Kenichi. "Nationalism and Preferences for Domestic and Foreign Animation Programmes in China." *International Communication Gazette* 75.2 (2013): 225–45.

Kononenko, Natalie. "The Politics of Innocence: Soviet and Post-Soviet Animation on Folklore Topics." *Journal of American Folklore* 124.494 (2011): 272–94.

Laitin, David D. *Identity in Formation: The Russian-Speaking Populations in the Near Abroad*. The Wilder House Series in Politics, History, and Culture. Ithaca, NY: Cornell University Press, 1998.

Leonard, Madeleine. "Us and Them: Young People's Constructions of National Identity in Cyprus." *Childhood* (2012).

Mikhail Baryshnikov's Stories From My Childhood, Vol. 1: The Snow Queen. Perf. Kathleen Turner, Kirsten Dunst and Laura San Giacomo. USA, 1999. Film.

Nikolaeva, Elena. "Ostorozhno—Mul'tfil'my! [Beware of Animated Films!]." *Russkoe Agentstvo Novostei*. Web. 27 March 2013.

Norris, Stephen M. *Blockbuster History in the New Russia: Movies, Memory, and Patriotism*. Bloomington: Indiana University Press, 2012.

Prince Vladimir [Kniaz' Vladimir]. Dir. Yuriy Kulakov. 2004. Film.

RIA Novosti. "Russian Billionaire Buys Soviet Cartoons from U.S. Film Company." 5 September 2007. Web. 25 August 2013.

Samarin, Stanislav. "Natsional'noe Vospitanie—Veter Panslavianskikh Parusov [National Education: The Wind in the Panslavic Sail]." *Panslavist*. Web. 27 March 2013.

Smith, Anthony D. *Chosen Peoples*. Oxford, New York: Oxford University Press, 2003.

———. *The Cultural Foundations of Nations: Hierarchy, Covenant and Republic*. Malden, MA: Blackwell, 2008.

———. *The Ethnic Origins of Nations*. Oxford: Blackwell, 1986.

———. *National Identity*. Reno and London: University of Nevada Press, 1991.

———. "The Problem of National Identity: Ancient, Medieval and Modern?" *Myths and Memories of the Nation*. Oxford: Oxford University Press, 1999. 97–124.

The Snow Queen [Snezhnaia koroleva]. Dir. Lev Atamanov. Russia, 1957. Film.

The Snow Queen [Snezhnaia koroleva]. Dir. Vladlen Barbe and Maksim Sveshnikov. Russia, 2012. Film.

Spyrou, Spyros. "Children's Educational Engagement with Nationalism in Divided Cyprus." *International Journal of Sociology and Social Policy* 31.9/10 (2011): 531–42.

Stephens, Sharon, ed. *Children and the Politics of Culture*. Princeton, N.J.: Princeton University Press, 1995.

———. "Editorial Introduction: Children and Nationalism." *Childhood: A Global Journal of Child Research* 4.1 (1997): 5–17.

Three Heroes on a Distant Shore. [*Tri Bogatyria Na Dal'nikh Beregakh*.] Dir. Konstantin Feoktistov. Russia, 2012. Film.

The Three Warrior-Heroes and the Shamanistic Czarina [*Три Богатыря И Шамаханская Царица*]. Dir. Sergei Glezin. Russia, 2010. Film.

Ushinkii, Nikolai D. *O Vospitanii: Dlya Pedagogov, Roditelei I Studentov Pedvusov [Ushinskii*

K.D. On Education: For Teachers, Parents and Students in Schools of Education]. Moscow: Shkolnaia pressa, 2003.

Waldron, Fionnuala, and Susan Pike. "What Does It Mean to Be Irish? Children's Construction of National Identity 1." *Irish Educational Studies* 25.2 (2006): 231–51.

Welcos, Robert W. "On, Workers! But Beware the Capitalist Sharks." *Los Angeles Times*. Web. 1 April 2013.

Xu, Xu. "'Chairman Mao's Child': Sparkling Red Star and the Construction of Children in the Chinese Cultural Revolution." *Children's Literature Association Quarterly* 36.4 (2011): 381–409.

Cosmopolitan Endurance: Migrant Children and Film Spectatorship

Stephanie Hemelryk Donald

Film, Migrancy, and Interruption

This essay discusses child responses to images of child migration in world cinema. It draws on recent research—the Australian Research Council funded Migration and Mobility project—with a group of young people in the United Kingdom, using their insights and choices to inform a preliminary discussion on what might be gained from participatory research in film studies, and how one might organize such research conceptually.[1] The project within which this activity was located is based on the growing realization of the impact of globalization, war and economic stress on millions of children worldwide who are forced to migrate. The work is primarily concerned with defining how and where their stories are narrated on film, but it also seeks to identify how a child's perspective might consolidate, or differ from, that of film-makers and adult audiences. The work develops from longstanding ideas of *glocality*, the relationship between global and local experience, and *grounded* or *ordinary* cosmopolitanism. The research is therefore historical, aesthetic and ethnographic in intent and methodology.

Theoretical discussions about children's subjectivity are increasingly nuanced away from the notion of children as perpetually innocent or passive, and towards an acknowledgment of complex and layered subjective states (Prout 2005). Children's studies, especially in relation to mass media and globalization, address class, ethnicity, identity and citizenship in the frame of competing intercultural expectations, and in respect to cross-cultural linguistic and political competencies amongst migrants (Ackers and Stalford 2004; Woronov 2004; Comaroff 2006; Buckingham 2007). However, despite the fact that, since the end of world wars in Europe and Asia in 1944 and 1945, child refugees and child migration have become ever more prominent features of global and especially urban life, the topic has not been prominent in considerations of social inclusion and exclusion, and cosmopolitanism and human flourishing (Nussbaum 1997; Beck 2009; Appadurai 2006; Benhabib et al. 2006; Sen 2006). Qvortrup, a scholarly "father" of children's studies, has pointed to the continuing "conceptual homelessness of childhood," and noted that the "structural analysis (class, race, caste, ethnicity, gender and so on)" were all "reserved for adults" (2007: 395). Furthermore, where children's subjectivity has been discussed, it is often from the perspective of the needs and fantasies of the adult subject. Castaneda's book (2002), on figurations of childhood, has argued strongly against the way that child subjectivity is invoked, in the work of thinkers such as Foucault, Deleuze and even Butler, to explain, prefigure and re-form the philosopher-adult. Castaneda observes that "working from one's own adult subjectivity to make claims about the child is fundamentally compromised by the fact that the child has been so consistently constituted as the adult's pre-subjective other" (152). This observation is pertinent to the following discussion in that the use of participatory methods in revealing child perspectives on cultural objects and social practices, is both a counterweight to the primacy of the adult subject and a valuable tool to developing a shared critical consciousness between adults and younger people (Hörschelmann and van Blerk 2012: 159 ff).

Although the terms *migrancy* and *mobility* are to some extent interdependent, each has its own parameters and applications. Migrancy is a heavily politicized concept, which encompasses the complexities of causation, settlement, pluri-cultural societies, and national identities. Migrancy entails mobility, but the condition of being a migrant does not necessarily require constant motion between places of origin and arrival, nor is the term a sufficient descriptor of those who have migrated. The migrant is also the emigrant, the settler and, as we argue here, the cosmopolitan. Mobility is a term that describes actual movements of people(s) and resources in a global context, whilst also drawing attention to the *uncertainties* of settled migrants; an internalized mobility, or a grounded cosmopolitanism. In the main it has been geographers who have broached the political ramifications of the concept *mobilities*, its connections to understanding settlement and migration, and the value of historically contextualized, local case studies based on age and class (Blunt 2007; Cresswell 2010). Such scholars have correctly noted that there are complex relationships between the movement of people in space and the socio-political journeys they take on arrival in a settler/receiving country, and indeed continue to take over decades of settlement and return. Disciplinary collaborations pursue the relationship between the identity and image of the city, human agency and citizenship, and the social politics of place (Bhabha 2009). At the root of these empirically founded approaches is Lefebvre's seminal work on the "right to the city" for the working poor (Lefebvre 2000). The arrival of the migrant child develops Lefebvre's claim that the "right to the city referred to the right to difference, the right to inhabit, and to participate in the city as a citizen, and was not reserved for the privileged few" (Donald, Kofman and Kevin 2012: 11), with childhood as one point of difference, and migration another.

Journeys from point of departure to an anticipated destination are not necessarily continuous or straightforward. Many migrations are fragmented, with several minor journeys embedded in what will become the perfected narrative of relocation. Recent films, *Le Havre* (Aki Kaurismäki 2011) and *Welcome* (Philippe Lioret 2009) are premised on an unwanted interruption to the flow of the migrant's journey, generally due to the policing of national borders. Set in French ports, these interruptions are visually as well as actually significant—given the sea border between France and Britain. In both films the main protagonists are young people, 13 and about 17 years old respectively,[2] seeking to reach the United Kingdom to be reunited with a loved one. The thirteen-year-old wants to rejoin his mother, and the seventeen-year-old is seeking to reunite with his girlfriend. In each case however, due to their protracted sojourn in France, they forge significant relationships with local people. These relationships are transitional in that they are based on the premise of escape, but the depth and intricacy of such relationships (for all parties) complicate the idea of a journey as a single object of experience. The films thereby concur that interruption is not simply a lacuna nor even necessarily a parenthesis, rather that every disruption, delay or rupture will be, for good or ill, intrinsic to migratory experience. As we found in working with the young people in our film workshops (discussed below), the continuities between the place of origin, journey, and the cultures of arrival merge very quickly although not unproblematically. Indeed one of the main findings of our work in London, was that children work hard to make sense of the differences through which they travel and across which they live.

Both the French "port" films interrogate the experience of child migration through the prism of interrupted mobility and transitory settlement. The child is the special case that brings the local population into a close connection with the asylum seekers, or as they term it, living dead (*morts vivants*), in their midst. The children are also a cinematic special case, providing an instant focus of affective attention within the film, even if the more developed characters are in fact adults with whom they come into contact. Their hunger, need for shelter, capacity for survival, willingness to take adult advice or assistance, renders them separate to the larger body of migrant men and women, but at the same time allows them to provide a comfortable metonymic structure of feeling by which the spectator engages with their status. The children's interrupted journeys give substance to the macro-observation that the experience of migrancy is pluri-temporal, pluri-spatial, and multi-locational. The narrative of a feature film represents only one stage (in *Welcome*, this turns out to be the final stage) of a journey, of which neither the origins nor other stages are essayed. This strategy underlines that such complexity involves everyone on the journey and not just the migrants themselves. Thus, the films enunciate a mutually responsive form of cosmopolitanism, which the migrant child cannot constitute alone.

In *Le Havre*, a young boy is stuck at the eponymous port when the police discover the shipping container in which he was hiding. The adults in the container are arrested, but the boy, Idrissa, escapes and is protected by a local man, Marcel Marx. Idrissa's final destination is London, and the story of the film is interested in how his presence in Le Havre affects a local community, bringing them together to help him embark on the channel crossing to Britain. While the film is arguably most interested in the emotional effect of the boy's predicament on a working-class French community coming to terms with new divisions between the State and those on the edges of society, a categorization that brings the poor into alignment with the migrant traveller, it also contextualizes the interruption to the boy's journey with scenes from informal migrant camps and formal state-run detention centers. Connection to the real world of state power and migrant disadvantage is underlined by news footage of the destruction of the so-called informal Jungle settlement in Calais.

In *Welcome*, a young Iraqi-Kurd seventeen-year-old is stuck at Calais, along with many other asylum seekers, trying to get to London to find his girlfriend. Again, it is the story of his struggle to escape and the help of a local man (a swimming instructor) that organizes the film's duration and plot. Here, too, the film explores the relationship between the local population and the asylum seekers, concentrating on an older man for whom the young man's plight offers a chance for personal redemption. *Welcome* does not share the fantasy or comic elements that characterize Kaurismäki's approach and design, with the result that the film gives somewhat more emphasis to the emotional impact and uncertainties of interrupted migration that the men in the Calais camps suffer as they wait for a chance to trick their way past the French and U.K. Customs officials. The desperation is most powerfully transmitted by the sequence in which men hiding in a truck to get through the French/British Channel tunnel, wear plastic bags to block their mouths and nose to prevent the Customs' sensors picking up the heat of human breath.

The fractures of geo-space and social space essential to telling stories of migrancy and mobility both must correspond (or not) to cinematic space and the ways in which this approximates or codes experience, and to its articulation to movement within the frame. Thus in *Le Havre* Kaurismäki employs formal techniques of set design and lyrical color-coding to define the district where the boy takes refuge. The dominant tone for most locations occupied by the boy or the working class community, are blue, and this saturation intensifies in the safest space—the yard and home of Marcel Marx—to the point that they resemble a children's picture book illustration or indeed a child's own drawing. By contrast, the most dangerous protagonist—a neighborhood snoop played by Jean-Pierre Léaud—is revealed at first only in shadow, his hand tweaking a curtain and then reaching for the phone. We later recognize him by his voice at the station when he again tries to have Idrissa arrested, reaching for his mobile to call the police and subsequently gripping the boy's arm, only for his hand to be overpowered by that of Chang—another migrant (a Vietnamese using documents belonging to an unknown Chinese "Chang") who is friends with Marcel Marx. The intervention saves the boy and the hand over hand sequence encapsulates the necessary relationships between people at various stages of their journey. Marx is an entertainer who used to live in Paris. Chang is a settled migrant and family man although forced to use an assumed name. Idrissa is in transit from the Gabon to find his Mother. Movement in the frame is also coded. The boy is often still in the frame, seated, working quietly at the kitchen sink, asleep, standing in water waiting for someone to bring him help, listening to adults talk in Marcel's house, lying with the dog, cleaning up the kitchen, and so on. He is the migrant and he is taking the greatest risks but it is the adults who move about him pursuing their own lives or acting on his behalf. Cinematically, Idrissa is regularly placed in the center of the frame emphasizing that, although transient, he belongs in this newly cosmopolitan space, and, although mobile, he is still.

In *Welcome*, Lioret uses the swimming pool as a metaphorical space of freedom and self-determination, as the boy trains to swim across the Channel. Again, as the teenager swims through the water, he occupies a central place in the framing of the relevant shots, and the Frenchman literally watches him from the sidelines. Yet, the pool is also a contradictory metonym for the wider seas that symbolize the perils of migration into Europe, and of this crossing in particular. The hopelessness of the asylum seekers' feeding centers at Calais' docks alternate with the apparent safety of the pool and the intermittent sanctuary of the local man's apartment. As in *Le Havre*, the French protagonist suffers from a neighborhood snoop willing to report him and his illegal house-guests to the local police. This recurring character provides the obvious resonance to France's history of wartime collaboration alongside the bravery of resistance, and to contemporary struggles around the politics of anti-immigration versions of nationalism.

Engagement and Grounded Cosmopolitanism

These two films are useful starting points for a discussion of work with young migrants today, as both are recent and deal explicitly with contemporary circumstances of forced migration, European political responses, historical resonances with other episodes of exclusion and imprisonment, and with the phenomenon of children travelling alone. Most importantly, however, both recognize through their structure and plotline, that migration is as much about interruption, stasis and settlement as it is about mobility per se. The central experience of forced migration is waiting; in a camp, at a border, in a port, in a detention center. Even for those who are fortunate and both travel and arrival is relatively easy, there is the sense of being stuck in a new place with rules and ideas that need a great deal of negotiation to survive emotionally and to prosper. Both these films describe plotlines and character development that exemplify the creation of relationships between those that travel, those that settle and those who can recognize their own habits of mobility and interruption in others. Finally, childhood on screen can be read as a metonym for adult anxiety or fear, re-read through Ahmed's cultural analysis of emotion as the "impressions left by others" (2004: 27ff). I have therefore offered a very brief analysis of these films simply to underline the problematic temporal and spatial characteristics of migration, and to suggest that the journeys attached to migration in general and child migration in particular may provoke cosmopolitan engagements of some intricacy.

The participatory research model is premised on an extended engagement with three groups of young people, and is designed to complement more formal film analyses, and historical contextualization. Below, I refer to the first stage of engagement with 16 young people in London, which focused on the narration of mobility and migration on screen. In practice when working with young people (8 to 14 years of age), that terminology has been simplified to journeys and then unpacked through watching and making film extracts on the topic. This allows those who have experienced a variety of more or less turbulent or disruptive or extended journeys to share a language with their peers, without having to divulge personal differences and experiences by dint of insensitive categorizations. Indeed, it was not even appropriate to suggest that children who are now ordinarily resident in the United Kingdom are migrants first and foremost, as that might serve to re-establish any feelings of deracination or multiple belonging which they may have been seeking to remediate (Doná and Veale 2011). As Doná and Veale have argued, an insistence on reifying migration also forecloses on subsequent experience. What we did seek to do was to valorize journeys as subjects of narration in film, and to indicate that films with children or young people as key protagonists were as important as any other kind of storytelling. The underlying premise in conducting the workshops was then not that all participants were simply migrants but that—due to their exposure to migrancy and relocation—all participants could lay clam to a status of grounded, active and visceral cosmopolitanism (Kofman 2005; Brosius and Yazgi 2007; Nava 2007; Morris 2010).

The workshops were conducted in three stages over three weeks: preparation and training, filmmaking, and feedback. There was also a follow up session where the group concentrated on editing one of the films to a standard suitable for screening. The participants were all attendees at a Saturday morning school for young people of Afghani backgrounds. Participants were aged between 8 and 15 years old. Approximately 95 percent were born in Afghanistan or overseas, whilst a few were born in the United Kingdom. The curriculum focused on core subjects (English, mathematics) but also taught specialist subjects such as drama. The film-group participants were self-selected from ages 8 to 15 (the younger members of the group were brothers and sisters of older children). Meetings took place in North London at the school on Saturdays, and participants were excused from ordinary classes to attend. It is fair to say that members of the group were academically talented as well as highly articulate. A few had clear ambitions and talents in acting and film-making (evidenced in the feedback session when we lost a few older group members to a drama class). In the first week we worked on building a shared vocabulary and visual database. Film as a storytelling medium was the baseline for everything we discussed: space, color, emotions, and journeys. The discussions were both conceptual and pragmatic. What colors show what emotions? How long is a journey? Are all journeys physical transitions from one place to another, or are there journeys that are more about the self, growing up, changing direction? How does space work on screen, and how can one work with small spaces to show greater truths about feelings and events?

The film used as an exemplar in Week One was the Australian film about the Stolen Generation,[3] *Rabbit Proof Fence* (Noyce, Australia, 2002). It is mainly an English language film but the main protagonists speak a simple English that makes the story accessible to all ages and to people for whom English is a second language. The film is based on the story of three girls, aged between about 7 and 14, who, in 1932, escaped the Moore River Children's camp in Western Australia (aka detention settlement for children taken from their Aboriginal mothers to be raised as domestic and agricultural laborers). The girls evaded capture for several weeks in order to reach their home in the far north of the state. The sequence that we watched concerned the decision to escape and the girls' first successes in avoiding capture. The film's tones are blue and brown in these scenes, which portray a landscape that is a beautiful but also demandingly tough space that the girls need to make their friend if they are to survive and move safely across it. The Tracker, an Aboriginal man who is deployed to pursue them, uses his understanding of the landscape to track them. They in turn use their intuition and in-country intelligence to outwit him. A fourteen year old boy commented to another that the Tracker was a spy, and the other boy agreed. Their certainty seemed likely to arise from the kind of behaviors that they could have observed, or heard discussed, in a civil war situation such as that which both had left behind in Afghanistan. In retrospect we might also have screened the clip of *Le Havre* where the neighborhood spy is seen phoning in Idrissa's whereabouts to the French police. The workshop participants also picked up on the drama of the escape but also on the betrayal evidenced by the Tracker, and the unreliability of law that did not protect children, but rather pursued them. In this regard one might see that the child philosopher sees the child subject of the law as integral and complete, not the pre-subjective other of assumed adult identities in the making (in that case young Aboriginal adults being prepared for low paid/slave labor), but young people deserving of full legal protection and respect.

This film was chosen on the spot, in an iterative response, from a number of possible texts that were prepared for screening in advance. This decision was based on observations made in the first hour of the workshop. The participants were of a wider age group than had originally been envisaged (the youngest was eight rather than eleven) as parents had asked that younger siblings could accompany older brothers and sisters into the workshop. This was beneficial in that the parents and families were happy, although a girl revealed in the last feedback session that she felt hampered from shooting the kind of film she was really interested in—a romance—with her younger brother present. It also suggested a film where kin sisters between the ages of 8 and 14 are the main protagonists. Furthermore, despite the mix of ages, and perhaps because of the familiarity of family groups, participants revealed some commonalities, which also made this film seem the most appropriate to start the discussion. The French port films were also considered but rejected because of the traumatic ending of *Welcome*, and because *Le Havre* was highly stylized and a series of clips would not convey the scope and emotional background of the story in the time we had available. Nonetheless, the final film made by the children reminded the researchers that there is a difficult line between their first-hand knowledge of violence and trauma, and acceptable boundaries of representation in a London school.

Also, the group responded well to the opening reference grid exercise in which they were asked to individually match colors and emotional states. Subsequent discussions centered on brown and green, both of which are dominant in the *Rabbit Proof Fence* palette. One girl (14 years) described brown as a serious color because it was grounded in the earth. A boy (12 years) suggested that it was more akin to despair, and told the group that brown was the color he associated with the feeling of not being understood, and not being able to communicate his frustrations. The group suggested after seeing *Rabbit Proof Fence* that the brown of the landscape was also ambivalent—it represented the warmth and traditional space of the Australian landscape which belonged to the girls and their ancestors, but it was nonetheless harsh terrain and dangerous to cross without the support of a tribe or a family. Second, the older members of the group showed an unexpectedly advanced philosophical and political awareness that they immediately brought to bear in understanding the unjust victimization of Aboriginal children in twentieth century Australia. They were particularly outraged that the Law was so ineffective in protecting minors but was instead used to imprison them. The connections between contemporary detention of child migrants was not explicit but it is not too much of a stretch to wonder how much they were linking these two experiences through personal experience of that of community members. *Rabbit Proof Fence* does not portray war and open conflict, but it evokes the simmering tensions and explosive violence of the twentieth and twenty-first centuries that are central to narratives of nationhood and post-colonial conflict across the world. The degree to which childhood has been implicated in these stories of abjection, triumph and survival is crucial to an analysis of the representation of migrancy and cosmopolitan responses in cinema. They became refugees, workers and soldiers. They have fled cities, countries and continents laid waste. So, it allowed a series of questions to emerge. How have these dramas been interpreted on film, and with what emphases? When does a child represent the stability of the nation, and when does her or his onscreen presence rather suggest adult anxiety? In what aesthetic, political or moral registers are their stories told? In addressing such issues, the workshop was drawing on theoretical attempts to conceptualize how we tread a line between fantasy, representation and social document. Stuart Hall's sympathetic reading of the energy of arrival, in the otherwise ordinary lives of migrants from former British colonies, is used by Nirmal Puwar to discuss social spaces in film (2007: 254). She reinforces a conception of publicness that allows us to relate historical and emotional experience within cinematic structures of fantasy. So, an otherwise hidden social phenomenon, the energy of new arrivals, becomes visible, legible and validated through film. I hope that the small work done on my Migration and Mobility project gives a space for such energy to break through.

Rabbit Proof Fence indicates how to use color to provoke emotional responses through film. This was immediately useful in the workshop as, whilst one group watched the film extract, the other learned to use the three media kits. Each kit comprised a highly portable Kodak Play-Sports digital movie camera, a memory card, and a small tripod. The cameras are straightforward to use and offer several color, B/W and sepia type settings, all of which the groups experimented with in their own films in Workshop Two. At the end of the first workshop we also screened an extract from *Jacquot le Nantes* (Varda 1991), where color and monochrome are used, respectively, to indicate the present and the past, but where color also evokes the strength of feeling in the main protagonist (the young Jacques Demy) towards cinema. Jacquot is not explicitly about child migration in the modern world, but it is about a child's journey through life, through film. Thus, while other films have been narratives about migration on film, Varda here shows how film can support that journey and both express and mitigate its challenges. The story is about Jacques Demy's passage from extreme youth to adolescence in times of war, and from innocence to maturity, expressed through cinema and through Jacques' own journey to become a film-maker. The aim of this screening was to inspire the workshop participants but also to give historical depth and perspective on children's experience of war. We also looked at a 1949 children's film from China, *Sanmao's Travels* (dir. Zhao Ming and Yan Gong), filmed in black and white. *Sanmao* concerns the story of a (approximately) ten-year-old boy living in the streets of Shanghai. Here, the child has travelled into the city and lives through begging and stealing. The film contrasts with the French films in that the adults in the story are *all* actively belligerent to the boy. It offers a mid–twentieth century example of a child having to know a great deal about survival, and as such validates the child's claim to knowledge and a say in his/her representation. *Sanmao*'s story resonates with rural-urban migrants around the developing world, but the film is a slapstick comedy, so we used it to think about genre and storytelling. The scene we looked at is where Sanmao salivates over food in the shops and eventually steals a bun, which results in a chaotic chase and a big fight involving lots of boys. The journey in question here was not the circumstances that had brought him to the metropolis, but the everyday journey of his life through the streets of Shanghai.

Workshop Two was all about making films. The brief had been to prepare a storyboard of three shots and to tackle the theme of a journey within that very short sequence. Participants were reminded that, given rules and ethical considerations, we would not be able to leave the school grounds, nor would we have much practical control over noise levels, set dressing, or timing. The Saturday school organizers could only let us work together for two hours, as the participants had to prepare for exams. Moreover, we would not be allowed to cause undue disruption to other classes. This attempt at film-making was always going to be a bit rough and ready but we agreed that we would do whatever we could and have fun. In the event, the group re-convened, presented their storyboards and then split into three smaller production teams to choose a storyboard to work from, to allocate roles start work. As expected, we were constrained by circumstances, but the teams worked with admirable focus and concentration each producing the shots they had determined on.

Genre

Three films of three shots were duly created. One was a highly comedic account of the theft of a wedding cake by two rich, fat and greedy men, their resulting stomach-aches, and their rough punishment by the wedding guests. The men were thin in the first shot but are shown to be fat and greedy after a lottery win. The implication is that sudden luck does not promote moral behavior. Indeed it leads to the abuse of a very important cultural event and custom: a wedding. The film was shot in black and white, used costume (fat suits made from cushions), and played with the joint thematic of slapstick humor and violence. There were some issues in general regarding gender stereotyping, with the girls being informed that all they could play were waitresses. In the event they played them rather brilliantly. The journey theme was at first hard to discern, but was probably selected by that team because of the strong personality of the boy who presented that storyboard. However, in the feedback session, the participants suggested that this was about a journey made too quickly, with the resulting consequences of poor acculturation to seeming good luck. The film was also workshopped in the fourth session to a presentable level of editing, with inter-titles explaining the action. The final scene shows relatives punishing the men by beating their stomachs. Although there was no real violence, and although in previous feedback the children suggested that violence is one solution but not the right one, this ending did provoke concern to teachers who felt that a more clearly moral ending would be more acceptable to them and to parents. In the end then, the edited film was not screened for parents (they saw a selection of clips on a PowerPoint instead), as the children had no time to discuss this request from their teachers (not from the researchers) and film an alternative ending before school closed for the summer. It left open a question around the extent to which children's own capacity to judge their decisions after the event, and thus the imaginative space available to them in the place of arrival (here, the United Kingdom) to express both the moralities and immoralities that they have observed in adult behavior across their own journeys of departure, waiting, settlement and so forth.

Another offering was a zombie film, in which a small brother transforms into a monster and kills his father and sisters. The use of a popular genre to make a first film was encouraged in the workshop as it presents the young filmmaker with a model. In this story, the zombie genre was deployed in ways similar to professional and adult film-makers—it inferred transition between one state and another, between life and death, and between safety and danger. The workshop film was highly effective in taking three shots and making these journeys explicit. The third film was a ghost-horror film, set in the girls' toilet block. The idea was that a safe space becomes a terrifying place because of a strange knocking behind a door. The film may have been derivative of the ghost in a toilet in *Harry Potter and the Chamber of Secrets* (the Moaning Myrtle episode) but this version of the theme was differently achieved. Instead of comedy and a highly characterized specter, their film managed to convey the transition between security (girls working in a classroom with their teacher—Shot One) and insecurity (the girl alone in the toilet frightened by the strange noise—Shot Two). Another film (zombie) achieved a shot that indicated true fear (a girl outside the classroom looking in through meshed wire—Shot Three). One of the three shots panned from the toilet doors, and indicated a sophisticated understanding of how to make familiar space uncanny.

In Week Three in the feedback session, three Hollywood films were cited as sources for their inspiration and films that I "should watch." The rationales were as follows:

- *Twilight*—the progress of a young woman who discovers she was born to be/destined to be a vampire. Her struggle against this and her eventual acceptance are the journey.
- *I Am Legend*—The protagonist is separated from his family, with whom he is desperate to be re-united. He is befriended by a family and their kind treatment gives him hope for the future. The journey is from despair to hope.
- *Home Alone 2*—There is a geographical journey and also a journey as the Protagonist encounters peril, challenges it and overcomes it (triumphing over the bad guys)

These are clearly films that they knew well, and despite the attention and pleasure derived from the clips that we used to discuss the journey and relocation themes in Week One, we felt that their sources made sense. These sources are genre films, none of which deal directly with a migration story but all of which tackle narratives organized around ontological and profound physical change, maturation of the child, adults feeling insecure (like children) and searching for safety, and both adults and children dealing with danger together. All of these themes are pertinent to migration experiences but all of them are also common to human fears and challenges whether or not marked by specific travel across borders. The decision by all the groups to go with a genre piece—comedy, horror and thriller respectively—was then highly instructive. The lesson to be drawn was, it seemed, that not only is genre highly successful in communicating complex ideas (obviously an observation which is a sine qua non of film studies), but that even comparatively young film-makers and audiences understand this complexity and use it with great sophistication. Further, it suggested that this particular group of young film-makers understood that cinematic communication through genre was an effective short-cut to expressing complicated stories of human experience. We regretted that we could not effectively communicate this quite profound morality on the children's part, to the teacher who felt deeply concerned about the ending of the wedding cake film. In retrospect, it may simply have been that the rawness of the script and of the shot composition laid bare the narrative and that the simple, direct enactment of violence caused the concern. In other words, it is less worrying to see staged horror than boys actually punching each other—even if they are punching a pillow and giggling as they do so. A boy punching is close to a man punching- and indicates that he knows what punching looks like in practice. It breaks open the discourse of innocence and vulnerability that might be used to frame teacher-child relationships and indeed to mask the transition from boy to man that anyone working with adolescents must countenance.

The conclusions from this short project (and I should note that this is only the first of a number of activities with these groups and others) are as follows. First, the use of genre in interpreting a narrative task (the journey) indicates a sophistication that brings together personal and emotional experience with global modalities. Second, this approach both distances the subject from the object of the study (migrant from migration), and reiterates the grounded cosmopolitanism of migrant children within general populations, and their easy manipulation of global and grounded flows of cultural materials and communicative action. Third, the capacity to see journeying within emotional matrices of despair, hope, and destiny suggests a maturity of vision and a depth of comprehension that challenges estimations of youth as pre-subjective, and recasts interruption as a cosmopolitan endurance. In practical terms, and as an addendum which I would like to retain within this piece to remind us why this work matters at all beyond the walls of film and genre study, these interpretations require that migrant and settling children deserve as much access to communicative technologies and audiences as possible. I also hope that this small project may give further ballast to the work of social scientists and lawyers arguing against detention of child migrants in Australia and Europe.

Notes

1. Thanks to professor Eleonore Kofman and doctoral candidate Tracy Mullan, both from Middlesex University, for their involvement in the project to date. Thanks also to the ARC for funding the work, and to the Paiwand team at Whitegates School for their hospitality, and to all participants for their time and talents.

2. Childhood ends legally at 18 under UN treaty, an individual being below the age of 18 years unless, under the law applicable to the child, majority is attained earlier (Art. 1, UN Convention on the Rights of the Child, 1989).

3. A concise account of this sorry and protracted episode in modern Australian history can be found in Graf (2012, 12–13). See also Buti (2007). In 2008, the Australian government apologized to the stolen generations of Aboriginal children for the utter dispossession visited upon them and their families in the twentieth century (Rudd 2008; Auguste 2009).

In 2010, the U.K. Prime Minister Gordon Brown apologized to British child migrants shipped around the Commonwealth in the same period, in the "memories of most of us here today," noting that "as children, your voices were not always heard" (CMT 2010; Hill 2007). Between June 1999 and July 2003, 2,183 children applied for refugee status in Australia, some seeking asylum alone (HREOC 2004; Crock, 2006). In 2013, children were again sent to mandatory detention, some offshore, again in contravention of the Convention on Human Rights.

Works Cited

Ackers, Louise, and Helen Stalford. *A Community for Children? Children, Citizenship and Internal Migration in the EU*. Aldershot: Ashgate, 2004. Print.
Ahmed, Sara. "Collective Feelings." *Theory, Culture & Society* 21.2 (2004): 25–42. Print.
Appadurai, Arjun. *Fear of Small Numbers: An Essay on the Geography of Anger*. Durham, NC: Duke University Press, 2006. Print.
Auguste, Isabelle. "On the Significance of Saying 'Sorry'—Politics of Memory and Aboriginal Reconciliation in Australia" *Coolabah* 3 (2009): 43–50. Print.
Beck, Ulrich. "Critical Theory of World Risk Society: A Cosmopolitan Vision." *Constellations* 16.1 (2009): 3–22. Print.
Benhabib, Seyla, et al. *Another Cosmopolitanism*. Oxford: Oxford University Press, 2006. Print.
Bhabha, Jacqueline. "The 'Mere Fortuity of Birth'? Children, Mothers, Borders and the Meaning of Citizenship." *Migrations and Mobilities: Citizenship, Borders and Gender*. Seyla Benhabib and Judith Resnick, eds. New York: New York University Press, 2009. 187–227. Print.
Blunt, Alison. "Cultural Geographies of Migration: Mobility, Transnationality, and Diaspora." *Progress in Human Geography* 31.5 (2007): 684–694. Print.
Brosius, Christiane, and Nicolas Yazgi. "'Is There No Place Like Home?' Contesting Cinematographic Constructions of Indian Diasporic Experiences." *Contributions to Indian Sociology* 41.3 (2007): 355–386. Print.
Buckingham, David. "Selling Childhood? Children and Consumer Culture." *Journal of Children and Media* 1.1 (2007): 15–24.
Buti, Antonio. "Bringing Them Home." *Sir Ronald Wilson: A Matter of Conscience*. Antonio Buti, ed. Crawley, Western Australia: UWA Press, 2007. 301–329. Print.

Castaneda, Claudia. *Figurations: Child, Bodies, Worlds*. Durham, NC: Duke University Press, 2002. Print.
CMT (Child Migrants Trust). "Apology to Child Migrants." 2010. Web. 10 March 2011. http://www.childmigrantstrust.com/news/number10govuk—apology-issued-to-child-migrants.
Comaroff, John. "Reflections on Youth, from the Past to the Post-Colony." *Frontiers of Capital: Ethnographic Reflections on the New Economy*. Greg Downey and Melissa S. Fisher, eds. Durham, NC: Duke University Press, 2006. 267–281. Print.
Cresswell, Tim. "Towards a Politics of Mobility." *Environment and Planning D: Society and Space* 28 (2010): 17–31. Print.
Crock, Mary. *Seeking Asylum Alone: A Study of Australian Law, Policy and Practice Regarding Unaccompanied and Separated Children*. Sydney: Themis, 2006. Print.
Doná, Giorgia, and Angela Veale. "Divergent Discourses, Children and Forced Migration." *Journal of Ethnic and Migration Studies* 37.8 (2011): 1273–1289. Print.
Donald, Stephanie Hemelryk, Eleonore Kofman and Catherine Kevin, eds. *Branding Cities: Cosmopolitanism, Parochialism, and Social Change*, 2d ed. New York: Routledge Academic, 2012. Print.
Graf, Christine. "Childhood Lost: Australia's Stolen Generation." *Faces: Peoples, Places, and Cultures* 29 (1 January 2013): 12–13. Print.
Le Havre. Dir. Aki Kaurismaki. France, 2011. Film.
Hill, David. *The Forgotten Children: Fairbridge Farm School and its Betrayal of Australia's Child Migrants*. New South Wales: Random House, 2007. Print.
Home Alone 2: Lost in New York. Dir. Chris Columbus. USA 1992. Film.
Hörschelmann, Kathrin, and Lorraine van Blerk. *Children, Youth and the City*. London: Routledge, 2012. Print.
HREOC. *Australian Human Rights Commission, The Last Resort? The National Inquiry into Children in Immigration Detention*. 2004. Web. 20 April 2013. http://www.hreoc.gov.au/human_rights/children_detention_report/report/index.htm .
I Am Legend. Dir. Francis Lawrence. USA, 2007. Film.
Jacquot le Nantes. Dir. Agnes Varda. France, 1991. Film.
Kofman, Eleanore. "Migration, citizenship and the Reassertion of the Nation-State in Europe." *Citizenship Studies* 9.6 (2005): 453–67. Print.
Lefebvre, Henri. *Writings on Cities*. Eds. and trans. Eleonore Kofman and Elizabeth Lebas, 5th ed. Oxford: Blackwell, 2000. Print.
Morris, Lydia. *Asylum, Welfare and the Cosmopolitan Ideal: A Sociology of Rights*. Oxford: Routledge, 2010. Print.
Nava, Mica. *Visceral Cosmopolitanism: Gender, Culture and the Normalization of Difference*. Oxford: Berg, 2007. Print.
Prout, Alan. *The Future of Childhood*. Abingdon: Routledge, 2005. Print.
Puwal Nirmal. "Social Cinema Scenes." *Space and Culture* 10.2 (2007): 253–270. Print.
Qvortrup, Jens. "Editorial: A Reminder." *Childhood* 14.4 (2007): 395–400. Print.
Rabbit Proof Fence. Dir. Philip Noyce. Australia, 2002. Film.
Rudd, Kevin. "Apology to Australia's Indigenous Peoples." 13 February 2008. Web. 16 April 2013. http://www.aph.gov.au/house/rudd_speech.pdf.
Sanmao liulangji [*Sanmao's Travels*]. Dir. Yan Gong and Zhao Ming. China, 1949. Film.
Sen, Amartya. *Identity and Violence: The Illusion of Destiny*. New York: Allen and Lane, 2006. Print.
Twilight. Dir. Catherine Hardwicke. USA, 2008. Film.
Welcome. Dir. Philippe Lioret. France, 2009. Film.
Woronov, Terry. "In the Eye of the Chicken: Space and Hierarchy among Beijing's Migrant Children." *Ethnography* 5.3 (2004): 289–313. Print.

Dubashi: *Indian Film, Cross-Cultural Communication and Screenings for Children*

SWARNAVEL ESWARAN PILLAI

The Tamil film *Dubashi* (*The Translator*, 1999) was produced by the Indian state owned organization Children's Film Society, India (CFSI), which was founded in the year 1955, as an autonomous body under the Ministry of Information and Broadcasting, when Jawaharlal Nehru was the first Prime Minister of India after its independence in 1947. Nehru, whose birthday on the fourteenth of November is celebrated annually as Children's Day in India, is known for his deep affection for children, and CFSI was his brainchild as he felt the need for an organization, which would focus exclusively on the production, distribution, and exhibition of a cinema for children, and cater to their need for entertainment and education.[1]

It is, therefore, significant that *Dubashi* was written by K. Hariharan on the fiftieth year of India's independence (1997), went into production the subsequent year, and was released in 1999. Being under production during the twilight years of the last century, *Dubashi* offers a possibility to read the expectations surrounding the new millennium from the vantage point of the history of a nation which is known for its multiplicity of languages and cultures. Even more important, *Dubashi* is a cultural artifact that records the changes/parallels in the mediums of mass entertainment: the growing popularity of the mythological in (early) Indian television, as exemplified by the serialization and the reception of the epic *Ramayana* in the film, which recalls the early days of Indian cinema when the epic was the preeminent genre. Furthermore, *Dubashi* reveals the changes in the industrial history of Indian cinema, due to the turn towards the digital during the last decade, through the seminal trajectory of its own distribution and exhibition.

Moreover, *Dubashi*'s narrative focuses on translation, as it is the chief occupation of its protagonists—the Rao family: Rama Rao, the father, and his two sons Raghu and Gopal. Rama Rao's wife, too, expresses her versatility in two languages, Marathi and Tamil, throughout the film. The very title, *Dubashi*, or *The Translator*, underscores the work of translation as the main theme of the film: the film abounds with literal translations from Tamil, Marathi, Hindi, English, and Japanese languages. We often hear a character talk in a language other than Tamil, and then it is translated in Tamil for the other character(s) and the audience. The narrative revolves around the changing fortunes of its central character Rama Rao, who belongs to a family of Dubashis known for their language skills and translating abilities. From the life and times of Rama Rao, who retires at the very beginning of the film from his official job as a translator, to that of his younger son, Gopal, who assists his father in translating the dialogues of the epic *Ramayana* that is broadcast in Hindi into Tamil, Dubashi uses translation as a metaphor for expanding interaction. For instance, right in the very first scene of Rama Rao's retirement we come to know through his colleague that he has been translating a very popular Tamil Novel, *Ponniyin Selvan* (The Son of Ponni) written by Kalki, into Marathi. From the translation of a novel from one regional language in India (Tamil, spoken in Tamilnadu in the south, to Marathi, spoken in Maharashtra in the west), the sphere of translation is expanded to the national when the *Ramayana* from Hindi—India's national language—is translated into Tamil. Later, toward the end of the film, when elder son Raghu is engaged with translation for a Japanese couple, *Dubashi* uses translation, from Japanese and Tamil into English, as a metaphor for the contemporary times of globalization and the transnational exchange of language and culture. Such an increase in scope points to the transition from the regional/feudal (through the patronizing of the King), to the national/industrial (through the technology of the satellite broadcast of the *Ramayana* to the entire nation through the state owned national network television: the *Doordarshan*) and the global (with Japanese tourists and their collection of antiques for the proposed museum at Hiroshima).

This essay, therefore, explores *Dubashi* as a children's film with its narrative centered on translation, to analyze its configuration of the child persona through the character of Gopal as it anticipates the new millennium, in the context of a globalizing world where mobility through the exchange of languages and cultures is privileged. Furthermore, by reconfiguring the circuit of distribution and exhibition for children's film through regular screenings at schools and community halls for a targeted group of audiences, with the help of digital technology driven distribution and exhibition through DVDs and LCD (liquid-crystal display) projectors, *Dubashi* mirrors the spirit of its hero Gopal, in seeking alternative avenues for communication across languages and culture, and successfully reaching its audience. This essay, therefore, studies in detail *Dubashi*'s exhibition over the last decade to foreground the changes brought in by digital technology, and analyzes in depth how the very localized and highly successful circulation of *Dubashi* became possible due to the characterization of Gopal whose innocence and matured outlook appealed to young and older children from middle to high schools. As the category "children's film" indicates, the targeted audience is of utmost importance as far as *Dubashi* is concerned, as it is the prerogative of educating and entertaining the children that dictates the funding from the state, and thereby, the production and reception of the film. This essay will foreground how the children's film as a category, as exemplified by *Dubashi*, is defined by the specificity of culture, and the particular context of its production, distribution, and exhibition.

Dubashi and the Exhibition of Children's Films in India

Dubashi's circulation over the last decade gives us an idea of the target audience for children's films in India, which are mostly produced by CFSI.[2] Right from the very beginning in 1955, the CFSI funded children's films were produced on celluloid, using the 35mm or 16mm stock, until 2012 when the digital mode of production was supported. Nevertheless, the distribution and exhibition of children's films over the last decade have been affected by the economy of digital technology which offers easy and affordable duplication, for instance, through the burning of DVD copies in a PC or a laptop, and enables wider exhibition because of the compactness and mobility offered by the lightweight LCD projectors. *Dubashi*, therefore, offers us a rare opportunity as it was made during the twilight years of the last century, and was shot on 35mm celluloid film, which was distributed and exhibited mainly during the new millennium, i.e., over the last decade, when digital technology made it possible to exhibit films in schools, colleges, and community halls, and easily reach a wider/targeted audience.

When we look at the history of the production and distribution of children's films in India, they have been generally produced by CFSI, and circulated through the venues of children's film festivals, and later exhibited through the public television channels; for instance, *Dubashi* was broadcast nationally through the state owned television—*Doordarshan*. But the last decade has seen a significant change in this routine: the exhibition of children's film has expanded beyond the spaces of major children's film festivals. The concept of children's film festivals has expanded to include the screenings of a few chosen films focused on subjects of interests to children in regional and local film festivals in diverse places, often in areas away from the metropolitan spaces where prestigious national and international children's film festivals are held on a regular basis.

Initially, *Dubashi* too opened up to audiences through its screenings in major children's film festivals like the 12th International Children's Film Festival of India (also called the Golden Elephant International Film Festival of India) held in Hyderabad, in November 2001,[3] and prior to that, at the Cairo International Film Festival for Children in March 2001.[4] The biannual International Children's Film Festival of India, arguably the most prestigious children's film festival in Asia, is hosted by the CFSI, and held every alternate year in Hyderabad, in South India, from November 14, the Children's Day, to November 20. The director of *Dubashi*, K. Hariharan, expected his film to just fold up after its initial showings in the festival circuit. But *Dubashi*'s continuous screenings have belied his expectations, and proven wrong his forebodings regarding the impossibility of reaching a targeted audience for a children's film.[5]

Since 1999, *Dubashi* has been one of the rare films to be regularly screened by the CFSI during its annual children's film festivals in various states of India. Additionally, private film society enthusiasts and film clubs have been able to take the film to its potential audiences, mainly the students in schools, through the possibilities offered by the new digital technology during the last decade. *Dubashi* had its traditional theatrical screening using film prints even prior to its official selection for the 12th International Children's Film Festival of India in 2001: It was screened in 2000 in the Children's Film Festival at Chennai in July (Kamath, "Merging with the Mainstream"). *Dubashi* along with Santhosh Sivan's *Malli* (1998) have been the most regularly screened children's films of the last decade by the CFSI mainly through its regional film festivals that have become increasingly popular during the new millennium.

For instance, in December 2004, *Dubashi* was one among the Indian films screened during a fortnight-long children's film festival that was held in Jamshedpur in North India. The festival was organized by CFSI along with the district administration of Eastern Singhbum, and a film club called the Celluloid Chapter of the city. Eleven films screened during the festival included three films in the local Bengali language, and three Iranian movies, which were subtitled in Hindi: *Maternal Love* (dir. Kamal Tabrizi, 1998), *The Father* (dir. Majid Majidi, 1996) and *Ebrahim* (dir. Hamid Mohseni, 1996). The inaugural film itself was screened at an auditorium in a school, Rajendra Vidyalaya (Soumya, "Reel Fantasy for Children"). Similarly in October 2007, *Dubashi* was screened by the CFSI along with the Coimbatore district administration in Coimbatore, Tirupur, and Pollachi, in South India. According to K.P. Ramakrishnan, southern regional officer and distribution officer of CFSI, the goal was "to take value based entertainment to children and expose them to quality films" by organizing 72 screenings in the district to "take such meaningful cinema about children to children" (Jeshi). The screening at the Shanthi Theater at Kattur indicates that it was a film print that was screened. The audience ranged from the middle to high school students. While the sixth grade students admired the "multi-talented" Gopal when *Dubashi* was screened, the tenth grade students appreciated Gopal because he "motivates his brother, co-operates with his father and acts as a source of inspiration" (Jeshi, "Metroplus Coimbatore"). Later in 2009, *Dubashi* again figured among the films when CFSI organized a children's film festival in Kottayam in the adjacent state of Kerala along with the local district administration. The district-level film festival screened films "simultaneously at 17 selected venues at the block panchayat (village) level and in the four municipalities" in an effort to educate and entertain children in cities as well as villages (Staff Reporter, "Children's Film Festival"). *Dubashi*, thus, was at the forefront of CFSI's attempts to reach audiences of about 100,000 people a year, mainly children, during the last decade, and catered to children's need for quality entertainment and education. The translation of *Dubashi* itself was what made such an attempt possible: *Dubashi*, the Tamil film, was dubbed in Hindi, and subtitled in English, to cater to a pan–Indian audience.

Nonetheless, CFSI's transition to the digital format has been slow and delayed. The last chairperson of CFSI, Nandita Das, an award-winning actress and a critically acclaimed film director, was mainly responsible for CFSI's adoption of digital technology.[6] In her tenure from 2009 to 2012, CFSI not only digitally restored fifty of its films but also started marketing the DVD copies of its films through well-known retailers like Shemaroo and Crossword Books. As far as the International Children's Film Festival of India was concerned, according to Das, "films could be submitted only in 35mm. With the digital revolution and a very limited budget of Rs. 4 crore (40 million Indian Rupees) 35mm was no longer possible" (Siddiqui, "Changing the Reel"). Therefore, Das was instrumental not only in the transitioning of the CFSI from its film-based productions/funding to productions on the more affordable digital format, but also in opening up the doors of the prestigious International Children's Film Festival of India to digitally produced films from all over the world in 2012. According to Das, her move to think beyond the box of CFSI produced films, and inviting the best films from all over the world to participate in the festival paid rich dividends: "(T)his week-long festival saw 152 films from 37 countries attended by over 1,75,000 children from all parts of the country, many of who [sic] had left their little villages and towns for the first time. Films made their entry for the first time even from the North East region and Kashmir. This was way above the expected estimate! South America and Africa were being represented for the first time in the festival" (Siddiqui, "Changing the Reel").

While CFSI's transition to the digital has certainly energized the production, distribution and exhibition of children's films in India, an equally significant role has been played by the Children's Film Society of Tamilnadu (CFSTN). CFSTN was founded by R.S. Rajan, the president of one of the oldest and prestigious film societies in India, Yadhaartha film society at Madurai, in South India. Rajan, as a coordinator and festival director of CFSTN, organized the screening of two critically acclaimed and popular films, *Dubashi* and *Halo* (dir. Santhosh Sivan, 1998) on November 14, 2002, at a theological seminary at Arasaradi in Madurai, to mark the inauguration of the CFSTN (Chandrasekar, "Life Madurai"). Thereafter, CFSTN, which came into being on the twenty-fifth anniversary of its parent organization, Yadhaartha, has established itself over the last decade as the most important children's film exhibitor in South India. Unlike the CFSI, the CFSTN is free of bureaucratic controls as Rajan and his friends who have been long standing lovers of good cinema (Rajan is presently the vice president of the internationally known Federation of Film Societies of India, whose ex-presidents include such luminaries as Satyajit Ray and Shyam Benegal) run the CFSTN as a non-profit organization that does not charge its members even the usual monthly fees.[7]

According to Rajan, any school, community, or social club like a film society interested in screening children's films could contact the CFSTN, and initially they charged only for the 16mm projectors that they had to hire for the screenings (Aravindan, "Budding with Creativity"). Later, when they got the projectors donated by friends, they could do away with those hiring charges as well. However, it was only during 2005/2006 when the CFSTN was into its third year of the dissemination of children's films that the real expansion of its activities took place (Rajan, R.S.). The organization of festivals/screenings with 35mm projectors in theaters, with very high rentals for the space or subsidized costs at odd hours of screenings, and/or the transportation of 16mm projectors and film prints back and forth from the community halls and school auditoriums, was replaced by screenings with the newer and user-friendly technology: easy to carry DVDs and lightweight LCD projectors and foldable screens. By 2007, many schools had installed the affordable LCD projectors in their auditoriums, and all that was needed was to carry the DVDs of children's films for projections during the festivals/screenings. Today CFSTN seeks the help of big schools like the schools run by the TVS group in getting the screening space of its well-designed auditoriums, when it wants to organize screenings for the children and their parents from nearby villages (Rajan, R.S.). The screenings are conducted when the schools are on vacation, and often the schools have come forward to help CFSTN by transporting its audiences with their buses. Presently, CFSTN has equipped itself through donations from well-wishers, and has its own projectors and LCD screens when it organizes screenings in remote areas where schools with projection facilities are far away (Rajan, R.S.). According to Rajan, Hariharan's children's films, *Wanted Thangaraj* (1979), *Crocodile Boy* (1986), and *Dubashi*, apart from Santhosh Sivan's *Malli* (1996) and *Halo*, have been the most screened among the children's films chosen by CFSTN, mainly because of their appeal to children in terms of their interesting screenplay, educational value, and the use of the local dialect in their dialogues. Rajan also points to *Dubashi* as singularly the most screened, and as the most popular film among children from the sixth to the twelfth grade in CFSTN's history (personal interview).

Being a non-profit organization which is reluctant to charge its patrons, CFSTN has to deal with some of the drawbacks and limitations of digital technology: the frequent fusing of the bulbs is one major cause of concern as replacing the old one with a new bulb is costly—it costs around 18,000 Rupees ($300 U.S. approx.). As Rajan is a trained projectionist, he could attend to any mechanical problems with earlier film projectors himself: however, the electronic LCD projectors do not lend themselves to repair-work so easily when they occasionally malfunction due to voltage fluctuation or other problems like excessive heat.[8] The other disadvantage with LCD projection is the intensity of light on the screen. According to Rajan, the higher throw/intensity of projected light in 35mm and 16mm projectors is good for bigger halls with larger audiences. The carbon-arc projection for the film print suits the conditions in community halls and schools, which are generally brightly lit and the films are screened not in ideal conditions of required darkness. Though the LCD projectors do not make the heavy sound that the 16mm projectors make while screening, the LCD projectors are generally good only for screening in smaller halls with a limited audience like in a classroom of 60 students (Rajan, R.S.). But with the rapid development in LCD technology and improvement in projection equipment, the CFSTN has been experimenting with increasing the capacity of its audiences.

The other major problem Rajan and CFSTN have been consistently facing concerns the screening schedule: evening times offer the best possible choice as most auditoriums and community halls are not air-conditioned, and keeping the doors and widows open during the evenings affords cooler conditions for viewing, particularly in the tropical heat of Southern India. Besides, the fading light after dusk does not interfere with the darkness inside the hall. However, the screening cannot be delayed till late evening as children have to get back home safely after the screenings with their friends, siblings, and/or parents.

Therefore, Rajan generally prefers the slot from 4 p.m. to 7 p.m. keeping the safety of the children as the priority (Rajan, R.S.). The scheduling of the annual CFSTN festivals around November 14 suits this schedule, as it is wintertime, and is relatively cooler around that time, and the mostly overcast sky and light too are generally favorable. CFSTN has earmarked the period from November 14 (Nehru's birthday) to November 19 (the birthday of his daughter, as well as the former prime minister, Indira Gandhi, who was a vice-president of the Federation of Film Societies of India too) as the main period of its children's film festival (Rajan, R.S.). Though the screenings of films are held simultaneously in many places around this time, the package of films are screened throughout the year in many places in South India in collaboration with local administrators, schools, and communities. According to Rajan, about 100,000 children, and some of their parents, watch the screenings of films by CFSTN every year (Personal Interview). *Dubashi*, being a prime film in the itinerary of the CFSTN, has been screened regularly by the CFSTN from November 14, 2002, onwards; *Dubashi*, thus, could be claimed to have been watched by at least a million children over the last decade in India. A detailed reading of its text is in order here, as it would shed light on the reasons for its enduring appeal.

Dubashi: Translation as a Metaphor

Straddling across diverse languages is a metaphor for hope and survival in *Dubashi*. It uses translation as a plot device to move its narrative forward, as its protagonist Rama Rao is a translator by profession. The central character is a *Dubashi*, a translator or literally the one who knows *du*/two *bashi*/languages, and this enables the narrative to focus on the problem of a family which is a minority community. Rama Rao's family is originally from Maharashtra in northwest India, and his ancestors have migrated to the Tamil speaking southern state of Tamilnadu.[9] *Dubashi*, alludes to this history when the film starts with Rama Rao retiring as a translator. We come to know from the office assistant in the opening scene that even at the time of retirement Rama Rao was actively translating the work of arguably the most popular Tamil writer Kalki into Marathi. Rama Rao's retirement also reveals the difficulties his family has to encounter, as a translator's job seems not to bring any retirement benefits or demands for his expertise. The times of the Maratha Kings like Serfoji II who patronized writers, poets, and singers seem to be a thing of the past.[10] *Dubashi*, nevertheless, uses the solemnity of such a situation to foreground how the strength of knowing multiple languages can help a family such as that of Rama Rao to find a way out of their sorrowful predicament.

Rao's elder son Raghu aspires to be a sculptor and is an introvert who is conscious of the stammer he suffers, whereas his younger son Gopal is vivacious and positive in his outlook. In fact, the narrative of *Dubashi* is centered on the joyful character of Gopal, who acutely longs for a bicycle of his own, but is able to prioritize the needs of his family over his desires. This aspect of his character is what endears him to children from the sixth to the tenth grades. When he senses an opportunity to correct the wrong usage of the Hindi language of North Indian tourists, his father diverts his attention by saying that they have been asked by the state to work on the local languages—the situation itself is created out of his father's playful convincing of Gopal of a (nonexistent) government policy on the purity of spoken language. This sequence is significant because it complicates the idea of "local" language, as Hindi, though the national language of India that is spoken mostly in North India, has an affinity to Marathi, the language spoken by Gopal at home, and that is the reason why he spontaneously reacts to the corrupted form of Hindi by the so-called native speakers from the North. From the local/national discourse surrounding Hindi, the narrative leaps to the regional/international when Gopal points to the awful English translation of Subbu, the local tourist guide. Gopal's mobility because of his knowledge of languages undergirds the narrative with hope, despite the trying circumstances of his family, and promise of solution to the problems.

Later, when escaping from the goons who are after him for trying to assemble a cycle from a dump yard, Gopal barges into the temple and takes over as a tourist guide, and explains in English the history of the Tanjore stone carvings to the eager audience in front of him. The effortless ease with which he gets into his new role and talks about the edicts of the Tanjore King Raja Raja Chozha attracts the attention of the present Tanjore King of the Maratha lineage who happens to visit the temple with his friends, a Japanese couple—Hiroshi and Nigo. This chance meeting with the King later enables Gopal to put his introvert brother Raghu in touch with the Japanese couple who are looking for rare collections from the culturally rich Tanjore city for the museum that is being planned at Hiroshima. Raghu not only comes out of his shell through this effort of Gopal, but also is able to fluently talk in English, and learn a few Japanese words from the tourist couple to his mother's pleasant surprise. Besides, Raghu's work as a tourist guide/translator for the Japanese couple enables him to fulfill Gopal's longing for a bicycle by buying him a new one at the very end of the film: *Dubashi* pays homage to *Bicycle Thieves* (Dir. Vittorio De Sica, 1948) through a scene wherein Gopal watches students in a classroom viewing De Sica's iconic film from a videotape, but opts for a happy ending in accordance with the buoyant spirit of Gopal, and the requirements of a children's film to educate, entertain, and instill hope.

The present King acting as a conduit to Raghu's friendship with the Japanese points to the contemporary times of global mobility, and in *Dubashi* it coexists with the traditional patronization of the arts by the King as he offers the job of translating his ancestor's literary works into Tamil to Rama Rao during the climax, when he asks him to pursue the work of translation in his palace itself where the originals are housed. Thus Rama Rao's anticipated visit to the palace symbolizes the continuing link with history while Raghu's presence in the house with his Japanese friends points to the globalizing world with its multiplicity of languages and culture. The film's attention to both history and globalization during the climax suggest the simultaneity of links to the past and links to the future of the Marathas in Tamilnadu. Like any migrant minority group, they want to hold on to the specificity of their language/culture, while surviving in a diverse and constantly changing world outside by adapting to it (they speak in their mother tongue at home and in other languages outside out of necessity). *Dubashi* celebrates the multilinguality of such marginalized groups as the best antidote to economically testing times in the contemporary global economy. Moreover, Gopal, who is instrumental for these movements back into the past and forward into the future, is also a figure at the cusp: he has the innocence of a child but has the maturity of a grownup—the reason for his joint appeal to children across ages (particularly from the sixth to the tenth grades) and to their parents.

Moreover, as we have seen from the observations of children during the screenings, Gopal's persona as an innocent child who is intelligent, lively, and worldly-wise is what makes *Dubashi* an interesting film for children of various ages. According to Rajan, children from villages are often accompanied by their older siblings for the screenings, as their parents are away working during the afternoon hours when the films are screened. Therefore, *Dubashi* became very popular with children as it appealed to both the young and the old among them due to its clear plot line, humor, and positive message. One of the sequences that reveals the essence of the film is the translation/interpretation of the popular television serial *Ramayan*, wherein the themes of translation, Gopal's positive outlook, and the changes in media during contemporary times is juxtaposed with the narration of an ancient epic.

Gopal enthusiastically joins his father in bank-manager Chari's house, translating *Ramayan*, the popular television serial which was (initially) telecast in Hindi and broadcast all over the nation by *Doordarshan*, the state television station of India, Delhi. As Gopal and Rama Rao alternately translate the lines from the television serial for the audience inside the frame inside Chari's living room, they do so for the larger Tamil audiences, too, that watched the film in many regions in Tamilnadu through the efforts of CFSI and CFSTN; the

English subtitles do the same for an audience who are not well-versed with either Hindi or Tamil. Gopal and Rama Rao, even as they inform us of the changing times when mythology, the primordial genre of the Indian cinema, is becoming the major attraction of Indian television, also recall the interpreters of early Indian cinema who narrated the story standing by the side of the screen when the silent movies were projected. *Dubashi*, thus, on the one hand pays homage to *Bicycle Thieves* and the potential of cinema to reach diverse audiences through translation/subtitles, and on the other, points to translation/interpretation as being central to the development of Indian cinema.

Notes

1. See the following for details of Nehru's profound affection and commitment toward children and a cinema for them, and Kedarnath's short film on Nehru and children: Children's Film Society of India, "Bachchon Se Baatein (1957)," http://cfsindia.org/bachchon-se-baatein/. Accessed 6 May 2013.

2. CFSI has produced 250 films in 10 languages over the last 58 years. For details see Children's Film Society of India, "Who We Are," http://cfsindia.org/about-cfsi/who-we-are/. Accessed 5 June 2013.

3. *Dubashi* was one among the 160 films from 40 countries that were screened at the festival. For details, see Rediff.com, Movies, "This One Is for the Kids," http://www.rediff.com/movies/2001/oct/22child.htm. Accessed 5 June 2013.

4. *Dubashi* was an Indian entry at the 11th round of the International Film Festival for Children at Cairo. See for details Weekly.Ahram.org, "11th Round of the Cairo International Film Festival for Children," http://weekly.ahram.org.eg/2001/525/cu5.htm. Accessed 5 June 2013.

5. In 2001, Hariharan was not very optimistic about the exhibition of *Dubashi*. He thought his film would be confined to festivals and special screenings alone. See for details Krithika, R. "Empowering Children," http://www.hindu.com/2001/11/17/stories/13171102.htm. Accessed 5 June 2013.

6. For Nandita Das's insightful interview when she was about to step down as the chairperson of the CFSI in 2012, after a three-year term, see Siddiqui Zaman, Rana. "Changing the Reel," http://www.thehindu.com/features/metroplus/society/changing-the-reel/article3640008.ece. Accessed 5 June 2013.

7. Rajan, R.S., personal interview in May 2013.

8. Rajan had his training as a projectionist at the iconic Gemini Studios in the early 1980s. Rajan, R.S., personal interview in May 2013.

9. The Maratha Kings, led by Vyankoji, ruled the Tanjore dynasty between AD 1674 and 1855. For the timeline, see "The History Files: Marathas (Thanjavur/Tanjore)," www.historyfiles.co.uk/KingListsFarEast/IndiaMarathasThanjavur.htm. Accessed 5 June 2013.

10. For the history of the Maratha King Serfoji II (AD 1798–1832) as a preeminent scholar and patron of arts, see "Saraswathi Mahal Library (Also Known as Serfoji Mahal Library)," tamilelibrary.org/teli/serfoji.html. Accessed 5 June 2013. Also see "Saraswati Mahal Library," saraswatimahallibrary.blogspot.in. Accessed 5 June 2013.

Works Cited

Aravindan, M.R. Hindu.com. "Budding with Creativity," 5 January 2004. Web. 5 June 2013. http://www.thehindu.com/thehindu/mp/2004/01/05/stories/2004010501530300.htm.

Bicycle Thieves. Dir. Vittorio De Sica. DVD. Image Entertainment. 1998.
Chandrasekar, Preethi. Hindu.com. "Life Madurai: Childhood Spirit on Celluloid," 13 November 2002. Web. 5 June 2013. http://hindu.com/thehindu/lf/2002/11/13/stories/2002111305350200.htm.
Children's Film Society of India. "Bachchon Se Baatein (1957)," Web. 5 June 2013. http://cfsindia.org/bachchon-se-baatein/.
Children's Film Society of India. "Who We Are," Web. 5 June 2013. http://cfsindia.org/about-cfsi/who-we-are/.
Crocodile Boy. Dir. K. Hariharan. Film. CFSI. 1986.
Dubashi. Dir. K. Hariharan. Film. CFSI. 1999.
Halo. Dir. Santhosh Sivan. Film. CFSI. 1998.
Jeshi, K. "Through the Eyes of Children." Hindu.com. 13 October 2007. Web. 6 August 2014. http://www.thehindu.com/todays-paper/tp-features/tp-metroplus/through-the-eyes-of-children/article2259251.ece.
Kamath, Sudhish. "Merging with the Mainstream." *Hindu.com*. 9 July 2000. Web. 5 June 2013. http://www.hindu.com/2000/07/09/stories/1309078m.htm.
Krithika, R. "Empowering Children." *Hindu.com*. 17 November 2001. Web. 5 June 2013. http://www.hindu.com/2001/11/17/stories/13171102.htm.
Malli. Dir. Santhosh Sivan. Film. CFSI. 1996.
Rajan, R.S. Personal Interview. May 2013.
Rediff.com. "This One Is for the Kids." Web. 5 June 2013. http://www.rediff.com/movies/2001/oct/22child.htm.
"Saraswathi Mahal Library (Also Known as Serfoji Mahal Library)." Web. 5 June 2013. tamilelibrary.org/teli/serfoji.html.
"Saraswati Mahal Library." Web. 5 June 2013. saraswatimahallibrary.blogspot.in.
Siddiqui Zaman, Rana. "Changing the Reel." Hindu.com. 16 July 2012. Web. 5 June 2013. http://www.thehindu.com/features/metroplus/society/changing-the-reel/article3640008.ece.
Soumya, Savvy. "Reel Fantasy for Children." Telegraphindia.com. Web. 5 June 2013. http://www.telegraphindia.com/1041201/asp/jharkhand/story_4069281.asp.
Staff Reporter. "Children's Film Festival Begins in Kottayam." Hindu.com. 24 November 2009. Web. 5 June 2013. http://www.hindu.com/2009/11/24/stories/2009112450880200.htm.
"The History Files: Marathas (Thanjavur/Tanjore)," Web. 5 June 2013. www.historyfiles.co.uk/KingListsFarEast/IndiaMarathasThanjavur.htm.
Wanted Thangaraj. Dir. K. Hariharan. Film. CFSI. 1979.
Weekly.Ahram.org. "11th Round of the Cairo International Film Festival for Children," Web. 5 June 2013. http://weekly.ahram.org.eg/2001/525/cu5.htm.

Branding Blackness: Disney's Commodification of Black Culture in Song of the South *and* The Princess and the Frog

Lydia E. Ferguson

In the 75 years since Walt Disney Studios released their first feature-length animated film, *Snow White and the Seven Dwarfs* (1937), the representations of race in major Disney productions have been nearly as white as the namesake of their first princess. It was not until the release of *Song of the South* (1946), the first of Disney's films to combine animation and live action, that audiences were greeted with an African American main character: Joel Chandler Harris's storytelling former slave, Uncle Remus, played by actor James Baskett. It was soon apparent that while the film attracted a large number of viewers by evoking pre–World War nostalgia, the frame narrative of *Song of the South* repelled many viewers with its romanticized depiction of slavery and plantation life. Now locked away in the (in)famous Disney vault, the film was rereleased in 1956, 1972, 1973, 1980, and for the final time, in 1986 to celebrate the film's fortieth anniversary.

Criticism emerging from the obvious lack of representation of African Americans plagued the Walt Disney Company for decades; yet, their response to this reproach seemed never to come. Finally, in 2009, sixty-three years after the initial release of *Song of the South* (*SotS*), Disney released its second animated feature film with an African American lead, *The Princess and the Frog* (*TPatF*)—and with it an abundance of merchandising ventures, including theme park rides, video games, cookbooks, and hair care products. Despite the long, impressive history of Walt Disney Studios, previous representations of blackness in their animated films have been minimal at least, and at worst, have been relegated to scavenger characters, or animals of the lowest esteem: the crows in *Dumbo* (1941), the trickster orangutans in *The Jungle Book* (1967), and the hyenas in *The Lion King* (1994). In his article on *TPatF* release, Sean Daly of the *Tampa Bay Times* condemned "the jive-pimpin' crows and faceless black carnies in *Dumbo*," while in *The Mouse That Roared*, cultural critic Henry Giroux censures the media giant for the racist allusions of the hyenas from *The Lion King*, who "speak with the voices of Whoopi Goldberg and Cheech Marin in the jive accents of a decidedly urban black or Hispanic youth," "the Amos 'n' Andy crows in *Dumbo*," and from *Mulan*, "the racialized low-comedy figure of Mushu, a tiny red dragon with a black voice [...] a servile and boastful clown" (106). And yet, the Disney Company's ostensible penchant for caricature managed to serve it well concerning the promotion of *TPatF*, as online news outlets, popular culture websites, and blogs by both loyal and disillusioned fans hastened to spread the word—free of cost—of Disney's history-making princess-to-be, along with speculations as to whether or not she would make the Disney Princess cut. Not surprisingly, *SotS* made its way into a good portion of these commentaries due to the lack of black Disney characters available for comparison.

The absence of positive characters of color in classic Disney films resulted in generations of black audience members having to look elsewhere for positive fairy-tale affirmations of their race and place in society; unfortunately, the rigorously high standards demanded by Walt Disney in the early days of Walt Disney Studios meant that few competitors approached the quality of their animated feature films. Hence, audiences and critics long wrestled with the ethical incongruities of the company's willingness to watch profits from African American consumers roll in, without ever providing admirable black characters in return.

The Walt Disney Company has always recognized and utilized the power that both their subtle and blatant depictions of race, gender, and social class signify to viewers; still, in order to achieve the desired bottom line, they have knowingly privileged white culture through synergistic marketing strategies that perpetuate traditional notions of social value—and they do so with the entire world as their captivated audience. Disney's "ever-expanding cycle of entertainment consumption [...] systematically planned and managed by the firm's marketing specialists," has enabled Disney to manipulate the majority of consumers and to commodify *blackness itself* to secure a profit (Roost 263). When Disney keeps Uncle Remus under wraps while showcasing Brer Rabbit, or incorporates Tiana's face onto every Disney Princess T-shirt, backpack, or toothbrush, the company is profiting merely by filling the marketing void it helped create. As Daly states so pragmatically, "money is no object when what you're buying is inclusion in mainstream culture." And for their exasperatingly sluggish turnaround in integrating the Disney canon, members of all colors have thanked them from the ticket window to the toy store to the theme park. According to Frank Roost, who studies the impact of global media on urban planning, "This strategy of cross-promotion among different entertainment products that included consumers' trips to a specific site of consumption was developed further over the decades and has become a basis for the Walt Disney Company's rapid growth" (263). For the millions of people who visit the Disney theme parks each year, the majority of which have likely never seen *SotS*, it is possible that a good portion of them (especially the children) perceive the Splash Mountain ride(s) to be the origin of the "Brer" characters. Hence, Disney can find financial solace in the fact that an inferior initial product does not necessarily equate to a failure on all accounts.

In *Walt Disney: The Triumph of the American Imagination*, biographer Neal Gabler relates how Walt "solicited comment from black Americans" on the script for *SotS* (435). The script eventually made its way into the hands of notable philosophy professor and cultural icon, Dr. Alain Locke of Howard University, who, as Gabler writes, shared with producer Walter Wanger, his concerns that "Walt had shown 'bad judgment' in not having contacted black leaders before having the script written" (Gabler 435). Not only would it have made logical sense to secure content editing suggestions prior to passing out the script for review, it would have made ethical and financial sense to hire writer Maurice Rapf, who Walt professed to have hired because he was "against Uncle Tomism and a radical," *before* he let notorious good ole boy Dalton Reymond draft an entire script chock full of racially insensitive content (Gabler 435).

Coincidentally, similar issues arose in the early stages of production for *TPatF*, in which Tiana, the lead character, was originally cast as a chambermaid named Maddy. Critic William Blackburn was quick to condemn the film's plot, issuing a scathing indictment in April 2007 that "Maddy" sounded too similar to "Mammy," and that the film's original title, *The Frog Princess*, was insulting to the protagonist.[1] Other potential viewers complained that Maddy's occupation as a chambermaid was too similar to that of a servant or slave; as a result, Tiana was altered again—this time into a budding restaurateur. Although Disney Studios conceded the need for such revisions, critics such as Scott Foundas and Fabio Parasecoli argue that the character of Tiana could have benefitted from further revision, as the final version of her character evokes the trope of the southern black cook, which remains an offensive stereotype to many African Americans.

According to critic Richard M. Breaux, the impetus behind the decision to transition Tiana from servant to server allowed some of the "cels of the Princess cooking, cleaning, and serving food [to] be saved and remain in the film" so that the "storyline could be reworked to salvage Disney's image in the eyes of critics and many African American parents who had longed for the day that a Disney animated feature would include non-stereotypical African Americans" (399). Given the backlash Disney received following each release of *SotS*, and (thanks to the Internet) the prolific amount of public scrutiny preceding the release of *TPatF*, audiences expected that the first black Disney princess would be nothing less, and in no way inferior to the most enviable of the established princesses. Revising the story to recycle cels, instead of scrapping the entirety of the original vision, was ultimately detrimental to the film's plot and Tiana's character development. Consequently, the company squandered its opportunity to ensure a truly profound impact on viewers.

For some, the lackluster effect of the less-than-enviable princess Tiana reinforced the Disney Company's failure to accurately represent the face(s) of America by featuring more characters of color in Disney films; for others, it was painful reminder of the problematic (mis)representations of African American life and culture in *SotS*—in which the brutal truths of slavery were glossed over by the smiles and songs of former slaves, happily living on and working for the plantation that formerly *owned* them. It was due to this romanticized frame narrative that *SotS* was boycotted by the NAACP and the National Negro Congress, and was met with a slew of scathing reviews from renowned *New York Times* film critic Bosley Crowther. Although the film grossed $3.3 million in its initial release (Gabler 438), "the studio was underwhelmed by the initial performance of *Song of the South*, which it hoped would be its big postwar smash" (Sperb 7). Notwithstanding the controversy surrounding the film's plantation myth narrative, the song "Zip-a-Dee-Doo-Dah" (Wrubel and Gilbert) was an instant hit with audiences, and took home the Academy Award for Best Original Song. One year later, in 1947, when James Baskett (who played Uncle Remus and voiced Brer Rabbit and Brer Fox) was in ill health, the Academy was persuaded by Walt Disney and other public figures to issue Baskett an honorary award for his performance (Gabler 438). Nearly 70 years and five subsequent theater releases later, the *SotS* film alone has managed to gross over $37 million, despite the film's relative absence from the market ("Song of the South [Reissue]").

Like *SotS*, ticket sales for *TPatF* did not meet studio expectations, yet the film generated financial success in other mediums. According to Disney exit polls, "Nearly one in five moviegoers came to the theater without children," prompting then president for domestic distribution Chuck Viane to claim, "That's the number that's sweetest[...]. We knew families were going to come. But we didn't know about the adults without kids" (qtd. in Bowles). It is surprising that Disney did not foresee theater attendance from adults without children, since African American women went without a Disney ideal created in their own image for over 70 years. It makes sense that black women of all ages would be intrigued to see the princess they may have wished for, but never received, in their own childhoods. Prominent members of the NAACP "gave the film a standing ovation after seeing the film at a screening in Los Angeles" (Merriman), later nominating Anika Noki Rose (who voiced Tiana) for Outstanding Actress, and the film for Outstanding Motion Picture at the 41st NAACP Image Awards ("The Pulse of Entertainment"). *TPatF* also went on to receive three Academy Award nominations: two for Best Original Song for "Down in New Orleans" and "Almost There," both with music and lyrics by Randy Newman, and the third for Best Animated Feature ("Princess Tiana"). To date, four years following its initial release, the film has grossed nearly $270 million worldwide ("The Princess and the Frog [2009]").[2]

Princess Tiana and *TPatF* merchandise remain widely available in stores and online, although not nearly to the extent of the products bearing the better-established princesses, such as Snow White, Cinderella, and Aurora (Sleeping Beauty). *SotS* merchandise, on the contrary, remains sparse, and can usually only be found in online auctions or the occasional collector's shop. Although vintage Little Golden Books, Disneyland Records, Read-Along Books, Sing-Along Songs, comic books, toys, and various other knickknacks still circulate, any new *SotS*-inspired merchandise features only the animated characters, usually omits the film's title, and *always* omits Uncle Remus, who, for obvious reasons, was never a focus for the company's marketing division. Since Disney could not make a noticeable profit from *SotS* and maintain its ethos with a significant portion of its fan base, the company decreased the visibility of the characters—at least, as they related to the original film. Eventually, Disney shifted its efforts into rebranding the Brer characters for the amusement park ride Splash Mountain, for which they recycled a multitude of animatronic "Dixie" minstrel critters from the Deep South portion of the once popular attraction, America Sings. Thus, the animatronic stereotypes, which had long perpetuated the minstrel show tradition by performing such staples as "Dixie," "Camptown Races," and "My Old Kentucky Home," were put back to work entertaining visitors ("America Sings").

To commemorate the twentieth anniversary of the Magic Kingdom's Splash Mountain ride in 2012, Disney offered a special anniversary pin in which *SotS*'s Brer Fox, with his razor-sharp teeth bared and his lip furled with devilish intent, is dangling a terrified Brer Rabbit by the ears over the menacing briar patch. The scene playing out on the pin is problematic in that it misrepresents the specific plot point being referenced. In other words, why does Brer Rabbit have a doomed expression on his face when the briar patch is his "Laughing Place"?

The representation would be truer to the famous trickster's character if he was grinning or smirking to the side to illustrate that he actually *wants* to be thrown in the briar patch, and that he is not in danger, but rather, in control of the situation and his fate. As it is, for Disney fans that have not seen *SotS* or the many reissues of the animated sequences, the cunning of Brer Rabbit—considered by many to be one of the film's few redeeming qualities—is subverted and lost in the narrative depicted on the commemorative merchandise.

Although Disney continues to profit from the film they wish they and the public could and would forget, the marketing for *TPatF* was drastically different for a number of reasons. Firstly, it was the first Disney animated feature-length film with a black lead. Secondly, the lead was also the first Disney African American princess. Thirdly, the online chatter that abounded regarding the film's release, both positive and negative, resulted in increased hype and free advertising. And fourthly, unlike the offensive *SotS*, which many black consumers boycotted or simply avoided, African Americans played a pivotal role in contributing to the success of all things related to *TPatF*. At $25 million, it managed to gross the highest ticket sales of any film the week of its release; yet ultimately, like *SotS*, it still failed to meet the studio's projected earnings (Bowles).

The merchandising ventures related to *TPatF*, however, were tremendously successful. Months before the theatrical release of the film, Princess Tiana products like the Just One Kiss Princess Tiana Doll were flying off physical and virtual shelves, and earning several consumer-marketing distinctions in the process. Many saw the incorporation of a black princess into the Disney Princess franchise as a step forward for the company, who would subsequently be supplying the long-awaited demand for a strong African American lead and more racially diverse products for children. Disney apparently timed Tiana's debut well, as the Target Market News report for 2009 found that African American consumers spent $3.1 billion on entertainment and leisure, $3.5 billion on toys, games, and pets, and $29.3 billion on apparel products and services in that year alone ("2010 'Buying Power' Report").[3] Despite having only two feature-length animated films with African American leads, The Walt Disney Company has succeeded in branding Disneyfied versions of blackness that have maintained their profitability.

Disney's animated films are logically what set the branding process in motion, yet it is becoming increasingly apparent that the films themselves are more valuable to the company as catalysts of consumer products and culture. Prior to the release of the actual film, Disney went all out in their promotion of *TPatF* and Tiana merchandise. The Disney Store "dedicate[d] all of its 229 windows in North America to *The Princess and the Frog*," with Tiana merchandise "out-selling other Disney Princess items by double digit percentages," and *TPatF* bedding selling "nearly triple the amount of regular Disney Princess bedding" (Bonner). Carol's Daughter, a distributer of hair and beauty products designed for African Americans, teamed with Disney to create a Princess Tiana Magical Beauty line, which sold out online in a matter of hours ("Princess Tiana"). The impressive sales of items such as bedding and hair products indicate the strong inclination of parents to purchase, not only the toys their children want to play with, but the practical merchandise they want their children to have.

When Tiana appeared in her own Magic Kingdom theme park attraction, Tiana's Showboat Jubilee—which had a limited engagement from October 26, 2009, to January 3, 2010 ("Disney and Florida Attractions")—she and the cast performed musical numbers from the film's soundtrack, which soundtrack critic Mark Morton praised for its "nice, lazy, laid-back, zydeco-inspired rhythm that would also not sound out of place on Splash Mountain." This connection between Tiana's world and that of the omitted Uncle Remus is telling, illustrating exactly why critics were unhappy with the decision to set the first African American princess's tale in the Jim Crow segregationalist south. This negative correlation did not stop parents wishing to pamper their daughters from spending "as much as $190" (Daly) for a Bibbidi Bobbidi Boutique makeover, where "Fairy Godmothers-in-Training sprinkle their pixie dust on aspiring princesses with three makeover packages ranging from a combination of hair, nails, and makeup to the royal transformation complete with Princess Tiana costume, tiara, wand and more" ("Disney and Florida Attractions").

The Disney Princess franchise link on Disney's Consumer Products (DCP) website reminds readers, "Little girls never forget their first encounter with a Disney Princess. Even long after they're all grown up, they continue to pass along their love for these heroines, introducing them to their own daughters" ("Disney Princess"). Certainly, for many Disney fans, all grown up with children of their own, this statement resonates strongly; however, the immediate and overwhelming popularity of Tiana merchandise around the country suggests that, with no Disney fairy tale fantasies to appeal to them directly, African American mothers were not passing along the princesses of their youth to their daughters at the same rate as white mothers. Well aware of this, when Tiana finally came along to supply that long-absent representation, adults, although apparently unexpected at theaters, were not forgotten in the film's merchandising efforts. Adults wanting *TPatF* items made exclusively for them could purchase the Princess Tiana Ball Gown, the Princess Tiana Bayou Wedding Dress, and items from Kidada Jones's (daughter of Quincy Jones) couture line of *TPatF* inspired jewelry (Matthews). With the inclusion of this adult role-play line, Disney was able to indoctrinate an older generation of consumers into the cyclical nature of their synergistic marketing strategy.

The proven success of the more diverse *TPatF*-inspired products illustrates the willingness of African American consumers to purchase products designed with them in mind. Dara Trujillo, "theme parks' manager of merchandise synergy," emphasizes a love of clothing over a love of culture, claiming, "Our guests love the princesses. It doesn't matter what their skin tone is [...] these are just gals in great gowns!" (qtd. in Daly). And yet, when Tiana role-play dresses became available in stores, they quickly became the "top selling dresses in the Disney Princess lineup at retailers nationwide," indicating that consumers had been awaiting such a product ("Princess Tiana"). Trujillo's rosy perception is problematic in that it values the commodity of the dress itself, symbolic of wealth and vanity, over the inherent beauty of the woman wearing it. Let us not forget that for the majority of *TPatF*, Charlotte, with her collection of nearly identical tailor-made (Disney role-playing) dresses and blonde-bombshell looks, is situated as the princess figure—not Tiana.

Tiana's own inadequacies are made evident in one of books released by Disney Press, following the more than 2.5 million books featuring Tiana that sold in just the first three months after the film's release ("Princess Tiana"). Helen Perelman's *Disney Princess Tiana: The Grand Opening* (2010) begins with the newly married Princess Tiana in her palace, which is the sugar mill—a symbol of an industry indelibly linked to slavery and the most brutal of working conditions—she and Prince Naveen have converted into her restaurant (where she works as a chef and he works as a waiter and entertainer). The narrator immediately informs young readers, "It may not have been the palace of every princess's dreams, but she loved it[...]. She had dreamed about this her entire life" (Perelman 1). Scott Foundas, amongst others, takes issue with this dream, asserting, "Disney's first black 'princess' lives in a world where the ceiling on black ambition is firmly set at the service industries, and Tiana and her neighbors seem downright zip-a-dee-doo-dah happy about that." The food service industry in particular is complicated by age-old stereotypes that drew the attention of critics. As Fabio Parasecoli maintains, although Tiana is driven, her "dreams of success as a restaurateur are constantly framed in terms of actual cooking, an occupation that has been historically connected with black women" (450).

Whether the majority of black viewers were troubled by this correlation is uncertain, but parents who wish their daughters to defy boundaries set by race and traditional gender roles should evidently look outside of the princess franchise, since, as Sheila Ullery of DCP claimed, "A local cooking school was actually doing recipes from the Tiana cookbook, and the instructor was already getting pent up demand for these cooking classes so that girls could learn how to cook like Tiana using the recipes from the cookbook" (qtd. in Matthews).

Obviously, many young girls want to transform themselves into princesses through their imaginations, and certainly, many young women, black or otherwise, dream of becoming chefs, but as Lee Artz asserts, "Disney creates its ideal world through an animated narrative realism. Each narrative tells a story of the way things are or are supposed to be. Each story (and every Disney product) represents the myth of how things are done, not then or now, but always in the life of the living being, group, or culture" (82). Considering the decades of criticism levied against Disney as a result of *SotS*, the company would have done well to take additional steps, prior to the film's release, to ensure Tiana would be a radical departure from any such humbling implications.

The extravagant, transformative payoff is part of the idealized princess experience, and the castle is the ultimate symbol of wealth, power, and fortitude gained through this upward mobility. As critics Dawn C. Chmielewski and Claudia Eller point out: "consider that a fairy tale castle is a landmark at Disney theme parks around the world and is embedded in the Walt Disney pictures logo." If the castle symbolizes success, then all Tiana and the audience gets as the payoff from her royal marriage is an extra "a" in the name of her dream business, which changes from "Tiana's Place" to "Tiana's Palace" at the film's end. As African American literature and culture scholar Neal Lester concludes, "Disney's efforts to breathe life into a Disney princess who is 'keeping it real' by keeping her feet planted firmly on the ground potentially diminishes Tiana's royal aura for those rightfully expecting the first black princess to live in the same world of fantasy and (im)possibility as do her other sister princesses" (297). At the end of Tiana's journey, neither she nor her prince project anything close to the viewer's idea of royalty; as such, she cannot vie with Disney's own, idealized princess archetypes, no matter how much merchandise they sell.

Ironically, many of the consumers who purchased *TPatF* products did so *because* of Disney's blatant lack of African American culture in their films and toys in the wake of *SotS*. Uncle Remus, the film's protagonist, all but absent from *SotS* merchandise, leaves the animal characters and songs as the sole focus of Disney's merchandising efforts for the film. While there is little representation of blackness in the toys and promotional products for *SotS*, the exact opposite is true for the merchandising efforts put forth for *TPatF*. Whereas Disney concealed Remus's blackness in favor of promoting the more positive images of Brer Rabbit for the film's merchandise, they minimized Tiana's amphibious "greenface," appearing to amplify her blackness for the "Just One Kiss Princess Tiana Doll" (which the DCP reports made *FunFare Magazine*'s 2009 Holiday Hot Dozen and ToysRUs Fabulous 15 List), the Sparkling Princess Tiana Doll, the Transforming Princess-to-Frog Tiana Doll, and the Princess Tiana Toddler Doll, which all appear to have darker skin tones than her character in the film ("Disney Princess"). Hence, in the case of the dolls, if not with the film, Disney is giving African American consumers products the type of products that they want to buy.

With the initial glow having worn off, merchandise related to *TPatF* film is less abundant than products featuring Tiana's face amidst the crowd. The princess-specific browsing offered online by Disney Stores and Target not only illustrates that the princesses of color have less merchandise dedicated the them, but also that they are most often situated in the rear or side of their white counterparts. The predictability of this placement reinforces complaints from critics that Disney films still—despite the appearance of a more diverse family photograph—privilege whiteness. Consequently, the bias evident in this pattern of placement implies that Jasmine, Pocahontas, and Mulan, even more than Tiana, appear to be supplemental to the Disney Princess brand, not significant to it. Thus, in the shift from character to commodity, visibility without individuality results in a Disney Princess Melting Pot, wherein Disney ensures the popular culture status and economic value of the "ethnic" princesses through their assimilation into the Disney Princess franchise. Unfortunately, as is the nature of assimilation, their royal status is achieved at the cost of losing much of the individuality that initially had such a significant effect on the eyes, minds, and wallets of the public.

With only two feature-length animated films with African American leads, The Walt Disney Company has managed to generate consistent profit from the marketing of these films and their black characters, despite the many criticisms levied against the characterizations of black culture in both films. The wide array of *TPatF* merchandise has helped diversify the Disney Princess brand, but because the film presents the viewer with a racially-ambivalent plot that glosses over the brutal reality of race relations in the 1920s Deep South, and because Tiana's "dream" is less a dream than an aspiration, it is unlikely that *The Princess and the Frog* will achieve the status of a "classic." Many die-hard Disney fans make the claim that popular culture is only entertainment to be enjoyed, and should not be put under a magnifying glass and overly scrutinized. However, with a popular culture machine like Disney, which specializes in generating entertainment for young, impressionable minds, it is up to parents to inform themselves about the products that will become indelibly linked with their children's formative years. Consumer culture is ever evolving, and for better or worse, Disney is at the forefront of that evolution. Thinking critically and questioning content meant for children is not an exercise in brand-bashing or exacting childhood vendettas; rather, it is a practice that ensures that we do not sacrifice our collective critical voice for the latest Disney sing-along.

Notes

1. Excerpts from Blackburn's original response to the early plans for *TPatF*, published in the *Charlotte Observer*, are available online in "The Princess and the Caricature."
2. Despite the source title, this number reflects revenue up to 2013.
3. These figures are updated from those cited in Breaux, 414.

Works Cited

"America Sings." *Yesterland*. Del Monte, 4 April 2012. Web. 11 May 2013.
Artz, Lee. "Monarchs, Monsters, and Multiculturalism: Disney's Menu for Global Hierarchy." *Rethinking Disney: Private Control, Public Dimensions*. Mike Budd and Max H. Kirsch, eds. Middletown, CT: Wesleyan University Press, 2005. 75–97. Print.
Bonner, Julie. "Disney's The Princess and the Frog Merchandise Is in High Demand." *Crushable*. Alloy Digital, 19 November 2009. Web. 6 May 2013.
Bowles, Scott. "'The Princess and the Frog' Ascends to No. 1." *USA Today* 14 December 2009. Print.
Breaux, Richard M. "After 75 Years of Magic: Disney Answers Its Critics, Rewrites African American History, and Cashes In on Its Racist Past." *Journal of African American Studies* 14 (2010): 398–416. Print.
Chmielewski, Dawn C., and Claudia Eller. "Disney Animation Is Closing the Book on Fairy Tales." *Los Angeles Times*. Los Angeles Times, 21 November 2010. Web. 9 May 2013.
Daly, Sean. "Disney's Princess Tiana Really Turns Heads." *Tampa Bay Times*. 5 December 2009. Web. 6 May 2013.
"Disney and Florida Attractions News Blog." *'Tiana's Showboat Jubilee!' at Walt Disney World*. AllEars.Net, 26 October 2009. Web. 6 May 2013.
"Disney Princess." *Disney Consumer Products*. Disney.com, 2011. Web. 6 May 2013.
Foundas, Scott. "Whitewash: Disney's The Princess and the Frog Can't Seem to Escape the Ghetto." *SF Weekly*. 9 December 2009. Web. 6 May 2013.
Gabler, Neal. *Walt Disney: The Triumph of the American Imagination*. New York: Random House, 2006. Print.
Giroux, Henry A. *The Mouse That Roared: Disney and the End of Innocence*. Lanham, MD: Rowman and Littlefield, 1999. Print.
Lester, Neal A. "Disney's The Princess and the Frog: The Pride, the Pressure, and the Politics of Being a First." *Journal of American Culture* 33.4 (2010): 294–308. Print.
Matthews, KJ. "The Marketing of a 21st-Century Princess." *CNN*. Cable News Network, 11 December 2009. Web. 6 May 2013.
Merriman, Helena. "Disney Draws Its First African-American Princess." *BBC News*. BBC, 28 November 2009. Web. 6 May 2013.
Morton, Mark. "Randy Newman Invokes the Deep South with the Soundtrack to Disney's 'The Princess and the Frog.'" Examiner.com. 11 December 2009. Web. 6 May 2013.
Parasecoli, Fabio. "A Taste of Louisiana: Mainstreaming Blackness Through Food in The Princess and the Frog." *Journal of African American Studies* 14 (2010): 450–68. Print.
Perelman, Helen. *Disney Princess: Tiana: The Grand Opening*. New York: Disney, 2010. Print.
"The Princess and the Caricature." *O-pinion*. Charlotteobserver.com, 11 June 2009. Web. 7 May 2013.
"The Princess and the Frog (2009)." *Box Office Mojo*. IMDB. Web. 9 May 2013.
"Princess Tiana Officially Joins the Disney Princess Royal Court." *Bloomberg*. 15 May 2010. Web. 6 May 2013.
"The Pulse of Entertainment: Precious, Invictus and The Princess and the Frog Lead in the 41st NAACP Image Award Nominations." *Eurweb.com Electric Urban Report*. Lee Bailey, 16 January 2010. Web. 14 May 2013.

Roost, Frank. "Synergy City: How Times Square and Celebration Are Integrated into Disney's Marketing Style." *Rethinking Disney: Private Control, Public Dimensions.* Mike Budd and Max H. Kirsch, eds. Middletown, CT: Wesleyan University Press, 2005. 261–98. Print.
"Song of the South (Re-issue) (1980)." *Box Office Mojo.* IMDB. Web. 9 May 2013.
Sperb, Jason. *Disney's Most Notorious Film: Race, Convergence, and the Hidden Histories of Song of the South.* Austin: University of Texas, 2012. Print.
"2010 'Buying Power' Report Shows Black Consumer Spend as Economy Improves." *Target Market News: The Black Consumer Market Authority.* Target Market News. Web. 13 May 2013.

The Commodification of Ms. Penny Proud: Consumer Culture in Fat Albert and the Cosby Kids and Disney's The Proud Family[1]

Debbie Olson

Media designed for children, particularly animation, "does not eliminate the subject or the self but finds it in operation as a series of bit parts in the concrete field of social relations" which is expressed in animation's slapstick type cuts and zooms between characters as they are propelled through the plot (McRobbie 606). Although Angela McRobbie here refers to feminist postmodernism, the point could be made that a child's identity is defined and constructed through real social relations that are mimicked in animation, usually with the aim of delivering an instructional or moral teaching. But social relations in today's children's programming often revolve around commodities and consumption.

There is an ongoing debate among media critics about television and film's effects on the child viewer and about visual media's influence on children in general, particularly in relation to images of sex and violence. But researchers disagree about how much effect, and what type of effect, television and film images have on the child viewer:

> On the one side are critics in the tradition of the Frankfurt school ... who contend that television kills children's imagination with limited colonizing narratives; violates their innocence in relation to sex, violence, and commerce; and like a narcotic, numbs their innate curiosity about the world. Basic to these claims is the assumption that children will mimic what they see.... On the other side, cultural studies has drawn attention to the varied ways in which audiences negotiate with, resist, or are co-opted by mass communication [Kapur "Out of Control" 122].

Though there are numerous studies that seek to gauge the effects of sex and violence on the child viewer, there is much less done on how children mimic, negotiate, or resist televised images and situations involving socialization. How do images of peer groups in children's programming help inform, construct, or motivate a child's real life socialization? And how do those images or situations, which may be race or gender coded, construct and/or inform broader ideological values, particularly their ideas about consumption? In this essay I will examine how African American children are placed in a subject position that naturalizes the desire for full participation in American capitalist consumer culture as constructed and presented by the white media industry. I will take a critical look at two successful, and rare, African American cartoon series and the later feature length films based on those series, that were written and developed by African Americans, but produced by dominant white media: Bill Cosby's *Fat Albert and the Cosby Kids* (1972–1985) and Disney's *The Proud Family* (2001–2003).

Part of what I argue the *Proud Family* cartoon does is present to the child viewer consumer culture in such a way as to reinforce its importance and desirability within African American social groups, which is a marked contrast to the consumer culture messages inherent in the '70s-era popular cartoon *Fat Albert*. The African American consumer demographic has not been a historically hot marketing target. According to Jacobson, persistent racist beliefs deem that "lacking both personal and family resources, black and other minority children [do] not attract the interest of national advertisers" (6). African American children have been either excluded from television advertising and programming altogether or were presented as stereotyped caricatures filled with racist assumptions about who African Americans really are. One advertisement from the 1930s for Little African licorice drops portrayed an African baby about to be eaten by an alligator with the slogan "a dainty morsel" (Kern-Foxworth). Black children were often portrayed in cartoons or live action shows as unintelligent, slow, lazy, "sambos," "pickaninnies," or "buckwheats." Black cartoon characters were consistently drawn with exaggerated features that reinforced the distinct boundaries between acceptable whiteness and unacceptable blackness.

But in today's niche market structures, advertisers have begun to at least attempt to attract minority consumers and the way to create a market is to create a desire for consumption that brings status or acceptance, whether real or imagined. Disney's *The Proud Family* works through Althusserian interpellation[2] in that the show's numerous images of consumption/exchange unconsciously "hail" the assumed African American child viewer, who, in the case of *The Proud Family*, is shown a social contextualization through the active participation in consumer culture. Fiske argues that "In responding to the call, in recognizing that it is *us* being spoken to, we implicitly accept the discourse's definition of 'us' ...

we adopt the subject position proposed for us by the discourse" (53). Assuming the viewer is placed in a particular subject position by television or film images and discourse, in what subject position might an African American child viewer be placed? As a marketing strategy, product advertisers work to "(re) define commodities as beneficial/functional for children. When goods become framed as 'useful' they become means to ends rather than intended for mere consumption or display" (Cook 115). Both the *Proud Family* and *Fat Albert* use commodities in such a way as to "hail" the viewer, but the two shows (and their associated films) differ greatly in their address to the viewer.

The Imagined Child

Since World War II, television and mass media advertisers have re-imagined childhood into a quasi–Victorian, untainted vision of innocence that works to seduce adults into desiring a nostalgic return to an imagined state of perfection. These idealized images of childhood are rooted in the angelic character Eva from Harriet Beecher Stowe's 1851 anti-slavery novel *Uncle Tom's Cabin*:

> Her form was the perfection of childish beauty.... There was about it an undulating and aerial grace, such as one might dream of for some mythic and allegorical being.... The shape of her head and the turn of her neck and bust was peculiarly noble, and the long golden-brown hair that floated like a cloud around it, the deep spiritual gravity of her violet blue eyes, shaded by heavy fringes of golden brown.... Always dressed in white, she seemed to move like a shadow through all sorts of places, without contracting spot or stain [Stowe 143].

The Victorian simulacrum of childhood is signified by numerous images of round, cherub-like, angelic faces with a halo of golden, curled hair and clear, sweet, wide blue eyes whose "spiritual gifts could rescue fallen adults" (Jacobson 3), as did Eva in Stowe's novel. But Stowe's novel also popularized another version of childhood embodied in the black child slave, Topsy, who is characterized as the unacceptable opposite of Eva's angelic purity:

> She was one of the blackest of her race; and her round, shining eyes, glittering as glass beads, moved with quick and restless glances over everything in the room. Her mouth, half open with astonishment ... displayed a white and brilliant set of teeth. Her woolly hair was braided in sundry little tails, which stuck out in every direction. The expression of her face was an odd mixture of shrewdness and cunning ... she was dressed in a single filthy, ragged garment.... Altogether, there was something odd and goblin-like about her appearance—something ... "so heathenish" [237].

Stowe's widely popular novel set the stage for later media representations of childhood. Eva's angelic whiteness became embodied in child actress Shirley

Temple, whose persona reached widespread popularity during the depression era, a time of mass social despair when such images of childhood freedom from adult pressures helped assuage social melancholia. Cook argues that childhood in the post-depression era became a "site for commercial activity" (112) with the rise of industrialization and over time evolved in such a way that "a child's value was measured less and less in economic—monetary terms and became constituted increasingly in sentimental—emotional ones" (113). Temple was the physical manifestation of Eva's purity and the social desire for the spiritual innocence that childhood represented—Temple's identity and body commodified in both film and real life.

Most of the Victorian images of perfect childhood are today represented by young cherub-faced golden-haired girls and are exhibited in a plethora of idealized nostalgia on postcards, in coloring books, picture books, commercials and advertisements, television and film. As a result, western media has created a naturalized collective memory of childhood as a "time that refers back to a fantasy world where the painful realities and social constraints of adult culture no longer exist," which is then embellished by advertisers who market a variety of products that promise to help return adults to that whimsical prelapsarian state (Spigel 185). Today, childhood as a site of consumerism has united with its romanticized emotional representation to create products that are marketed effectively to both adults, for nostalgic reasons, and to children, who, by consuming the products that represent "ideal" childhood, become active participants in the creation of their own commodified mythology.

Child as Consumer

Throughout the post-war years, the television industry increasingly shifted the notion of children as influencing agents used to persuade their parents to purchase goods and services that were marketed to children, to "sovereign, playful, thinking consumers" who are now one of the fastest growing market demographics, particularly in this age of niche markets and kids-only networks like Nickelodeon, Nickelodeon's TV Land, the Cartoon Network, Noggin, Discovery Kids, and the Disney Channel (Kapur "Out of Control" 125). As Vivian A. Zelizer has argued, the nineteenth-century child who labored for the good of the family was transformed throughout the early Industrial Age into a child consumer—the child's value became sentimentalized rather than connected to how much money that child could produce: "Children stopped working just as the rise in consumerism and mass advertising created tantalizing new opportunities for spending" (13). As media technology advanced, so too has the reach of advertisers into children's lives. The advent of children's cable networks afford advertisers "a ripe environment through which to address children as consumers" (Spigel 204) in both programming and advertisements. Early attempts by television and Hollywood film to "mass market childhood ... childhood got branded sweet and cuddly, cute and tiny" and very, very *white* (Kapur 57).

As Ellen Seiter and Vicki Mayer argue "many aspects of children's toy and media worlds have remained unchanged since the 1950s; white, affluent children are the most desirable demographic group" (Seiter and Mayer 120) and are the most visible in children's television. Children's consumer culture often excludes children of color and consistently presents idealized childhood as white and middle to upper class. According to Kapur, "The luxury of childhood, of time spent in play and learning safe from the factory and the market, was, of course, practically available only to the bourgeois child.... The fear of slipping down the class hierarchy and finding oneself part of the hordes of working-class children ... continued to haunt these mainstream celebrations of childhood as an Edenic state"(49–50). This Edenic image of childhood is closely aligned with Christian beliefs in a white Christ, as the spiritual, otherworldly state of pure childhood is portrayed as angelic and divine, as Stowe's Eva. The divinity and purity of a prelapsarian state is "at the heart of the bourgeois cult of the beautiful child ... [because] childhood itself was [is] a privilege of class" (Kapur 49). Though slavery has been non-existent since 1865, Jim Crow laws[3] and separate-but-equal attitudes have historically kept the image of the African American child reminiscent of Stowe's Topsy, the heathenish imp, as an unconscious social conception of black childhood. One only needs to compare the visual aesthetic of the Bratz dolls (MGA Entertainment) with that of Mattel's Barbie to confirm a modern notion of the heathenish child of color.[4]

The Color of Money

American society has thankfully moved, albeit slowly, towards blurring the boundaries between people of color and the myth of white superiority. However, in areas of production and consumption, the media industry still believes money only comes in one color: white. One example is the media's belief that African Americans have limited purchasing power, a notion that conflicts with the mainstream media celebration of hip-hop/rap culture: "The spectacle [of black hip-hop culture] presents itself as something enormously positive, indisputable and inaccessible" (Debord 141). Though arguably, there is debate about whether or not hip-hop images are "enormously positive," the point I am making is that the trappings of African American culture have become appropriated by white mainstream society to such an extent that it presents back to African American viewers, particularly African American children, an acceptable "blackness" [i.e., social identity] that is in some cases economically inaccessible to the very group that created the images in the first place.

How does consumer culture play out in children's programming? In the case of white appropriation of hip/hop/rap culture, such appropriation then defines the African American child's own culture (particularly through Disney's appropriation), which is then recycled (re-defined) back to the African American child through mainstream children's media. This re-presenting of African American culture to the African American child positions the child in such a way that acculturates her into accepting the "hail" by the consumer culture featured in the show, or film, as a boundary from which the African American child's subjectivity is then constructed. The child's subjectivity is therefore defined by the media images as existing only in relation to something else—namely money/consumption—a groundwork from which to build the consumer "subject" based on the social call and the child's response . As Jacobson argues, when programmers and advertisers envisioned the child consumer "they typically envisioned a white, middle-to-upper class child, somewhere between nine and nineteen" (5), and though television and film images today are much more diverse than they were a mere ten or fifteen years ago, children's animated television programming has been conspicuously slow to catch up. How do all-black cartoons for children position the African American child viewer? And, most importantly, do those cartoons position the child in such a way as to foster belief in an equal, and necessary, consumerist participation in order to achieve an acceptable "blackness," an economic equality which has historically been denied to African Americans?

Hey Hey Hey! It's Fat Albert!

The 1970s ushered in a new, but sadly brief, era in broadcast television with the introduction of three all-black cast cartoons. *Fat Albert and the Cosby Kids* (1972–1985), written by Bill Cosby, was the third African American children's cartoon to appear on network television, preceded by *The Harlem Globetrotters* (CBS 1970–1973) and *The Jackson 5ive* (ABC 1972–1973).

The *Fat Albert* television series, and the later 2004 live-action film of the same name, were created by comedian Bill Cosby and are partly autobiographical about Cosby's childhood growing up in Philadelphia. The show takes place in the inner city, as do the majority of media films and television programs featuring young African Americans, and does not shy away from its educational purpose.

In the opening sequence of each show, Bill Cosby states "and if you aren't careful, you just might learn something!" The show is structured in such a way as to incorporate African American traditional storytelling techniques in that it is narrated and "told" by Bill, who always opens the show from his junkyard worktable (in which he is most often shown fixing some item or building something), and who interjects with narrative commentary throughout the episode. The characters include a motley assortment of very distinctive personalities: Fat Albert, Mushmouth, Rudy, Dumb Donald, Weird Harold, Bill (as himself), Russell (Bill's younger brother), Mudfoot, and Bucky. Their playground is a Philadelphia junkyard full of an infinite number of broken, cast-off commodities, which society deems worthless. But these objects are used throughout each episode to create play and foster imagination among the gang. The underlying analogy in the visual setting is that poor black kids from the inner city are analogous to social "junk," cast-offs with no economic usefulness, but the show delivers the message that everything is useful and has a purpose; it just takes creativity and mind-power to free the object (or child) from what society says it is or should be. It is the character's creative interactions with these commodities that provide a compelling vantage point from which to view the shift in the attitudes of programmers towards consumption and consumer culture among African American children viewers from the 1970s (which was the beginning of the end of industrial age Fordism) to the 2000s (the post-industrial age) and how that shift in attitude, as imagined in *Fat Albert and the Cosby Kids* and *The Proud Family*, influences their subject position in American consumer culture.

Throughout the first season's twelve episodes of *Fat Albert*, money and images of exchange are only shown in one episode: "Creativity" (first aired September 30, 1972). In this episode, Rudy shows up at the junkyard with a brand new guitar. Rudy is the big-talking rich kid of the gang, and always tries to get out of work or find the easy way out of things, but usually gets into trouble for his efforts. More importantly, Rudy's rich status is not played up in the show. He may be rich but he still hangs out in the junkyard with his friends. He is constructed as a know-it-all who really has a lot to learn. He flaunts his guitar playing and the gang teases him that he doesn't play very well. The gang then decides they want musical instruments too, and in close-ups of each member, they all state that they will ask their parents who "will get it for me." The next scene finds the gang all sitting against the wall of a junkyard shack moping because none of their parents "have the money to buy musical instruments." Fat Albert then gets the idea that they can work and earn the money to buy the musical instruments. What follows next is a montage of each of the boys working odd jobs to gain money. At the end of the montage, the gang goes to the music store and they each pick out their instrument. When the music store clerk adds up all the prices it comes to over $400—Fat Albert puts their hard-earned sixty-four cents on the counter and asks what can they get with that? The clerk sells them a broken drumstick. When the kids go back to the junkyard, Russell, who is tapping on a piece of pipe, inspires them to use their imagination and make musical instruments out of the things they have. The rest of the episode shows the gang using various junk: an old bedspring, empty cans and bottles, an old radiator, pipes, and garbage cans and lids to create musical instruments. They proudly form the Junkyard Band.

This episode reinforces the ideologically traditional American work ethic, that the way to consume is to produce, to work for the dollars/capital that will allow consumption. But the kids' imagined extravagant consumption is not realized despite their hard work; instead their hard-earned money only permits a very modest purchase. As Cosby says in the shows' narrative, the gang learns to "make do with what they have," an important message for poor kids from the inner city. But, for the African American child viewer the message also reinforces a healthy skepticism of consumerisms' seductiveness. The gang worked very hard for that sixty-four cents, but it did not buy music; in fact, they were really only able to purchase a piece of "junk." On one hand, it could be argued that the show's underlying assumptions to the African American child viewer could be to not desire those things that are unattainable and instead, work hard, know your place, make do with what you have, and be thankful. But, the episode does not disparage the gang's dreams and desires for musical instruments that are above what they can afford—in fact, quite the opposite, as the show makes a point of allowing each character to voice his dreams about the type of instrument he wants and how he would play it.

The message here is that it is ok to desire and dream about purchasing, but the reality is that it is not *necessary* in order to fulfill desires: a message that is not a part of the consumer culture displayed in *The Proud Family*. Consumption and production (in the form of music) for the Fat Albert gang can be utilized without monetary exchange, and is in fact, shown to be preferable and more fun to consume and recycle the things already available, that it is not necessary to always purchase something new to bring happiness. The junkyard objects in *Fat Albert* also demonstrate the virtue of recycling, which was a part of social consciousness of the '70s, as the waste products from consumerism become, for the gang, the trappings of childhood. Most importantly, the gang's activities do not revolve around the purchase of things/commodities through exchange, but rather, through the gang's re-use of cast-off objects they find in the junkyard, they produce and create the experiences of childhood: music and play. All the characters learn and grow personally, not through the objects they create or interact with, but through their interactions with each other and the adults.

The Proud Family

Disney's *The Proud Family* (2001–2003) is the first animated Disney television cartoon to feature an all-black cast. The show is structured like a sitcom and was created by Bruce W. Smith, one of the few African American animators, who joined Disney in 1990. *The Proud Family* is set in suburban Americana and contains a large list of characters: Penny Proud, a fourteen-year-old girl and the main protagonist of the show; her father Oscar Proud, who sells snack foods and is arrogant but henpecked; Trudy Proud, Penny's mother; Suga Mama, Penny's hip but cranky grandmother; Bobby Proud, Penny's lazy uncle; the twins Bee Bee and Cee Cee; Dijonay Jones, Penny's best friend; Zoey, Penny's geeky white friend; LaCienega, Penny's vain and popular friend; the Gross Sisters, the representative "gang" girls who are colored light blue and bully everyone around them; and Wizard Kelly, Jr., who is the rich kid of the group. His dad, Wizard Kelly, owns and controls practically everything in town. The show does not pretend to be educational, but instead presents the "typical" problems that many teens face: jealousy, peer pressure, fitting in, the ins/outs of friendships, having parties, dating, boyfriends, etc. The show's tone is sardonic and the antics between Oscar and his mother, Suga Mama, are at times over the top in their meanness. Suga Mama hates her son Oscar and the two are constantly hitting each other or doing mean things to each other. In fact, there is an underlying tone of rivalry and competition between each of the characters that seems to function as a visual reaffirmation of "natural" capitalist competition; you must always try to outdo someone else. Of the shows first twenty-five episodes, ten featured storylines that revolved around money and the affirmation of the joys of competition and materialism. In the feature length film based on the show, *The Proud Family Movie* (2005), consumption and money play a key role in the film's plot. The DVD extras include an alternate ending, deleted scenes, and a little driving game that encourage the young viewers to actively participate in the film's consumption.

In the show's forty-first episode, entitled "It Takes a Thief" (air date September 12, 2003), LaCienega's new boyfriend, Wiz Jr., gets the girls a job at his father's upscale department store, Wizingdales. In contrast to the *Fat Albert* episode, the girls do not work towards a specific goal; in fact, the reason for getting a job is never discussed. During the episode's second scene, Penny asks her father for some money because she hasn't been paid yet. Oscar denies her request, but is then bullied by Suga Mama into giving Penny a wad of cash. The bullying of Oscar by either Suga Mama or Trudy, or both, into giving Penny money functions as an ongoing plot element within the show. When Penny asks her Dad for money, he usually questions her about why she needs it, but is then bullied by Suga Mama and/or Trudy into giving her money regardless of her reasons. This episode of *The Proud Family* also presents large differences in social attitudes towards money and consumption when compared to *Fat Albert*. Penny is given cash merely for the asking, in direct contrast to the Fat Albert gang, who are not given cash just because they've asked. During the *Fat Albert* episode, each member of the gang is shown doing odd jobs and working hard (or trying to) whereas Penny and her friends are at their job dancing and "hanging out." Zoey actually asks "Shouldn't we be working?" as the store's manager, Randi, appears.

In the next segment, Randi teaches the girls how to "sell" things to customers, an action which involves flattering the customers by flirting with them and validating the customer's sense of sexual appeal. Randi asks a young male customer, using a very sexy tone: "is everything to your satisfaction, Handsome? Have you seen our sale rack?" to which the young man replies, "Now I have, Mama; I'll take everything," and the young man buys the entire rack. The girls then practice their flattery on other customers; each using a soft, low, sexually suggestive tone (except Zoey, who uses a gruff tone) and each girl makes a sale. But the message is to *sell*, and to use sex to do it. It also reaffirms the value of buying excessively, as the young man, who is so flattered by Randi's flirtation with him that he buys *all* of the clothes on the rack, is seen strolling out of the store whistling.

The conflict in the episode arises when one of the store's expensive watches is missing and the girls are fired, all except LaCienega because she is Wiz Jr.'s girlfriend. The watch is eventually found: the young twins BeeBee and CeeCee were the culprits—even the babies desire goods and are found at the end of the episode to have made off with other objects and a number of zoo animals they hid in their closet. At one point, after the watch is discovered missing, LaCienega is faced with choosing between loyalty to Penny and the girls, or to Wiz Jr. and all his "limousine rides, expensive gifts, fancy restaurants." LaCienega chooses to stay with Wiz Jr., with the gifts and status that his money can buy. Friendship and loyalty are not as valuable as wealth and all that it can provide, which the girls learn from each other as they negotiate between desired wealth vs. friendship. At the end of the episode, LaCienega does break up with Wiz Jr. (involuntarily with a little help from Penny, who falsely accuses Wiz Jr. of stealing the watch) but she comforts herself by stating that *she* broke up with him because he "wasn't cute enough."

In *The Proud Family Movie* (2005), the plot revolves around Oscar, who accepts an offer of a million dollars to partner up with the evil villain who only wants Oscar's failed "everlasting multiplying" formula so he can take over the world with his "peanut soldiers." In the film, money exchanges hands freely and often, in particular one scene where Oscar seeks help from Suga Mama, but she will only help him for money. The film highlights a rap star—15 Cent—who flashes bling and drives a stoked up Hummer, accouterment that attracts Penny and her friends: they want to be dancers in his upcoming music video. While it is unfortunate that so many stereotypes abound in this film (rap star, dancing, bling), it *does* position all the black characters as solidly middle-class or affluent. Yet, like the series, the film's rhetorical strategy of relating money and exchange to a character's importance and worth is ever-present.

A Penny Wise

Both television series, and their film adaptations, offer differences in social contexts and aesthetics. In *Fat Albert*, narrator Bill Cosby also functions as a father figure to the gang and, in a sense, to the viewer. His "character" is wise and thoughtful, jokes around and acts silly, and most significant to my analysis, Cosby is often shown fixing things or building things with the junk items that surround his worktable. He demonstrates industriousness and frugality in the way he repairs and produces new commodities from the old. The gang has learned from Cosby's humble creations and repairs, the passing down of valuable knowledge about non-excessive and responsible use of commodities. Oscar Proud, in contrast, depends completely on production/consumption. His entire character's focus is trying to sell his snack foods to become rich, yet he takes no part in their production, and when he does attempt to produce, the product is inedible. Getting rich is uppermost in his mind. Because his character is belittled and ridiculed on the show, emasculated by his wife and his own mother, he is not taken seriously and his fathering abilities are effective only when reinforced by Suga Mama or Trudy. Oscar also does not engage in any sort of building or creative activity like Cosby does; rather, Oscar's activities usually result in injuries to his person.

Aesthetically, *Fat Albert and the Cosby Kids* is much more ethnically rich than the characters in *The Proud Family* and *The Proud Family Movie*. Though *The Proud Family* is a product of modern racial sensitivities, the drawings have "whitened" features, which are consistent with Disney's historical whitening of other characters of color, namely Pocahontas, Mulan, and Aladdin. *The Fat Albert* kids all have the same skin tone, but their facial features and hair are more distinctly African American. *The Fat Albert* show is not afraid of the Afro. In contrast, *The Proud Family* characters have more uniformly white facial features—some of the characters noses are almost non-existent, and though most of the characters have different skin shades, none of the characters are as dark as those on *Fat Albert*.

Another interesting detail about the girls on *The Proud Family* is their supposed age: the show advertises them as teenagers, about fourteen years old. But the girls on the show are drawn as much younger, about ten or twelve. Penny Proud always wears pigtails and her hair is dark, but very white in appearance. All of her friends have some sort of ponytail or pigtails and all have at least shoulder-length hair whose texture is flowing and straight. Their dress is also very "little girl," rather than teenager, which renders them sexless when compared to other Disney female characters who are supposedly the same age: Pocahontas, Ariel, or even Cinderella.

There are a number of significant differences between the ways the characters in the two shows deal with production and consumption. Penny and her friends often relate to each other through consumption activities. In another episode, Penny and Wiz Jr. are competing for class president. Wiz Jr. tries to buy the election by giving away free CD players and throwing parties. During the scene when he gives away the CD players, the other students push and fight for them in a mall-like shopping frenzy. Penny tries to compete, but is just not rich enough, so she finally resorts to hiring the Gross sisters to dig up dirt on Wiz Jr., which they do for a price. Neither wins the election, but not because of trying to buy the election; it was because of the *polls*. Zoey had told her helpers to only poll the cool kids, who said they would all vote for Penny, but cool kids don't vote. So, the school's non-cool kids voted for Myron, the geek candidate. But the point is made that if you are cool you don't vote, and that it is money that makes the campaign—and correct polling—not the issues.

The Proud Family's consistent images of consumerism in every facet of life, most importantly in the pursuit of happiness, works in a way that Debord describes as "nothing more than 'that which appears is good, that which is good appears.' The attitude which [consumerism] demands in principle is passive acceptance which in fact it already obtained by its manner of appearing without reply, by its monopoly of appearance" (141) which is never questioned nor inverted in *The Proud Family,* where no one is ever told they can't afford something. The *Proud Family* kids construct and negotiate through their world in relation to capitalist consumption and production in a way that defines their status and acceptance by others. Their playground is the mall. Material goods and the power of capital define and construct their relationships to each other and to the world around them in ways that naturalize, for the child viewer, the importance of consumption to all aspects of life. The girls learn that their power as women can be achieved through the act of *selling* goods, i.e., selling themselves, by flaunting their budding sexuality. Penny, whose very name denotes monetary value, learns only that the *lack* of money prohibits achieving happiness, not the value of hard work in order to gain money. Penny and her friends constantly evaluate boyfriends based on their wealth, never their character. When Penny asks for money from her parents it is given to her, in contrast to the Fat Albert gang. *The Proud Family* girls' adventures most often are negotiated paths through abundant consumerism.

Fat Albert The Movie

In 2004, nearly 20 years after the end of the animated *Fat Albert* series, Bill Cosby teamed up with director Joel Zwick (*Family Matters* [1989–1998], *My Big Fat Greek Wedding* [2008]) to create the live action film *Fat Albert*. That the film is produced in the post–Fordist context puts a unique spin on the original Fordist-era narrative. In the live-action film, Fat Albert (Kenan Thompson) and the gang magically escape from the television set in order to help a teen girl who is having problems making friends. But as so many critics of the film noted, it is an odd trip down memory lane located in a modern world full of cell phones, DVDs and rap music. It is the incompatibility of these two eras forcibly jammed together in this film that reinforces the notion that the only viewer position for the black child is as a consumer.

There are numerous scenes in the film where Fat Albert and the gang come face to face with consumerism, which they then reject: in the department store Fat Albert racks up $10,000 worth of clothing, but when presented with the bill states they have no money; they visit the mall but do not buy anything; they visit a CD store (and show shock and upset at the language of the song they are listening to) but do not purchase anything; and when they have to pick up Doris and her friend for their date, the gang finally visit the junkyard and build a car out of cast-off items. But rather than highlight the reusability of the junk they made the car with, or the innovation and creativity of having Bill and Old Weird Harold pedaling, Flintstone style, in the engine compartment, the reaction of the girls is one of embarrassment. In fact, throughout the film, the gang walks the streets singing, dancing, and constantly smiling—an odd contrast to the snarling, grumpy, and coarse teens and adults that they interact with. No one smiles as much as the Fat Albert gang, which only works to highlight for the modern audience how silly and uninspiring "innocence" really is.

Conclusion

It could be argued that Penny's self-identity as displayed on *The Proud Family* is created by her relations to others through consumption, which also places the African American child viewer into the subject position of consumer, one who witnesses the power and desirability of capital and value exchange: "the commodification of experience under capitalism, an outcome of the absurd expectation generated by consumer culture that life should be an endless procession of opportunities to expand the self through the acquisition of things" (Kapur *Coining* 127). Within each of the episodes discussed, it is the interaction with commodities that shapes the discourse among Penny's friends and between the children and adults. The child viewer, who may not consciously understand, is an observer of the spectaclization of Penny as bearer of monetary value, who represents "lived reality ... materially invaded by the contemplation of the spectacle [consumption] while simultaneously absorbing the spectacular order, giving it positive cohesiveness ... reality rises up within the spectacle, and the spectacle is real" (Debord 140). Penny's identity on screen is defined, negotiated, and signified by the joys and opportunities that commodity exchange brings, and as such Penny and LaCienega and the other girls, are commodified by the desire for exchange, for the accouterments of consumer culture that shapes and validates their social identity. But what is this consumerist identity's effect when the African American child viewer comes from a lower economic class? *The Proud Family's* images of wealth and social status hail the black child to desire commodities that are presented as essential to shaping his or her social identity and acceptance by others, commodities that effortlessly "appear" from parents who are never shown working or engaging in their production. Within the larger context of achieving an ideological "Americanness," the ability to secure goods that allow for full participation in society becomes a significant message of the show to young African American viewers, which is demonstrated by Penny and her friend's ability to participate fully in social activities only *after* they secure the money or goods needed to take part.

In contrast, the *Fat Albert* gang rarely negotiates capital or the acquisition of new things, most particularly in the film version. Their relationship to each other and to the world around them does not require monetary exchange but instead, demonstrates an appropriation and creative use of commodities that were thrown away or deemed useless by dominant society. The kids on *Fat Albert* learn about handling real life issues not through *purchasing*, like when Penny "purchased" the services of the Gross Sisters to help her win the election, but by their own ingenuity and creativity in their consumption and appropriation (without cost) of junk. The Fat Albert gang espouses a divinity of behavior towards each other, which counters the "Topsy" stereotype that informs beliefs about black childhood. The gang learns through real experience that is lived and negotiated using such psychological commodities like loyalty, respect, creativity, and friendship that are not purchased with money. Gottdiener argues that "self-identity through consumption relies on all the complex aspects of social interaction" (24), which is true for Penny Proud and friends, but self-identity is not constructed through consumption in *Fat Albert*. In *Fat Albert* the character's identity formation is dependent upon the negotiation within their inter-personal relationships and with any peripheral characters with which they interact. The shared experiences of life that, in the show, do not depend on, nor are informed by, monetary exchange play a much more significant role in the formation of each member's identity as they learn and grow from experiences that are outside of consumer culture, though, admittedly, *Fat Albert's* positioning of the gang outside of consumer culture reinforces the framing of African American's as separate and excluded from dominant white society.

However, that exclusion can also be interpreted as a site of Black resistance to the shallowness of white consumer culture. Unlike the shallow characters on *The Proud Family*, who have been incorporated into white consumer culture, the character's identities on *Fat Albert* are constructed by their negotiation of complex social issues and behaviors; not through capitalist consumption, but through the creative use of throw-away commodities and positive social reaffirmations of the simple forces of friendship, love, and respect for fellow human beings, and perhaps most important, through the fatherly guidance of Bill Cosby. In the film version of *Fat Albert,* it is Fat Albert and the gang who must teach Doris how to negotiate with other people. She learns through them the value of being a full participant in inter-personal skills. Many of the teen characters in the film are displayed as self-absorbed or worse, bordering on juvenile delinquency.

Interestingly, the *Fat Albert* series, whose context is located at the end of industrial age Fordism, presents only *males* who create and produce, while *The Proud Family,* located in the context of the post-industrial age features no production at all—as a father, Oscar is totally inept at production (and parenting) while all the girls consume, never produce. These subtle gender divisions in *The Proud Family* converge with cultural beliefs about the incompetent black male who is more likely to be absent or incarcerated than a responsible father and provider.[5]

The subject positioning of the African American child viewer of *Fat Albert and the Cosby Kids* encourages the development of a child's inner status and good character, as opposed to the outward trappings of materialism that *The Proud Family* so "proudly" embraces. The absence of consumer ideology in the original *Fat Albert* series does reinforce beliefs in the lack of African American social mobility and status, and in fact, encourages young black children to be happy with what they have and to not *try* to enter consumer society. But that message is perhaps less damaging to young viewers than the Proud Family's message: that the only way to achieve good character is through active participation in uninhibited consumerism, that a child's value it directly related to their cash flow. In fact, the character's names in the two series and their films reflect the differing attitudes towards personhood and production: one refers to the actual body as the basis of identity—"FAT" Albert—while the other suggests full assimilation into consumer society—Penny [coin] Proud [of having coin/money] as the way to achieve acceptable identity. It is this modern message of assimilation into consumer culture that suggests *The Proud Family* is not really a visual resistance to earlier perceived racist depictions; but rather, is a hegemonic, commodifying narrative masquerading as a resistance narrative—a message that is not so progressive after all.

Notes

1. My sincere thanks to Stacy Takacs, director of American Studies, Oklahoma State University, for her invaluable guidance and suggestions in the writing of this essay.

2. According to Althuser, "ideology 'acts' or 'functions' in such a way that it 'recruits' subjects among the individuals (it recruits them all), or 'transforms' the individuals into subjects (it transforms them all) by that very precise operation which I have called interpellation or hailing, and which can be imagined along the lines of the most commonplace everyday police (or other) hailing: 'Hey, you there!'" (174). The subject then, is "hailed" by the ideological message and because she turns around, she listens, she believes the message was intended for her alone. And because she believes the message was for her, that places her in the subject position.

3. Jim Crow laws were local and state laws in the United States, almost exclusively in the Deep South, that enforced separation between blacks and whites in all aspects of society after the Civil War ended in 1865. Jim Crow laws reinforced the inferior status of blacks in state and local institutions, in commerce, and in social practices. Jim Crow laws provided "separate but equal" services, which in practice were never equal to services or conditions for whites. Blacks during Jim Crow were restricted to using only those businesses or services marked for "colored only." For more information on the Jim Crow laws see Leslie V. Tischauser's *Jim Crow Laws,* 2012; Jerrold M. Packard's *American Nightmare: The History of Jim Crow,* 2003.

4. The Bratz doll differs significantly from Mattel's Barbie doll. (There is an on-going legal battle between MGM Entertainment and Mattel over who actually owns the Bratz line. Mattel argues that the Bratz designer, Carter Bryant, was working for Mattel when he designed the doll.) Barbie has soft features, wide pale eyes, small nose and small mouth. The Bratz dolls have oversized heads, come in a variety of dark skin shades, and the facial features are much more prominent than the Barbie dolls. Bratz dolls have large, almond-shaped eyes with very dark eye shadow, large and pouting mouths, and are usually dressed in spike heels and urban hip-hop outfits. The differences in the two dolls mark the changes in social conceptions about urban children, particularly girls of color. The Bratz dolls are advertised as having "attitude" in contrast to the much more conservative and "properly" dressed Barbie doll. The Bratz dolls are the "street" version of Barbie. For more on Bratz and Barbie, see Margaret Talbot's "Little Hotties," in *New Yorker* December 4, 2006 (http://pez5009.pbworks.com/f/IIIC%26P%3ATalbot.pdf) and Angharad N. Valdivia's "Living in a Hybrid Material World: Girls, Ethnicity and Mediated Doll Products," *Girlhood Studies* 2.1 (2009): 73–93.

5. For more about stereotypes of black males, see Daniel J. Leab's *From Sambo to Superspade: The Black Experience in Cinema* (1975); Dennis Rome's *Black Demons: The Media's*

Depiction of the African American Male Criminal Stereotype (2004); Michelle Alexander's *The New Jim Crow* (2010); and Leslie V. Tischauser's *Jim Crow Laws* (2012).

Works Cited

Austin, Regina. "'A Nation of Thieves': Consumption, Commerce, and the Black Public Sphere." *The Black Public Sphere*. The Black Public Sphere Collective. Chicago: University of Chicago Press, 1995. 229–252.

Baker, Jr., Houston A. "Critical Memory and the Black Public Sphere." *The Black Public Sphere*. The Black Public Sphere Collective. Chicago: University of Chicago Press, 1995. 5–37.

Berry, Gordon. "Black Family Life on Television and the Socialization of the African American Child: Images of Marginality." *Journal of Comparative Family Studies* 29.2 (1998): 233–242.

Cook, Daniel Thomas. "The Rise of 'The Toddler' as Subject and as Merchandising Category in the 1930s." *New Forms of Consumption: Consumers, Culture, and Commodification*. Mark Gottdiener, ed. Lanham, MD: Rowman and Littlefield, 2000. 111–129.

DeBord, Guy. "The Commodity as Spectacle." *Media and Cultural Studies: Key Works*. Meenakshi Gigi Durham and Douglas M. Kellner, eds. Malden, MA: Blackwell, 2001. 139–143.

Fiske, John. *Television Culture*. New York: Routledge, 1987.

Gottdiener, Mark. "Approaches to Consumption: Classical and Contemporary Perspectives." *New Forms of Consumption: Consumers, Culture, and Commodification*. Mark Gottdiener, ed. Lanham: Rowman and Littlefield, 2000. 3–31.

Graves, Sherryl Browne. "Television, the Portrayal of African Americans, and the Development of Children's Attitudes." *Children and Television: Images in a Changing Sociocultural World*. Gordon L. Berry, and Joy Keiko Asamen, eds. Newbury Park, CA: Sage. 179–190.

Greenberg, Bradley S., and Jeffrey E. Brand. "Cultural Diversity on Saturday Morning Television." *Children and Television: Images in a Changing Sociocultural World*. Gordon L. Berry and Joy Keiko Asamen, eds. Newbury Park, CA: Sage. 132–142.

Jacobson, Lisa. *Raising Consumers: Children and the American Mass Market in the Early Twentieth Century*. New York: Columbia University Press, 2004.

Kapur, Jyotsna. *Coining for Capital: Movies, Marketing, and the Transformation of Childhood*. New Brunswick, NJ: Rutgers University Press, 2005.

____. "Out of Control: Television and the Transformation of Childhood in Late Capitalism." *Kids Media Culture: Console-Ing Passions*. Marsha Kinder, ed. Durham, NC: Duke University Press, 1999. 122–138.

Kern-Foxworth, Marilyn. *Aunt Jemimia, Uncle Ben, and Rastus: Blacks in Advertising*. New York: Greenwood, 1994.

McRobbie, Angela. "Feminism, Postmodernism, and the 'Real Me.'" *Media and Cultural Studies: Key Works*. Meenakshi Gigi Durham and Douglas M. Kellner, eds. Malden, MA: Blackwell, 2005. 598–610.

Seiter, Ellen, and Vicki Meyer. "Diversifying Representation in Children's TV: Nickelodian's Model." *Nickelodeon Nation*. Heather Hendershot, ed. New York: New York University Press, 2004. 120–133.

Spigel, Lynn. *Welcome to the Dreamhouse: Popular Media and Postwar Suburbs*. Durham, NC: Duke University Press, 2001.

Stowe, Harriet Beecher. *Uncle Tom's Cabin*. 1851–2. New York: Bantam, 1981.

Zelizer, Viviana A. *Pricing the Priceless Child*. New York: Basic, 1995.

About the Contributors

Karin **Beeler** is a professor and chair of the English Department at the University of Northern British Columbia (Canada) where she teaches television genre and film studies courses. She is the author or editor of several books in the areas of film and television studies.

Stan **Beeler** is a professor of English at the University of Northern British Columbia (Canada). His areas of interest include film and television studies, popular culture and comparative literature. His books are about television shows and club culture.

Michel **Bouchard** is an associate professor of anthropology at the University of Northern British Columbia. He has been studying Russian-speaking populations for close to two decades, examining the roots of nation in discourse, articulated in cultural practice and through time. His work focuses on how the meaning of nation is contested using shared symbols.

Noel **Brown** is an independent scholar, and his primary research interests are classical and modern Hollywood cinema. He is the author of *The Hollywood Family Film: A History, from Shirley Temple to Harry Potter* and has written for *The Historical Journal of Film, Radio and Television*, the *Quarterly Review of Film and Video*, and *Scope: An Online Journal of Film and Television Studies*.

Julian **Cornell** teaches film and media studies at New York University and Queens College–CUNY and is a visiting assistant professor in film studies at Wesleyan University. His interests are in the ideologies and politics of American, Scandinavian and Japanese popular culture and genre cinemas. He is researching representations of race, class and gender in contemporary American science fiction, animation and disaster films.

Lydia E. **Ferguson** is a doctoral student in the Auburn University English Department, where she teaches American literature and composition. Her primary research focuses on late nineteenth and early twentieth century realist fiction and regional performances of cultural identity.

Lincoln **Geraghty** is a reader at the School of Creative Arts, Film and Media and director of the Centre for Cultural and Creative Research at the University of

Portsmouth. He is an editorial advisor for several journals, including *The Journal of Popular Culture*, *Reconstruction* and *Atlantis*. He edited *The Influence of Star Trek on Television, Film and Culture* (McFarland, 2008), and, with Mark Jancovich, *The Shifting Definitions of Genre* (McFarland, 2008).

Naomi **Hamer** is an assistant professor at the Department of English, University of Winnipeg, affiliated with the Centre for Research in Young People's Texts and Cultures. Her research examines the adaptation of picture books across media from feature films to interactive mobile applications.

Stephanie **Hemelryk Donald** is a future fellow and professor of comparative film and cultural studies at the University of New South Wales. Her research covers film, the media, and children's experiences in the Asia-Pacific region, with a particular focus on visual culture. Recent work on cultural history located in art and film is published by *Theory, Culture and Society and, New Formations*.

Dan **North** teaches film and media at Webster University in Leiden, Netherlands. He is the author of *Performing Illusions: Cinema, Special Effects, and the Virtual Actor* and coeditor, with Bob Rehak and Michael S. Duffy, of *Special Effects: New Histories, Theories, Contexts*.

Debbie **Olson** is a lecturer at the University of Texas at Arlington. Her research interests include West African film, images of African and African American children in film, cultural studies, and new Hollywood cinema. She is the editor-in-chief of *Red Feather Journal: An International Journal of Children's Visual Culture* and coeditor of *Lost and Othered Children in Contemporary Cinema* and *Portrayals of Children in Popular Culture: Fleeting Images*.

Swarnavel Eswaran **Pillai** is an assistant professor at Michigan State University. His documentaries include *Thangam*, *The Indian National Army*, *Villu (The Bow)*, *Quagmire*, *Unfinished Journey: A City in Transition*, and *Migrations of Islam*. His research includes the history, theory, and production of documentaries, and the specificity of Tamil cinema and its complex relationship with Hollywood as well as popular Hindi films.

Tatiana **Podyakova** is a native of the northern Russian city of Arkhangelsk, where she is pursuing her graduate degree in the Department of Russian Language and Oral Culture at the Northern Arctic Federal University. Her research interests include the application of the tools and methods of folklore to contemporary political discourse, notably that of the liberal opposition in Russia.

Heather **Rolufs** is a doctoral student at the University of British Columbia Okanagan in Kelowna studying representations of doubling and the doppelgänger in science fiction television. She received a master's degree in Victorian literature and a bachelor's degree in literature from the University of Northern British Columbia, in Prince George, Canada.

Index

ABC network 177
Aboriginal children, Australia 139–140, 146n3
Academy Awards, Oscars 29, 163–164
Ackers, Louise 134, 146
Adams, Ernest 66, 75
Adamson, Andrew 44, 56, 73
advertising *see* consumer products, merchandising; franchises
Afghanistan 6, 139–140
African Americans: in film and media 7, 24, 113, 160–188; Jim Crow laws 166, 176, 187n3, 187n5
Africans, stereotypes 120–122; in films 153
Ahmed, Sara 138, 146
Aitken, Stuart C. 68, 75
Aladdin 18, 26, 182
Alesha Popovich and the Turagin Snake 121, 130
Alexander, Michelle 187n5
Alexander Nevsky 123
Alice in Wonderland 4, 17, 37–48
Alice's Adventures in Wonderland 37, 42
Althusser, Louise Pierre 173, 187n1
Altman, Rick 10, 26
American Beauty 31, 34, 36
American (U.S.) films: family films 4, 10, 29, 51–52, 105, 117–118; film industry 3, 7, 120, 129; foreign distribution, Europe 50, 55; foreign distribution, Russia 110, 115, 129; foreign films, Americanization of 81, 83–84, 86; made in Canada 94; subtitles and dubbing, aversion to 55; *see also* Disney; DreamWorks; Hollywood; Miramax; MGM
American Idol 70
Amos 'n' Andy 161
amusement parks *see* parks
Anderson, Benedict 111, 129n1, 130
Andersen, Hans Christian 65, 116
androids 16

animal rights 79
animation *see* CGI; DreamWorks; Pixar
Antarctic 25, 33
Appadurai, Arjun 134, 146
Arabs, stereotypes 127–128
Arasardi, India 153
Aravindan, M.R. 153, 158
Arctic 19
Aronofsky, Darren 31
L'arrivée d'un train en gare de La Ciotat 103
L'arroseur arosé 105
art, paintings 34, 116
The Artist 59
Artz, Lee 168, 170
Asians, stereotypes 113, 120–122, 127; wars in Asia 134
Astérix & Obelix 4, 49–61
Atamanov, Lev 116
Attebery, Brian 47
Auguste, Isabelle 146n3, 146
Austin, Guy 60
Austin, Regina 188
Australia 139–141, 146, 146n3; Australian Research Council 133; Sydney 25
avatars 67
The Aviator 100, 107
awards: Academy Awards, Oscars 29, 163–164; Emmy Awards 30; Gérard du Cinéma 59; NAACP Image Awards 164; Razzies 59

Babe 15, 19, 22, 25–26
Baccilega, Cristina 44, 47
Back to the Future 35
Badham, John 34
Baer, Edouard 59
Baker, Jr. 188
Barbie dolls 176, 187n4
Barcelona 104
Baryshnikov, Mikhail 117, 131
Baskett, James 160, 163

191

Baum, L. Frank 83–84, 87*n*7
Baynes, Pauline 72
Bazalgette, Cary 9, 13–14, 21, 26, 38, 47
BBC 63, 103, 130, 117
Beach Boys 33
Beatles 33, 60*n*1
Beauty and the Beast 41
Beck, Ulrich 134, 146
Beckham, David 73
Beckham, Victoria (Posh Spice) 73
Bee Gees 34, 36
Beeler, Karin 5, 8*n*2, 89–97, 189
Beeler, Stan 4, 28–36, 189
Bell, Anthea 60
Bellucci, Monica 56–58
Benegal, Shyam 153
Bengali 151
Benhabib, Seyla 134, 146
Benigni, Roberto 53
Bennett, James 3
Bercoff, André 55
Bergery, Benjamin 54, 60
Berri, Claude 53, 55–56, 58–59
Berry, Gordon 188
Besson, Luc 59
Bettelheim, Bruno 80, 88
Bhabha, Jacqueline 135, 146
Bibbidi Bobbidi Boutique 166
Bibigon 117
Bichevskaia, Zhanna 121
Bicycle Thieves 7, 156, 158–159
Billig, Michael 111, 130
Bing, Jonathan 29, 36
Black Swan 31, 36
Blackburn, William 162, 170*n*1
BlackMoonWhiteSun 74–75
Blacks *see* African Americans; Africans
Blunt, Alison 134, 146
Blu-ray 2–3, 5, 9–10, 20, 89–90, 110
Bogatyrs (painting) 116
Bonner, Julie 166, 170
bonus features, special features 2, 5, 63, 70, 89–90, 95
books *see* cartoons; comics; literature
Bordwell, David 102, 107
Bouchard, Michel 6, 109–132, 130, 189
Boulting, John 99
Bowers, David 96
Bowles, Scott 163, 165, 170
Boyer, Robert 40
Branch, Michelle 74, 76
Brand, Jeffrey E. 188
Bratz dolls 176, 187*n*4
Brazil, soap operas 109
Breaux, Richard M. 162, 170
Britain *see* United Kingdom
British Film Institute 107

Broadway plays 29
Bronx 99
Brosius, Christiane 139, 146
Brown, Devin 68, 76
Brown, Gordon 146*n*3
Brown, James 57
Brown, Noel 4, 49–61, 189
Brown, Tom 3, 93, 96
Brown, William 45–47
Brubaker, Rogers 130
Bryant, Carter 187*n*4
Buckingham, David 26, 13–14, 38, 47, 79–80, 88, 134, 146
Buckley, Jeff 32
Buckley, William F. 18
Buena Vista Games 66
Bunyan, John 68, 76
Burch, Noël 103, 107
Burger King 29
Burn, Andrew 76
Burrows, Andy 67, 76
Burton, Tim 4, 37–48
Bush, George H.W. 10
Buti, Antonio 146*n*3, 146
Butler, David 39–40, 45, 47, 134

cable *see* television
Cabot, Meg 76
Cairo International Film Festival for Children 151, 158*n*4
Calais 136–137
Cale, John 31–32
cameras, motion picture 99
Cameron, James 9
Canada, Canadian 1, 94, 112
Canadian Broadcasting Corp. (CBC) 112
Canal Plus 50, 56
Cangia, Flavia 130
Cannes Film Festival 118
capitalism 7, 173, 185–186
Capron, Robert 91
Caputi, Jane 30, 36
cards *see* trading cards
Carnavale, Rob 99, 107
Carol's Daughter (retailer) 166
Carroll, Lewis 37, 42
Cartoon Network 175
cartoons, cartoon novels 2, 5, 30, 34, 80, 89–97, 119, 172–188
Casetti, Francesco 90, 96*n*1–2, 96
caste, class 134
Castenada, Claudia 134, 147
Cave, Nick *see* Nick Cave and the Bad Seeds
CBC 112
CBS network 177
cell phones 7, 184; iPhones 89; smartphones 90; in theatres 96*n*2

Celluloid Chapter film club 151
censorship 124–126, 128; film ratings 45
Centre for Research in Young People's Texts and Cultures (CRYTC) 1
Cetinic, Nina 60
CFSI *see* Children's Film Society of India
CFSTN *see* Children's Film Society of Tamilnadu
CGI computer generated animation, special effects 4, 12, 15–16, 19–20, 22, 40, 45, 54, 58, 102, 118, 129
Chabat, Alain 49, 56
Chandrasekar, Preethi 153, 159
Charlotte Observer newspaper 170n1
The Cheat 107n3
Cheburashka 117
Chechnya 124
Chennai, India 151
Child Migrants Trust (CMT) 146n3, 147
Childhood journal 111
children: as filmmakers 6, 138–147; childhood innocence 9, 11–15, 18–19, 23–25, 38, 64–69, 71, 74–75, 105, 113, 142, 145, 150, 157, 172, 174–175, 184; coming-of-age tales 15, 44, 68–70, 74, 111; migrant 6, 133–147; orphans 105–106; rebellion against authority 23; *see also* heroism
Children's Day, India 148, 151
Children's Film Society of India (CFSI) 7, 148, 150–153, 157, 158n1, 158n2, 158n6, 159
Children's Film Society of Tamilnadu (CFSTN) 153–155, 157
children's literature *see* literature
China, Chinese 137; Cultural Revolution 112; films 112, 142; limiting foreign films 112
Chmielewski, Dawn C. 168, 170
Christian images, values 85, 119, 176; mythology 64; utopia 75
Christmas 9, 12; Father Christmas 66
Christou, Miranda 130
The Chronicles of Narnia 5, 51, 63–77
Cinderella 41, 164, 183
Cine-Journal 107
cinemas *see* theatres
Cinématograph shows: Lumière Brothers 103–105
Citizen Kane 31–32, 36
Civil War, Afghanistan 140
Civil War, American 187n3
Civil War, Spanish 40
Clark, Vivienne 96n6, 96
Clarkson, Kelly 70, 76
Clavier, Christian 53, 56, 59
Claymation 19
Clinton, Bill 10, 36n1

CMT *see* Child Migrants Trust
Cohen, Leonard 19, 26, 31
Coimbatore, India 151
Coleman, Warren 33
Comaroff, John 134, 147
comics, comic books 29, 40, 49–61, 69, 101, 164
coming-of-age tales *see* children
computer games *see* games
computer generated animation, special effects *see* CGI
Connell, R.W. 106–107
Constantinople 119, 126–127
consumer products, merchandising 2, 6–7, 21, 51, 56, 80, 109, 113, 118, 122, 165–166, 169, 172–173, 175–179, 183–187; branding 7, 51, 65, 78, 86, 103, 165, 169; *see also* franchises
Convention on Human Rights 146n3
Convention on the Rights of the Child, U.N. 146n2
Cook, Daniel Thomas 174–175, 188
copyright, digital rights management 89; in Russia 109–110, 114, 117, 128–129
Cornell, Julian 4, 9–27, 189
Cosby, Bill 173, 177–179, 182, 184, 186
cosmopolitanism 6, 133–147
Council of Europe 50
Cresswell, Tim 134, 147
Crock, Mary 146n3, 147
Crocodile Boy 154, 159
Crossword Books 152
Crowther, Bosley 163
CRYTC *see* Centre for Research in Young People's Texts and Cultures
Cukor, George 51
culture, cultural dissonance 35; cultural pedagogy 22, 25; cultural values 10–13, 51, 83, 87, 129, 173; popular culture 1, 13, 18–19, 34, 73, 87, 110–112, 115, 161, 169, 189–190; transmedia culture 2–3; *see also* nationalism

Daly, Sean 161, 166–167, 170
Dargaud Films 52
Darnell, Eric 33
Das, Nandita 152, 158n6
Davidson, John E. 101, 107
Dawtry, Adam 58, 60
Debbouze, Jamel 56
DeBlois, Dean 26
DeBord, Guy 141, 183, 185, 188
De Certeau, Michel 69, 76
Deleuze, Gilles 134
Delhi 157
del Toro, Guillermo 40
De Mille, Cecil B. 107n3

Democratic Party 10, 36n1
Demy, Jacques 142
Deneuve, Catherine 59
De Niro, Robert 18
Denmark, film industry 52
Depardieu, Gérard 53, 56, 59
The Departed 100, 108
Depp, Johnny 43
Depression era 83, 175
De Sica, Vittorio 156
Diamond, Neil 32, 36
Diary of a Wimpy Kid 2, 5, 89–97
didactic *see* education, didactic
digital rights management *see* copyright
digital technologies *see* technologies
Digital Trends (journal) 96n4
disability, diversity in films 3
Discovery Kids network 175
Disney Channel 175
Disney Consumer Products (DCP) 166–167
Disney Corporation, productions, Walt Disney 2–3, 5, 7, 9, 13, 18, 41–42, 46, 51–52, 63, 65–67, 69, 89–90, 96n4, 109–110, 112, 116–118, 129, 160–188
Disney Movies Online 2
Disney Press 167
The Disney Store 165, 169
Disney/Walden Media 5, 63, 65–67
Disneyland 18, 52; *see also* Parks, theme
Dobrynia Nikitich and the Dragon 123, 130
Dole, Robert 9–12, 19
dolls 122, 165, 168–169, 176, 187n4
Dona, Georgia 139, 147
Donahue, Dierdre 106, 108
Donald, Stephanie Hemelryk 6, 133–147, 190
Doordarshan television network 149–150, 157
Do Rozario, Rebecca-Anne 65, 76
DreamWorks Animation 56, 89
Druhot, Leon 107n3
Dubashi (The Translator) 6–7, 148–159
Duel in the Sun 99
Dumbo 161
Dunkley, Cathy 29, 36
DVDs 1–3, 5–7, 8n2, 8n4, 9, 20, 28, 63, 65, 70, 78, 89–90, 92, 95, 96n3–4, 110, 113, 114, 117, 128–129, 149–150, 152–153, 180, 184

Easen, Sarah 99, 108
Eastern Singhbum 151
Ebert, Roger 99, 108
ebooks 3
Ebrahim 151
Edenic image of childhood 176
Edensor, Tim 111, 130

Editions Albert René 58
education, pedagogy 2, 4, 9–11, 13–14, 19–26, 60, 68, 86; didactic, moral lessons in film 7, 10–17, 19–20, 22–24, 64, 66, 68, 72, 78–79, 86, 112, 141, 143, 172; school as film location 90, 93; schools used for screening films 7, 148–159; teaching about film and media, media literacy, workshops 2, 5–6, 94, 100, 135, 139
Edutopia 100, 108
Edwardian novels 75
Egoff, Sheila 47
Egypt 56, 58, 127; Cairo 151, 158n4
Eleftheriotis, Dimitris 105, 108
Eller, Claudia 168, 170
Elley, Derek 55, 60
Emmy Awards 30
environmental themes, in film 23, 25, 33, 79, 84–85; recycling 179, 185–186
EOFA Journal 52
ethnicity *see* culture; nationalism
Eurimages 50, 53
Europe, European culture 50, 56, 120, 122; films 4, 49–50, 52–53, 55, 58–60; literature 41; migration, migrant children 137–138, 146, 146n3; stereotypes 122; wars 134
European Children's Film Association 52
European Community 50
European Union 50
Ezard, John 66, 76

fables 12
Facebook 129
fairy tales 4, 17, 38, 40–42, 44, 46–47, 65, 82–84, 115–117, 130, 161
Fairy Tales from Far Off Lands 117
Family Matters 184
fantasy 2, 4, 9, 12, 15–16, 19, 21–23, 25–26, 38, 40–42, 45–47, 53, 65–66, 68, 72, 74–75, 80, 85–86, 141; fantastic media, tales 2, 4, 37–40 (defined), 41–47
Fat Albert 7, 184
Fat Albert and the Cosby Kids 7, 172–188
The Father 151
Federation of Film Societies of India 153
feminism *see* gender
Ferguson, Lydia E. 7, 160–171, 189
Festival of Britain 99
Fidélité Films 59
Fielding, Connor 91
film: preservation, restoration 5, 99–100, 104, 117, 152; screen studies 1–2; workshops on film-making for children 6, 138–147; *see also* education; technologies
Film Foundation, Scorcese 100
Film Societies of India 155
Filmoteca de Catalunya 104

films: African 153; Chinese 112, 142; European 4, 49–50, 52–53, 55, 58–60; French 4, 49–61; Indian 6–7, 148–159; Iranian 151; Japanese 5, 78, 80–81, 83, 86, 87*n*5, 112; Russian, Soviet 6, 109–132; South American 153; *see also* American
Films by Jove 117
Fiske, John 81, 88, 188
Fleming, Victor 51
Florida 166
folklore, folk tales 41; Russian 81, 113, 115–117, 119, 122
Ford, John 18
Fordism 178, 184, 186
Forestier, Frederic 49
Foucault, Michel 134
Foundas, Scott 162, 167, 170
fourth wall, term 93, 96*n*6
Fox *see* 20th Century-Fox
Fox, Michael J. 35
France, French films 4, 49–61; migrant children 135–137, 140, 142; Paris 52–53, 59, 98, 101–103, 106, 137
France Soir 55
franchises, multimedia 4–5, 49, 52, 58, 60, 63–67, 69, 71–72, 74–75, 79–80, 86, 165–167, 169; *see also* consumer products; Disney
Frankfurt school (media criticism) 172
Freud, Sigmund 11
Freudenthal, Thor 91, 96
Friese-Greene, William 99
FunFare Magazine 168

Gabler, Neal 162–163, 170
Gabon 137
games, computer, video 2, 5, 16, 20, 63–67, 78–80, 86, 87*n*4, 89–91, 94, 160, 180; *see also* trading cards
Gandhi, Indira 155
Gaul 53–54, 56, 60
Gellner, Ernest 111, 130*n*1, 130
Gemini Studios 158
gender 3, 6, 12, 41, 44–46, 66, 92, 106, 109, 120, 134, 143, 161, 167, 173, 186; feminism 40, 172–173; same-gendered 72; *see also* sex
Genette, Gerard 65, 76
Geraghty, Lincoln 5, 78–88, 189–190
Gérard du Cinéma 59
Germany, German: actors 53; film coproductions 49, 55, 59; stereotypes 122
Gilbert *see* Wrubel and Gilbert
Girlhood Studies journal 187
Giroux, Henry 13, 21, 26, 112–113, 130, 170, 161
globalization 50, 115, 133, 149, 157
glocality (term) 133

Goldberg, Whoopi 161
Golden Elephant International Film Festival 151
Gong, Yan 142
Goodfellas 99, 108
Gordon, Zachary 91
Gore, Albert, Jr. 10
Goscinny and Underzo 52–53, 56
gothic elements in film 42, 46
Gottdiener, Mark 185, 188
Graf, Christine 146*n*3, 147
Grand Rapids, Michigan 12
graphic novels 3, 29, 101
Graves, Sherryl Browne 188
Greece, Greek 65, 71
Greenberg, Bradley S. 188
Greenfeld, Liah 130
Greenhill, Pauline 42, 47
Grimm Brothers 41, 72, 116–117
Gulliver's Travels 17
Gypsies, stereotypes 121

Haenni, Sabine 102, 108
Hall, Arsenio 18
Hall, Stuart 141
Halo 153–154, 159
Hamer, Naomi 5, 63–77, 190
Happy Feet 4, 18–19, 21–26, 28, 33, 36
Hariharan, K. 148, 151, 154, 158*n*5
The Harlem Globetrotters 177
Harris, Anita 66, 76
Harris, Joel Chandler 160
Harry Potter 51, 72, 106, 144
Hart, Jason 130
Hartley, John 80, 88
Hashmi, M. 40, 47
Hays, Will 9–12, 19
Hazanavicius, Michel 59
Hecht, Ana Carolina 131
Henley, Georgie 5, 69, 73, 75
Hergé 52
Hermans, Gert 52, 60
heroes, heroines 11–12, 19, 23–24, 44, 54, 79–84, 86, 106, 112–114, 116, 119–123, 125, 127–129, 149, 166; quests 37, 66, 68, 79–87, 98
Higgins, Scott 101, 103
Hill, Benny 57
Hill, David 146*n*3, 147
Hills, Matt 2, 8*n*3
Hindi 149, 151–152, 156–158
Hiroshima 149, 156
Hispanic stereotypes 161
Hobsbawm, Eric J. 111, 129*n*1, 131
Hollywood 4–5, 9–10, 15, 21–22, 28, 49–61, 90, 129, 144, 176
Hollywood North 94

Home Alone 144, 147
Homer 65
Hörschelmann, Kathrin 134, 147
Houston, A. 188
How to Train Your Dragon 19, 21–23, 26
Howard University 162
HREOC (Human Rights and Equal Opportunity Commission, Australia) 146n3, 144, 147
Huber, Veronique Pache 131
Hugo 5–6, 98–108
Human Rights: Commission, Australian 146n3, 144, 147; Convention, European 146n2; Convention, United Nations 146n3
The Hunchback of Notre Dame 106
Hutcheon, Linda 29–30, 36, 90, 93, 95, 96n5, 96
Hyderbad 151

I Am Legend 144, 147
Ice Age films 4, 16, 18, 21–22, 25–26
Ilia Murometc and the Nightingale Robber 124–128, 131
immigration *see* migration
Independence Day 9–10, 26
India, Indian films 6–7, 148–159
Indonesia 112
innocence *see* children
International Children's Film Festival of India 151, 152
Internet *see* websites
The Invention of Hugo Cabret 6, 98, 101–102
iPhones 89
iPods 89
Iran, films 151
Iraq 136
irony, in film 18, 57
Irwin, W.R. 39, 47
Ishii, Kenichi 112, 131
Italianamerican 107n1, 108
Italy, Italian: actors 53; actresses 56; directors 107n1; films 7; film co-productions 49, 53–56, 59
iTunes 1, 28

Jäckel, Anne 53, 60
Jackman, Hugh 33
Jackson, Kathy Merlock 11, 26
Jackson, Rosemary 39, 47
Jackson 5 33, 177
Jacobson, Lisa 173–174, 177, 188
Jacquot le Nantes 142, 147
James, Alison 58, 60
Jameshedpur 151
Japan, Japanese: films 5, 78, 80–81, 83, 86, 87n5, 112; language 149, 156–157

Jefferson Lecture 99
Jenkins, Henry 2–3, 8n1, 63, 65, 69, 76, 80, 88–90, 96n1, 96
Jenson, Vicky 44, 56
Jeshi, K. 152, 159
Jim Crow laws 166, 176, 187n3, 187n5
John, Gottfried 53
Jones, Kidada 166
Jones, Quincy 166
Jones, Terry 54
The Jungle Book 161

Kalki 149, 155
Kamath, Sudhish 151, 159
Kapur, Jyotsna 172, 175–176, 185, 188
Kashmir, India 152
Katsuno, Hirofumi 81, 88
Kattur, India 152
Kaurismaki, Aki 135–137
Kedarnath 158n1
Keionna 76
Kenya 25
Kerala, India 152
Kern-Foxworth, Marilyn 173, 188
Kevin, Catherine 135, 147
Kidman, Nicole 33
Kiev 116, 119–128, 130n3
Kimball, Melanie A. 106, 108
Kincheloe, Joe L. 21, 25, 27
Kinder, Marsha 78, 88
Kinescope 18
King-Smith, Dick 15
Kinney, Jeff 5, 89–97
Kirk, E.J. 65, 76
Kirkpatrick, B. 40, 47
Klaussmann, Liza 58, 60
Klimchuk, Marianne Rosner 65, 76
Klinger, Barbara 3, 8n1, 90, 96n1, 96
Knobel, Michele 63–64, 70, 76
Kofman, Eleanore 135, 139, 146n1, 147
Kononenko, Natalie 112–113, 119, 122, 131
Koops, Wendy 60
Kottayam, India 152
Krasovec, Sandra A. 65, 76
Kress, Gunther 64, 76
Krithika, R. 158n5, 159
Kurds 136

Lacayo, Richard 10, 26
Laitin, David D. 131
Lane, Nathan 93
lang, k.d. 32
Langmann, Thomas 49, 59
Lankshear, Colin 63, 70, 76
Lanzoni, Rémi Fournier 50, 60
The Last Battle 75
Latino characters 24

Law, Jude 100
Leab, Daniel J. 187*n*5
Léaud, Jean-Pierre 137
LeBeau, Vicky 105, 108
Lefebvre, Henri 135, 147
Le Guin, Ursula 40, 47
Le Havre 135–137, 140, 147
Leonard, Madeleine 131
Lester, Neal A. 168, 170
Lewis, C.S. 5, 63–77
Libération 55
libraries 100, 119–120, 129, 158*n*10, 159
The Life and Death of Colonel Blimp 99
The Lion King 2, 9, 26, 93, 161
The Lion, the Witch and the Wardrobe 63
literacy *see* education; literature; New Literacies
literature, children's 11, 72, 85, 89, 95, 99, 164, 167; bestsellers 29; ebooks 3; Edwardian and Victorian classics 75, 85, 175; movie companion books 5, 65, 69, 73, 90, 94–95, 96*n*6; reading motivation 95, 99; re-writing texts 20–21; *see also* cartoons; comics; graphic novels; fairy tales; fantasy; folklore; mythology
Little Red Riding Hood 72
Little Women 51
LiviaEvans 77
Lobster Films 104
Locke, Alain 162
Locke, John 11
London 135–136, 138–140
Longstocking, Pippi 106
The Lord of the Rings 54
Los Angeles 164
Los Del Rio 36*n*1
Lucas, George 51, 57
Lukasiewicz, Tracie 47
Lumière Brothers, Cinématograph shows 103–105
Lurie, Alison 85, 88
Lury, Karen 3
Lyons, Charles 28–29, 36

Maastricht Treaty 50
Macarena (dance) 32, 36*n*1
Madagascar 4, 15, 25–26, 28, 33–35, 36
Madurai, India 153
The Magic Box 99, 108
Maharashtra 149, 155
Majidi, Majid 151
Malli 151, 154, 159
Manlove, C.N. 39, 47
Mao Tse-Tung 112
Maratha, Marathi 149, 155–158, 158*n*9
March of the Penguins 33, 36
Maret, Jeffrey 81, 88

Marie, Laurent 50, 55, 60
Marin, Cheech 161
marketing *see* consumer products, merchandising
Marriner, Katy 108
Marx, Groucho 18
Marx, Marcel 137
Masters, Kim 10, 26
Maternal Love 151
Matrix, Sidney 42, 47
Mattel 176, 187*n*4
Matthews, K.J. 166–167, 170
Mauclair, Jean-Paul 107*n*3
Mayer, Vicki 176
McAvoy, James 73
McDonald's 29
McGrath, Tom 26, 33
McHugh, Molly 96*n*4, 96–97
McRobbie, Angela 172, 188
media literacy *see* education
MEDIA program, European Union 50
medium as message 94
Medusa 65
Medvedev, Dmitri 124
Meet Me in St. Louis 51
Méliès, Georges 98, 100–104, 106, 107*n*1, 107*n*3
Mendes, Sam 31, 34
La Mer 105
Mercury, Freddy 19
Merman, Ethel 18
Merriman, Helena 164, 170
Mexico, soap operas 109
Meyer, Vicki 188
MGM Entertainment 176, 187*n*4
Michigan 12
Mickey Mouse 109, 116
Mid-Atlantic Popular and American Culture Association 1
Middlesex University 146*n*1
Migration and Mobility project 133, 141; migrancy 134; migrant children 6, 133–147; mobility 134
Mikhail Baryshnikov's Stories from My Childhood 117, 131
Miller, George 33
Miller, Toby 50–51, 60
Ming, Zhao 142
Minnelli, Vincente 51
Miramax 58
Mr. Dressup 112
mobility *see* Migration and Mobility project
mogi93 77
Mohseni, Hamid 151
Le Monde newspaper 55
The Monkees 32, 36
Monroe, Marilyn 33

Montreuil 100
Monty Python 54
Moore, Perry 69, 73
Moorhead, Agnes 31
morals *see* education, didactic and moral lessons
Morocco 56, 58
Morris, Lydia 139, 147
Morrison, Donald 50, 61
Mortenson, Norma Jean 33
Morton, Mark 166, 170
Moscow 12, 116
movie houses *see* theaters
MTV 29
Mueller, Greg 67, 77
Mulan 182, 161
Mullan, Tracy 146*n*1
multimedia *see* technologies
multimodal design, multimodality 64–65
The Muppets 93
Murdoch, Rupert 10
Murphy, Eddie 32
music, in film 4, 7, 18–19, 28–36, 57–58, 70, 74, 121, 163–164, 166, 176–179, 182–184; in television 7, 176–179, 182–184; videos 70–71, 93, 182, 184
Musker, John 26
Muslims, stereotypes 121
My Big Fat Greek Wedding 184
myths, mythic 5, 12, 68, 78–83, 86–87, 175; Christian 64; Greek 65, 71; Nordic 65; Roman 71, 158; Russian 129

NAACP (National Association for the Advancement of Colored People) 163–164
NAACP Image Awards 164
National Endowment for the Humanities 99
National Film Archives, U.K. 107*n*1
National Negro Congress 163
nationalism 2, 4, 6, 10, 50, 83, 112, 109–132, 134
Natural Born Killers 9, 26
Nava, Mica 139, 147
Nehru, Jawaharlal 148, 155, 158*n*1
Nel, Philip 106
Netflix 1, 28, 90
New Literacies 63–64
New York City 12, 25, 34, 99, 102; Broadway plays 29; Bronx 99
New York Times 163
New Yorker magazine 187*n*4
Newman, Randy 164
newsreels 30
Nicholson, Jack 18
Nick Cave and the Bad Seeds 19, 26
Nickelodeon 29, 175

Nikolaeva, Elena 115, 131
Nintendo 78, 89
Nodelman, Perry 46, 47
Noggin (television network) 175
Nordic mythology 65
Norris, Stephen M. 113–114, 118–119, 131
North, Dan 5–6, 98–108, 190
North Pole 12
Novaia Gazeta newspaper 124
novels *see* literature
Novgorod 116, 119
Noyce, Philip 139, 147
Nu, pogodi series 117
Nussbaum, M.C. 134

Odyssey 65
O'Hehir, Andrew 103, 108
O'Keefe, Deborah 80, 85, 88
Oklahoma State University 187*n*1
Olson, Debbie 7, 172–188, 190
Olson, Scott Robert 51, 61
online *see* websites
orphans *see* children
Oscars, Academy Awards 29, 163–164

Packard, Jerrold M. 187*n*3
Paiwand team 146*n*1
Pan's Labyrinth 40, 47
Paranorman 3
Parasecoli, Fabio 162, 167, 170
Parc Astérix 52
Paris 52–53, 59, 98, 101–103, 106, 137
Parker, Tony 59
parks: amusement 16, 20; theme parks 3, 29, 52, 160, 162, 164, 166–168
parody, in film and literature 6, 17–18, 32, 35, 52, 59, 110, 124–128
patriarchy 15, 17, 24, 42, 106
patriotism *see* nationalism
La pêche aux poisons rouges 105
pedagogy *see* education
People magazine 73, 77
Perelman, Helen 167, 170
Perrault, Charles 72
A Personal Journey with Martin Scorcese Through American Movies 107*n*1
Peter Pan 106
Philadelphia 178
phones *see* cell phones
Piéplu, Claude 53
Pierce, Tamora 46, 47
Pike, Susan 132
The Pilgrim's Progress 68
Pillai, Swarnavel Eswaran 6, 148–159, 190
P!nk 19
Pirates of the Caribbean 90
Pitof, Jean-Christophe 54

Pixar 89
Pocahontas 169, 182–183
Podyakova, Tatiana 6, 109–132, 190
Pokémon 5, 78–88
The Polar Express 4, 9, 12, 16, 19, 26
political aspects of film 11, 13, 28, 32, 39–40, 50–51, 53, 57–59, 83, 105, 110–111, 113–114, 124–146, 128, 133–134, 138, 141; "Family Values" platform 10–11; *see also* capitalism; Democratic Party; nationalism; Presidents; Prime Ministers; Republican; socialism
Politkovskaia, Anna 124
Pollachi, India 151
Ponniyin Selvan 149
popular culture *see* culture
postmodern 12, 56, 172
poverty 14, 83, 135–136, 178–179
prejudice *see* race; stereotypes
Presidents *see* Clinton; Medvedev; Putin; Yeltsin
Presley, Elvis 18–19, 26, 33, 36, 127
The Primary Chronicle (document) 119
Prime Ministers *see* Brown, Gordon; Gandhi; Nehru
Prince (musician) 18–19, 27, 33, 36
Prince Vladimir 114, 118–119, 122–123, 129, 131
princes, in film 41, 46, 71, 167–168
The Princess and the Frog 7, 160–171
The Princess Diaries 69–70, 77
princesses 7, 30–31, 69–70, 160–169
Propp, Vladimir 79, 81–82
The Proud Family 7, 172–188
The Proud Family Movie 180–182
Prout, Alan 133, 147
puppets 19
Putin, Vladimir 109, 113–114, 123–124
Puwal, Nirmal 141, 147

Les quatre cents coups 105, 108
Queen (band) 33
quests *see* heroes
Qvortrup, Jens 134, 147

Rabbit Proof Fence 139–142, 147
Rabkin, Eric 39, 47
race, prejudice 3, 7, 12, 22, 24, 113, 134, 138, 160–171, 173, 187; *see also* stereotypes
radio play 63
Raffi (musician) 36
Rajan, R.S. 153–155, 157, 158*n*7, 158*n*8, 159
Ramakrishnan, K.P. 151
Ramayana 148–149, 157
Randolph, Boots 57
Ranger, Terence 111, 130*n*1
Rapf, Maurice 162

ratings, film: FV (fantasy, violence) 45; PG (parental guidance) 45
Ray, Brian 42, 44, 47
Ray, Satyajit 153
Razzie Awards 59
reading *see* literature
realism 22, 40, 54, 116, 119, 168
recycling *see* environmental
The Red Shoes 99
Rediff.com 159
refugees *see* Migration
Reiniger, Lotte 41
religion, as a cultural force 111; clergy 10; Christian 64, 75, 85, 119; Christmas 9, 12, 66; Hallelujah song 31–32; in *Pan's Labyrinth* 40; replaced by nature 85–86; Russian Orthodox 114, 119, 122, 129; spiritual welfare of children 11
re-mixing, defined 70
Renn Productions 56
Repas de bébé 105
Reymond, Dalton 162
RIA Novosti 117, 131
Rich, Claude 56
Richards, Jeffrey 83, 88
Riding, Alan 55, 61
Rieder, John 44, 47
Rise of the Guardians 9, 12, 14–15, 18–19, 21–22, 27
Robinson Crusoe 17
robots 16
Rock, Chris 34
Rolufs, Heather 4, 37–48, 190
Romantic era, themes 65, 67–68, 71–72, 74
Rome, Dennis 187*n*5
Rome, Roman 53–54, 56; mythology 71, 158
Roost, Frank 161–162, 171
Rose, Anika Noki 164
Rose, Jacqueline 11–12, 17–19, 22, 27
Rosen, Lisa 34, 36
Rostov 121
Rousseau, Henri 34
Rousseau, Jean-Jacques 11
Rowling, J.K. 72
Rudd, Kevin 146*n*3, 147
Rushdie, Salman 21–22, 27
Russia, Russian films 6, 109–132; folk tales 81; Moscow 12, 116; mythology 129; Russian Federation 114, 122, 128; Russian Orthodox church, religion 114, 119, 122, 129

Sabella, Ernie 93
Safety Last! 105, 108
St. Nicholas 9, 15
Salt-n-Peppa 19
Samarin, Stanislav 114–115, 131

Sandifer, Philip 103, 108
Sanmao liulangji (*Sanmao's Travels*) 142, 147
Santa Claus 9, 12–13, 15
satire, in film 6, 58, 101, 128
Saturday Night Fever 36
Savage, Mark 103, 108
Schatz, Thomas 40
Schickel, Richard 100, 108
Schumacher, Michael 59
Schwarzenegger, Arnold 9–10
Scorcese, Charles 107*n*1
Scorcese, Francesca 100, 107*n*1
Scorsese, Martin 5–6, 98–108
Screech, Matthew 52, 61
Screen Education journal 100
Screen journal 1
screen studies *see* film, screen studies
Screening the Past (journal) 96*n*3
The Searchers 99
Sefton-Green, Julian 79–80, 88
Seiter, Ellen 176, 188
self-reflexivity 93–94, 96
Selznick, Brian 6, 98, 101–102, 108
Sen, Amartya 134, 147
Serfoji II (King) 155, 158*n*10
sex, sexuality in films 3, 9, 11, 19, 28, 34–35, 58, 65, 69, 71–75, 118, 127, 172–173, 181, 183; *see also* gender
Shanghai 142
Shary, Timothy 105, 108
Shavit, Zohar 11, 17–18, 27
Shemaroo (retailer) 152
short films, as bonus features 2, 8, 87*n*1, 89, 116
Shrek films 4, 8*n*4, 18–19, 21, 27–32, 36, 44, 47, 51, 56, 113, 115, 118
Shrek the Halls 8*n*4
Shull, M.S. 30, 36
Siddiqui Zaman, Rana 152–153, 158*n*6, 159
Silvestri, Chris 87–88
Sinyard, Neil 21, 27
Sivan, Santhosh 151, 153–154
Slavic countries 115, 121
Sleeping Beauty 41
Slotkin, Richard 82–83, 88
Smash Mouth 30, 32, 36
Smith, Anthony D. 111, 131
Smith, Bruce W. 180
The Snow Queen 116–117, 131
Snow White and the Seven Dwarfs 51, 160
socialism 83, 112, 116
Society for Cinema and Media Studies 2
Soiuzdetmultfilm 116
Soiuzmultfilm 116–117
Song of the South 7, 160–171
Soumya, Savvy 159
The Sound of Music 51

South American films 153
South Korea 112
Soviet Animated Film Studio 114
Soviet Union, films 6, 109–132; *see also* Russia
Spacey, Kevin 31, 34
Spain 40, 84; Barcelona 104
Sparkling Red Star 112
special features *see* bonus features
Sperb, Jason 163, 171
Spigel, Lynn 175–176, 188
Spyrou, Spyros 130–131
Stalford, Helen 134, 146
Staples, Terry 9, 21, 26
Star Trek 18
Star Wars 51, 57
Startz, Jane 29
Steig, William 29
Steinberg, Shirley R. 21, 25, 27
Stephen, John 3, 108
Stephens, Sharon 110–111, 131
stereotypes, in film and television 3, 7, 24, 59, 66, 72, 113, 120–122, 127–128, 143, 160–171, 173; *see also* gender; race
Stoller, Nicholas 93
Story of Movies teaching resources 100
Stowe, Harriet Beecher 174, 176, 188
streaming video *see* websites
subtitles, dubbing 7, 54–55, 92, 109, 116–117, 129, 151–152, 158
Sullivan, Ed 18
supernatural *see* fantasy, fantastic
Suvin, Darko 39, 47
Swinfen, Ann 40, 47
Sydney, Australia 25

Tabard, Rene 107*n*3
tablets 2, 89
Tabrizi, Kamal 151
Takacs, Stacy 187*n*1
Talbot, Margaret 187*n*4
Tamil 148–149, 155, 157–158
Tamilnadu 149, 153, 155, 157
Tampa Bay Times 161
Tanjore 156, 158*n*9
Target (store) 169
Tatar, Maria 42, 47
Tatars, depicted in film 113
technologies *see* cameras; cell phones; CGI; DVDs; games; Kinescope; Nintendo; tablets; television, cable; 3D; transmedia; Ultraviolet; websites; Xbox
television: cable, multi-channel 10, 20, 176; Emmy awards 30; MTV 29; as paedocratic 80; programs, series 2, 7, 29, 32, 63, 70, 79–80, 83, 86, 87*n*1, 87*n*4, 87*n*6, 110, 112, 148–150, 157–158, 172–188; soap operas 109; video on demand 10, 20, 90, 96*n*4

Index

Temple, Shirley 174–175
Thacker, Deborah 20–21, 27
theaters: cinemas, movie houses 2–3, 6, 28, 30, 52, 59, 89–90, 98, 100, 105, 110, 113–114, 118, 150, 152–153, 163, 166; stage 29, 63
theme parks *see* Parks
Thompson, Kenan 184
3D films, format 2, 4, 37, 45–46, 59, 98, 102–104, 110, 117
3 *Godfathers* 18, 27
Three Heroes on a Distant Shore 122, 131
Three Warrior-Heroes films 113, 116, 119–123, 125, 129, 131
Through the Looking Glass 37, 42
Thurmeier, Michael 26
Thus Spake Zarathustra 18
Time magazine 9, 50
Tintin 52, 55
Tirard, Laurent 49
Tirupur, India 151
Tischauser, Leslie V. 187*n*3, 187*n*5
Todorov, Tzvetan 4, 37–47
Tosenberger, Catherine 72, 77
Toy Story films 14–16, 18–19, 21–22, 24, 27, 51
toys 12, 14, 18, 25, 29, 66, 78–80, 98, 162, 164–166, 168–169, 176; *see also* consumer; dolls; games
Toys "R" Us (store) 168
trade agreements 50–51
trading cards 5, 78–79, 83, 86
The Translator see *Dubashi*
transmedia 2–3, 5, 63–108; defined 63
Travolta, John 34
Trim, Mary 68, 77
Trotter, James 106
Trousdale, Gary 8*n*4
True Lies 9–10, 27
True Romance 9, 27
Trujillo, Dara 167
Tsar 122
Turkey 127
TVS group, India 153
20th Century-Fox 9–10
Twilight 144, 147
2001: *A Space Odyssey* 18, 27

Underzo *see* Goscinny and Underzo
U.K. *see* United Kingdom
Ukraine 120–123, 130*n*3; stereotypes in film 113
Ullery, Sheila 167
Ultraviolet format 89
Uncle Tom's Cabin 174
Union of Children Animated Films 116
United Kingdom, U.K., Britain 1, 6, 28, 59, 68, 99, 107*n*1, 133, 135–136, 138–139, 141, 143, 146; BBC 63, 103, 117, 130; London 135–136, 138–140
United Nations Convention on the Rights of the Child 146*n*2
United States *see* American
U.S. *see* American
Ushinkii, Nikolai D. 115, 132
Usmanov, Alisher 117
utopias 24, 75, 79, 83–86

Valdivia, Angharad N. 187*n*4
van Blerk, Lorraine 134, 147
Vancouver 94
van Leeuwen, Theo 64, 76
Varda, Agnes 142, 147
Variety magazine 28, 55
Vasnetsovi, Viktor 116
Veale, Angela 139, 147
Vermillion, B. 40, 47
Vernon, Conrad 27
Viane, Chuck 163
Victorian life 37, 45, 174–175; novels 75
video games *see* games
video on demand *see* television; websites
videos, music *see* music
Vidov, Oleg 117
Vietnam, Vietnamese 137
Vikings 23
violence 6, 9, 45–46, 54, 58, 72, 98, 113, 118–119, 140–141, 145, 172–173
Le voyage dans la lune 104
Vyankoji (King) 158*n*9

Wainwright, Rufus 32
Waldron, Fionnuala 132
Wallace & Gromit 19, 27
Walt Disney *see* Disney
Wanger, Walter 162
Wanted Thangaraj 154, 159
war 133–134, 142; American Civil War 187*n*3; Spanish Civil War 40; World War I, II 99, 174–175
Washington, D.C. 99
Wasikowsak, Mia 37
Watson, Victor 68, 77
websites, Internet, online distribution 1, 3, 5, 28–29, 63, 89–90, 93–95, 110, 129, 166; fan videos 5, 70–71; streaming video 2, 6, 10, 20, 90, 96*n*4, 110; video on demand 10, 20, 90, 96*n*4
Wedge, Chris 26
Weekly.Ahram.org 159
Weintraub, Steve 93, 97
Welcome 135–137, 140, 147
Welkos, Robert W. 116, 132
Welles, Orson 31

Whitegates School 146*n*1
The Wiggles 36
Williams, John 57
Williams, Robin 18, 24
Willie Wonka and the Chocolate Factory 14, 27
Wilt, D.E. 30, 36
Wise, Robert 51
The Wizard of Oz: books 83, 87*n*7; film 21, 51
Wojik-Andrews, Ian 3, 18, 21, 27
women *see* gender; sex
Wonder, Stevie 33
Wood, Aylish 102, 108
Wood, Elijah 33
Woodson, Stephani 12, 24, 27
Worley, A. 40, 48
Woronov, Terry 134, 147
Wrubel and Gilbert 163

Xbox 94
Xu, Xu 132

Yadhaartha film society 153
Yazgi, Nicolas 139, 146
Yeltsin, Boris 123, 130*n*5
Young, Paul 108
YouTube 69, 94, 110, 117, 129, 130*n*4
Yuyama, Kunihiko 88

Zahorski, Kenneth 40
Zelizer, Viviana A. 175, 188
Zemeckis, Robert 35
Zidane, Zinedine 59
Zidi, Claude 49, 53–54
Zipes, Jack 21, 27, 40–42, 48, 72, 77, 82–84, 88
Zwick, Joel 184